691

MATERIALS FOR BUILDING
VOLUME 3

A

MATERIALS FOR BUILDING
VOLUME 3

Water and its Effects—2

LYALL ADDLESON, B.Arch., A.R.I.B.A., Dip.T.P., A.M.T.P.I.

Head of Design Section
Faculty of Environmental Science and Technology
Polytechnic of the South Bank, London

London
Iliffe Books

THE BUTTERWORTH GROUP

England
Butterworth & Co (Publishers) Ltd
London: 88 Kingsway, WC2B 6AB

Australia
Butterworth & Co (Australia) Ltd
Sydney: 586 Pacific Highway Chatswood, NSW 2067
Melbourne: 343 Little Collins Street, 3000
Brisbane: 240 Queen Street, 4000

Canada
Butterworth & Co (Canada) Ltd
Toronto: 14 Curity Avenue, 374

New Zealand
Butterworth & Co (New Zealand) Ltd
Wellington: 26–28 Waring Taylor Street, 1
Auckland: 35 High Street, 1

South Africa
Butterworth & Co (South Africa) (Pty) Ltd
Durban: 152–154 Gale Street

First published in 1972 by
Iliffe Books, an imprint of
the Butterworth Group

© Lyall Addleson 1972

ISBN 0 592 00237 3

Printed in England by Chapel River Press

contents

preface

Materials for Building uses a considerable amount of the material that originally appeared in the series of articles of the same name in *The Architect and Building News* between 1964–68. The decision to publish the articles in book form provided an opportunity to correct mistakes, add or delete, and as important, to bring everything up-to-date, including complete metrication. In the light of present practice, some may find the metric values 'too accurate'. Generally speaking the metric equivalents of imperial values rather than sensible metric values are given. In many cases experimental or test results have had to be converted, and here too much rounding off or over-simplification would have been inappropriate.

Materials used in buildings have to meet a number of different functional requirements while they are exposed continuously to a wide variety of destructive agencies. Factors associated with both of these include strength, water, heat, fire, sound and production. In building practice materials have to be selected to meet specific functional requirements and to ensure that harmful deterioration is delayed for as long as is practicable.

In order to obtain the best out of the materials available it is necessary to have an understanding not only of the properties of the materials themselves but also of the factors which influence their performance and durability. This series of books aims to provide a systematic coverage, on a comparative basis, of the relationship between materials for building as a whole and the factors against which materials are expected to perform. Consequently each of the factors in terms of its nature and characteristics are explained separately and then related to a specific range of materials. The properties of all materials relative to each factor are also included.

In this study an attempt has been made to gather together a considerable amount of diversified information from a number of sources and to relate it in a particular way. It is to be hoped that the form of presentation used particularly the graphics and the extensive use of photographic examples will facilitate an understanding of the problems involved and of their possible solution. Perhaps even stimulate further study.

This volume deals mainly with the deleterious chemical effects of water on materials. (The basic problems associated with water are covered in Volume 2). The causes and effects of efflorescence together with precautions that may be taken to avoid its occurrence are considered first. Chemical attack, including unsound materials, acid action, alkali action, sulphate attack and fungal attack in timber, follows. The causes and effects of the chemical reactions involved are explained and precautions which can be taken to avoid deleterious results are noted. A special section is devoted to the corrosion of metals with particular emphasis placed on electro-chemical theory, but including the effects of polluted water. Again the causes and effects of corrosion and protective methods and procedures are discussed in detail. Frost action, a physical phenomenon, is explained separately on the same lines as the other chemical effects. The final section 'Weathering', is intended to serve as a summary of all the preceding sections (including those in Volume 2) and consists of groups of annotated photographs related to specific problems. All the examples are of failures rather than successes.

Many people and organisations have made this series possible and I am extremely grateful to all of them for their help and co-operation. Specific acknowledgment to publishers, authors, firms or organisations for permission to use their material is given where the material appears. I owe special thanks to George Mansell, formerly editor of *The Architect and Building News*, for his faith in me and for his unceasing encouragement. All the staff at *The Architect and Building News* were always helpful but Geoffrey Lee who attended to all arrangements for the articles deserves special mention. The photographic department at Dorset House never failed to develop and print my films on time and as required. Istvan Fenyvesi worked hard and conscientiously on the diagrams and charts and proved to be invaluable in the conversion to SI units.

I was fortunate enough to have had Mrs. Sheila Todd to do all the original typing so accurately and quickly.

I am always grateful to my students for their helpful criticisms and for their willingness to co-operate in teaching experiments. The things they have found out themselves and their penetrating questions have always encouraged me to explore further.

Last but not least, thanks to my wife for her patience and understanding while I was searching, writing or photographing, and for her secretarial and checking assistance.

London 1971   L.A.

3.05 efflorescence

Deposits of soluble salts at or near the surface of a porous material as the result of evaporation of the water in which the salts are dissolved, is usually known by the term *efflorescence*. On evaporation the concentration of salts in solution increases until they finally crystallise out. In general, efflorescence is harmless, the superficial white deposits often contributing more to a temporary change of appearance of the surface on which it forms. Butterworth has aptly described efflorescence as *usually* being 'a skin trouble and not a deep-seated disease'. However, it is the exceptions which require, if not repay, a deeper consideration, not only of the physical processes involved but also of the derivation of the soluble salts.

Under certain conditions the soluble salts may be responsible for deleterious effects on materials. These effects are included in *3.06 Chemical attack* later. The main purpose of this section is, in addition to discussing efflorescence, to outline the sources, behaviour

In general, efflorescence is harmless, the superficial white deposits usually causing a temporary change in appearance of the surface on which it forms (right), but occasionally soluble salts can be responsible for deleterious effects (bottom picture)

References

(1) BS 3921 : 1965, *Bricks and Blocks of Fired Brick-earth, Clay or Shale. Note*: This new British Standard incorporates information previously contained in four other standards. Within the context of this section, it is important to note that the methods of analysing soluble salt content and tests for liability to effloresce previously contained in BS 1257 : 1945, *Methods of Testing Clay Building Bricks*, have been superseded. (2) *The Selection of Clay Building Bricks: 1 & 2*, BRS Digests (2nd Series) Nos. 65 and 66, HMSO, December, 1965, and January, 1966, respectively. A useful appraisal of BS 3291 : 1965. (3) Butterworth, B., *Efflorescence and Staining of Brickwork.* Reprint from the Brick Bulletin, amended December, 1962, published by the National Federation of Clay Industries. (4) *Principles of Modern Building, Vol. 1*, 3rd Ed., HMSO, 1959. (5) *Some Common Defects in Brickwork*, National Building Studies, Bulletin No. 9, HMSO, 1950. (6) *Clay Building Bricks*, National Building Studies, Bulletin No. 1, HMSO, 1948. (7) Butterworth, B., *Bricks and Modern Research* (Crosby Lockwood), 1948. (8) Schaffer, R., *The Weathering of Natural Building Stones.* Building Research Special Report No. 18, HMSO, 1932. *Note*: This report, now over 30 years old, has been out of print for some time, but is nevertheless still in demand. It is understood that a revised up-to-date edition may be published in the future. In the meantime the two BRS Digests included in (9) bridge the gap in time since the report was last printed. (9) *The Weathering, Preservation and Maintenance of Natural Stone (Parts I & II)*, BRS Digests (1st Series), Nos. 20 and 21, HMSO, July, 1950 (revised March, 1965), and August, 1950. respectively. (10) Lea, F. M., *The Chemistry of Cement and Concrete*, revised edition of Lea & Desch, Arnold, 1956. (11) Eldridge, H. J., *Concrete Floors on Shale Hardcore*, Building Research Current Papers, Design Series No. 30.

Two groups of comparative photographs (above, and those on the opposite page) illustrating that efflorescence is usually transient, although it may persist for a few years after the completion of the building. Unless there are external sources of soluble salts the efflorescence usually disappears completely. The

photographs showing the efflorescence (top in each group) were taken a few months after completion; the others about a year later. The buildings are all from the same comprehensive development. Above, the efflorescence had disappeared completely after a year and has not reappeared

and *basic* effects of soluble salts. For purposes of explanation it is more convenient to sub-divide the various aspects of the whole problem. However, in practice, it should be remembered, one or more of the separate aspects usually operate together.

In order to cover efflorescence in particular and soluble salts in general the following headings are used:

(1) General considerations, which will include an outline of the whole problem so that the significance of the individual aspects dealt with separately under the remaining headings may be better appreciated; (2) Nature of soluble salts; (3) Sources of soluble salts; (4) Physical processes involved in the formation of efflorescence; and

(5) Precautions. Certain aspects included under these headings, it should be noted, have already been outlined or discussed in detail in *Part 1.00* generally and *Sections 3.01, 3.02, 3.03 and 3.04.* This section has, however, been made as self-contained as possible. Consequently aspects previously covered in detail are only outlined here but are nevertheless referred to as necessary.

general considerations

1. Basic effects of soluble salts

Depending on their nature, distribution and quantity in the materials, including complete constructions, in which

they occur, soluble salts may produce effects of five kinds.

(a) They may cause temporary, although unsightly, white efflorescences on the exposed surfaces of materials, whether these are external or internal (mode and direction of drying out is relevant).

(b) They may crystallise out within the surface pores of a material, with the resultant expansion caused during crystallisation sometimes capable of disrupting the surface of the material. Expansion may, however, take place as a result of a change of state of the salt deposited below the surface. Efflorescence within a material is often referred to as 'crypto-florescence'.

(c) They may cause efflorescences that give more or less permanent coloured stains (see *Section 3.06*).

(d) They may form a hard glassy skin on the surface of the material which usually causes deterioration of the surface due to blistering or exfoliation (see *Section 3.06*).

(e) They may react in solution with certain compounds in Portland cement or hydraulic limes (in mortars, renders, plasters or concrete, for example) causing expansion, ultimate softening and possible disintegration of the material as a result of what is commonly known as 'sulphate attack' (see *Section 3.06*).

2. Variable factors

It is understandable that the phenomenon of efflorescence, together with the behaviour and effects of soluble salts in solution, often present a baffling problem. As an example consider superficial efflorescence. The precise position of its occurrence is no clear indication of its origin. In many cases salts derived from what can best be termed 'external sources' are usually significant. On the other hand, only very small quantities of salts are required to form even a prominent efflorescence. In brickwork the small quantities required usually occur in the bricks and mortar.

Among other factors which must be taken into account, two are closely interrelated. These are:

(a) The porosity of the materials concerned, particularly the difference in behaviour between fine-pored and coarse-pored materials as these relate to the drying out pattern in which the wetting and drying cycle is also important (see particularly Vol. 2, *Section 3.03*, under 'General influences, 1. Capillarity'). This raises the significance of the problems associated with what Schaffer has called 'selective decay'. This often occurs when a material is not homogeneous or when materials with different physical properties are used with one another.

(b) The precise distribution of the salts, rather than their quantity, within a material. The significance of this may be understood if it is realised that to be dissolved the salts require water; to be transferred the salts require water as the 'transfer' medium. Consequently the salts will remain in a sense innocuous provided water cannot reach them. Although obvious, cognisance of this particular aspect can help greatly in an understanding of the precautions which should be taken when trying to prevent the effects of soluble salts. This may be extremely relevant when trying to prevent the more deleterious effects of soluble salts.

3. Tests

Variations in the properties (porosity and soluble salt content are notable) of materials that are commonly affected, in one way or another, by soluble salts in solution, also contribute to the difficulties often encountered in dealing effectively with the problem.

It is possible to test samples of materials either for their soluble salt content or for their liability to effloresce. Despite this, none of these tests, within the context of the materials involved, is conclusive evidence that there will be no efflorescence or other deleterious effects, when *other* samples of the same material are used in a building. Among other things, the precise relationship between the material under review with other materials in the construction and the factors which influence the behaviour of the salts, is important, and these are difficult to simulate for test purposes.

In brickwork, for example, there have been no deleterious effects when bricks with a high sulphate content (according to tests carried out on samples) have been used, while the converse has been true when bricks of low sulphate content have been used. Examples such as these do not, however, necessarily invalidate the usefulness of tests. They only help to reinforce two things. Firstly, the importance of correlating test results with actual experience of the particular material in practice. Secondly, the necessity for an understanding of the behaviour of soluble salts in solution, the importance of the context of the *whole of a construction* and the advisability of taking, wherever practicable, reasonable precautions. Many, though not all, of these are associated with preventing a construction from either becoming excessively damp (Vol. 2, *3.03 Moisture content* is relevant) or remaining damp for excessively long periods of time (Vol. 2, *3.04 Exclusion* is relevant).

It may be noted here that cognisance of the 'misleading confidence' which test results *alone* can engender, has been taken into account in BS 3921 : 1965 for bricks and blocks of brick-earth, clay or shale. As explained in the references, this standard now supersedes a number of existing standards. Except for special quality bricks, the standard does not attempt to set any limits of the soluble salt content of ordinary bricks. Far from discouraging tests, the standard advises manufacturers in particular to carry out tests regularly as part of general quality control of their products. The results

There were still some traces of efflorescence after one year, but these had disappeared completely after a further year and have not reappeared

of these tests may, at least, highlight any significant changes in a particular material. Remedies may then be taken during subsequent manufacture.

4. Apparent transient nature of efflorescence

Another aspect of efflorescence which often encourages what may be termed a certain degree of cynicism, is its apparent transient nature in a great many cases. For some it would appear to be a phenomenon which must be associated only with new buildings (brick, unfairly at that) on which it usually occurs, sometimes to the temporary annoyance of owners, architects and builders, soon after completion, but usually disappears within a comparatively short period of time as the result of the combined effects of wind and rain. In other cases, the efflorescences may persist for a little longer, when it seems to be a seasonal phenomenon ;

appearing prominently in the spring and summer but disappearing by the autumn. The cycle may persist for a number of years, but usually (unless there is a perpetual supply of salts from external sources) the amount of the deposit recurs with decreasing intensity, until it finally disappears after a few seasons.

Despite these 'fortunate' occurrences, which probably take place in the majority of cases, it is still possible, under certain conditions, for the efflorescences to remain hidden behind the surface probably causing slow but eventual damage. If, on the other hand, the salts remain in solution for long enough within the material, damage due to chemical attack could also be taking place slowly. Consequently there may be a considerable time lapse from the completion of a building until the deleterious effects of the soluble salts are 'suddenly' made apparent.

3

It is obviously extremely easy to over-estimate or exaggerate the effects of soluble salts, while many of the precautions, which could be taken to try and prevent some of its effects, are sometimes seen to be tedious. Nevertheless, it may be noted that, even when every precaution has been taken, it is still possible for some isolated damage or disfigurement to occur. As in most cases in building practice, the effects which result when no precautions at all have been taken, are usually extremely pronounced, and sometimes regretted.

5. Materials commonly affected

The problems of efflorescences and salts in solution can take place in any porous material in which water transfer is possible. However, in the past brickwork and stonework, including the constituents of the relevant jointing and/or surfacing materials used, have received the greatest attention. In fact, the major part of research, carried out in all parts of the world, has been devoted to these two materials. The effects of soluble salts may equally well be produced on or within other porous materials such as tiles, faience and concrete, while they may also damage finishes such as paint or weaken the bond of adhesives.

In many ways the effects of soluble salts on some materials, hitherto regarded as 'immune', may not become pronounced until the material is used in new ways or, as important, it is more widely used. As will be seen later, the increased use of Portland cement in mortars, for example, is now seen as one of the more important sources of salts in brickwork.

6. Importance of sources of salts

It cannot be emphasised too often that salts, other than those initially present or inherent in a particular material, derived from external sources and transferred through a construction or from one part of a construction to another, are of fundamental importance in all considerations. An analysis of any particular situation aimed at assessing the necessity for any precautions should, therefore, always take these external sources into account. It may be as well to note here that, although fairly obvious, it is surprising how often, particularly in stone plinths, the soil (including hardcore under any adjacent paving) has been overlooked as a source of salts. Illustrations of these kinds of examples have been included in earlier sections; some others are included in this section.

nature of soluble salts*

1. Composition

The composition of the soluble salts which may be encountered is to a large extent determined by their sources

*A general discussion of *solutions* is given in Vol. 1, *1.06 Solutions*, particularly 'True solutions' and 'Solids in liquids', and of *salts* in Vol. 1, *1.10 Chemical reactions*.

('Sources of soluble salts' later). As the latter are numerous, the composition of the salts are also numerous. However, soluble salts more commonly associated with the materials, including the jointing and surfacing materials, making up a construction, are the sulphates and carbonates of calcium, magnesium, sodium and potassium.

Some common salts are: calcium sulphate (gypsum); magnesium sulphate (Epsom salt); sodium sulphate (Glauber's salt); potassium sulphate (sulphate of potash); ferrous sulphate (sulphate of iron or copperas); calcium carbonate (lime); magnesium carbonate; sodium carbonate; and potassium carbonate.

The presence of nitrates and chlorides is usually indicative of salts derived from ground water, although sulphates and carbonates may also be present. Chlorides may also be derived from sea spray although they may also be present in some polluted atmospheres.

2. Solubility

In general, the sulphates constitute the more commonly found salts in most materials. (Any carbonates present can be converted into sulphates.) All, except calcium sulphate, are very soluble in water. Although generally regarded as an insoluble compound, calcium sulphate does dissolve in water to an appreciable extent. (Soluble to the extent of 1 part in 500.) Its solubility cannot, therefore, be entirely overlooked. The important point is that the other sulphates are soluble to an even greater extent.

3. Significance and effects

Only the sulphates, for the reason given in 2 above and because they are generally the most aggressive of the salts, are included here.

(a) Calcium sulphate

Calcium sulphate mainly because of its relatively low solubility does not normally give rise to efflorescence. However, its innocuous character only persists provided (i) there are no appreciable quantities of other soluble matter present, *or* (ii) that materials are not maintained in a damp condition for long periods, *or* (iii) a hard glassy skin is not formed. Solutions of calcium sulphate may give rise to sulphate attack if dampness persists for long enough. Calcium sulphate may form a hard glassy skin on sheltered areas of a building not freely washed by rainwater. The skin is not protective and may lead to disruption of the surface of the material on which it forms.

The solubility of calcium sulphate may be increased if potassium sulphate is present. Calcium and potassium sulphate combine to form a double salt which is more soluble, and appreciable amounts may be found in efflorescences.

Calcium sulphate may occur in

stonework as a result of decomposition. In brickwork its presence is, as explained later (see 'Sources of soluble salts'), a consequence of manufacture. Consequently calcium sulphate is unavoidably present and over one-third of all bricks produced in this country contain upwards of 3·0 per cent of it. But for the reasons already given such quantities may not necessarily be detrimental to the brick.

(b) *Magnesium sulphate*

This salt is probably responsible for most of the failures caused by soluble salts, despite the fact that it is rarely present in appreciable quantities (in brickwork the amounts present rarely exceed 0·5 per cent). In stonework magnesium sulphate results from the decomposition of magnesium carbonate exposed to the atmosphere. The failures caused by magnesium sulphate may take various forms. However, once it has gained a foothold and suitable conditions persist, its destructive effects may be serious—some building stones are particularly susceptible to attack.

The salt may crystallise out at or near the surface of a material. On external surfaces, because of its solubility, the magnesium sulphate is readily washed away. This does, to a large extent, minimise the possibility of destruction of materials. Thus sheltered parts of a building are more vulnerable.

When magnesium sulphate appears on the surface of plaster, decoration may be impracticable or disintegration of the surface may occur. Under certain conditions, when lime is present in the plaster, crystal growth at the interface of the background and the plaster may exert sufficient pressure to separate the plaster (and sometimes the surface of the brick as well).

(c) *Potassium sulphate and sodium sulphate*

During crystallisation, potassium sulphate tends to assume a hard glassy form, while sodium sulphate gives a fluffy deposit.

Decay is usually likely to be most severe where the salts concerned can exist in more than one state of hydration. Externally, the transition temperature between the two states is within the range of outdoor temperatures. Sodium sulphate, for example, at temperatures below 32·5°C crystallises with ten molecules of water of crystallisation (Na_2SO_4 10 H_2O). Known as sodium sulphate decahydrate, this compound changes into the anhydrous salt (Na_2SO_4) at 32·5°C even under water. In air it begins to lose water below this temperature. Heat from the sun can change it to the anhydrous form, but a subsequent shower of rain may convert this to the decahydrate which will occupy four times the volume. Consequently, if the salt is deposited in the pores of a material, the dimensional changes can lead to destructive pressures in the pores, and powdering of the surface.

4

(d) *Ferrous sulphate and vanadium*

Rusty stains, particularly on mortar joints in brickwork, are usually due to iron salts which are changed to ferric oxide by oxygen and lime. Yellowish green stains are due to an efflorescence of a coloured salt which contains vanadium.

sources of soluble salts

The sources from which salts may be derived can, for convenience, be grouped into three classes, namely, (1) salts originally present in a material before its incorporation in a building ; (2) salts derived from the decomposition of a material exposed to the atmosphere after its incorporation in a building; *and* (3) salts derived from external sources. Each of these will be discussed separately, including their own sub-divisions, but, as pointed out earlier, it is as well to remember that, within the context of building practice, all sources are usually closely inter-related.

1. Salts originally present in a material

In this class, the salts which may be present in a material before its incorporation in a building are chiefly those which result from what may best be termed the manufacture (either natural or man-made) of a particular material. Solid state materials, e.g. fired clay products, quarried and dressed stone or concrete, are implied. Any salts which may find their way into a particular material after manufacture are regarded, for the purposes of this study, as being derived from external sources.

It is convenient to consider groups of materials separately.

(a) *Clay bricks*

The origin of salts is attributed to *three* main sources, namely, the clay itself (including the tempering water), pyrites, and the action of sulphur from the fuels used in firing. The relative importance of any of these three sources has not been established conclusively. Each of the main sources is dealt with separately. As firing temperature is significant, particularly as regards the quantity and nature of salt which may be present, it is also discussed. Table 3.05/1 sets out the results of soluble salt analyses and efflorescence tests (after Butterworth). The results, it should be noted, were obtained before the publication of BS 3921 : 1965.

(i) *Clay.* Although not considered to be a major origin of salts, when salt is present it is usually gypsum. The reason for its presence is usually due to the fact that it may not be in a form that can be easily separated from the clay before it is used for making bricks. Where, however, the gypsum does occur in massive form, separation is not difficult. Butterworth has noted that there is at least one works in England where gypsum for plaster and clay for bricks are dug from the same quarry, and yet the soluble salts content of the bricks is in no way abnormal.

(ii) *Pyrites* (iron sulphide). This may

The origin of salts in clay bricks may be attributed to three sources, the clay, pyrites and sulphur from fuels used in firing—see text

be present in certain clays. The salts are formed during heating of the clay in air when the pyrites take up oxygen, giving gaseous oxides of sulphur which further react with bases in the clay to form sulphates.

(iii) *Sulphur action.* Sulphur in fuels (coal and oil (see *3.02 Exposure,*

	Fletton		London Stock		Colliery Shale Stiff-plastic-pressed Common		Keuper Marl Wirecut Common	
Type of brick	Sample 1	Sample 2	Sample 1	Sample 2	Sample 1	Sample 2	Sample 1	Sample 2
Total Soluble (per cent weight) Composition:	3·70	2·39	0·20	0·77	0·96	0·29	0·86	5·70
R_2O_3*	0·06	0·02	nil	0·02	0·11	0·02	nil	nil
Ca·· (calcium)	0·97	0·62	0·06	0·18	0·06	0·03	0·21	1·40
Mg·· (magnesium)	0·01	<0·01	<0·01	<0·01	0·03	0·03	0·03	0·04
Na· (sodium)	0·02	0·06	0·01	0·02	0·01	0·01	0·04	0·08
K· (potassium)	0·02	0·02	0·01	0·05	0·03	0·03	0·05	0·17
SO″₃ (sulphate)	2·13	1·42	0·11	0·42	0·29	0·08	0·49	3·38
SiO″₃ (silicate)	0·04	0·06	nil	0·05	0·01	0·02	0·04	0·03
Liability to Efflorescence	nil	slight	nil	slight	heavy, iron and potassium sulphates	moderate, magnesium and alkali sulphates	slight	variable, slight to heavy alkali and calcium sulphates

Table 3.05/1. Results of soluble salt analyses and efflorescence tests on clay building bricks

* R_2O_3 is a conventional symbol for the sesquioxides of iron and aluminium (Fe_2O_3 and Al_2O_3) which are precipitated together in the course of analysis, and are not separated when there is too little to justify the trouble involved.

Reference: Butterworth, B., *Clay Building Bricks*, National Building Studies, Bulletin No. 1, Table 5, p. 18, HMSO, 1948.

Notes:
1. Two analyses are given for each type of brick in order to show that there may be a variation, sometimes a wide one, between different samples from the same district or of the same variety.
2. Because of the variations likely, it is unwise to attach too much importance to *small* differences in analytical results. This is not a reflection on the accuracy of the analytical methods used, but rather an emphasis on the variability of the material. The results of periodic analyses would enable some idea of the usual variation to be obtained. This would make comparison of different makes of brick valid.
3. The results given in the table have been based on the analytical method given in BS 1257:1945 which is now superseded. The methods of analysis now included in BS 3921:1965 are aimed to improve the extraction of the more soluble constituents (magnesium, potassium and sodium). These, although the minor constituents, are the most aggressive. Analyses made by the old method should not be used in conjunction with the limits specified for soluble salts for special quality bricks in the new standard.
   For the present purposes, and bearing in mind the allowable tolerance (see note 2), the analyses given in the table are considered adequate.
4. The analyses do not report the presence of salts, such as calcium sulphate or sodium silicate, but record instead the bases and acids of which they are composed. This is due to the necessities of the analytical method.
5. The accuracy of extraction is limited by the fact that the samples used contain both powdered brick and the salts. The former must first be removed before the latter can be analysed. Both the old and the new British Standards specify a method of extraction which enables analysts 'to steer a course between inefficient extraction and too violent a treatment'.
   It is wise to check that the results of analyses have been obtained by the standard method, particularly if they show phenomenally low results.
6. A wide range of data is given in Bonnell, D. G. R. and Butterworth, B., *The Properties of Clay Building Bricks made in the United Kingdom.* HMSO, 1950.

'Sulphur dioxide', Vol. 2) used for firing the bricks are the most general source of salts. During firing, sulphur burns forming oxides capable of reacting with the clay. During the early stages of firing there is an increase in the amount of salts, but these begin to decompose again at the temperatures usual in the firing of bricks. Decomposition proceeds further as the firing temperature is raised.

(iv) *Firing temperature.* In part, the soluble content of particular types of brick varies over such wide limits, because certain salts tend to be decomposed and expelled from bricks by hard firing. For example, magnesium sulphate is more easily decomposed in the firing of bricks than is calcium sulphate. A firing temperature of between 1 000 and 1 500°C is sufficient to get rid of magnesium sulphate. However, magnesium sulphate is often absent even from lightly fired bricks and as many bricks fired at temperatures below 1 000°C appear quite satisfactorily hard, it is possible for a manufacturer to be taken unawares if there is a local change in the composition of the clay (isolated seam or pocket of clay in a pit containing either magnesium sulphate or carbonate). This sort of experience underlines the importance of regular analyses at works. After the first discovery of the change in the composition of the clay, for example, a higher firing temperature should be used. This will guard against any further local changes that may occur, but will also mean a change in colour in the bricks, as lighter coloured bricks are fired at lower temperature.

Variations in the soluble content of bricks of a particular type may, then, occur in those kilns where close temperature control is not exercised. Higher soluble contents will generally occur in those bricks coming from the cooler parts of the kiln. For the reasons already outlined under 'General considerations', apart possibly from magnesium sulphate, the soluble content of any particular type of brick is not necessarily indicative that either efflorescence and/or chemical attack will result. However, some *under-fired* bricks may be badly attacked and these should, therefore, be carefully considered before use in building.

Although ferrous sulphate, like magnesium sulphate, is not found in the majority of bricks, when it does occur it is present in very small amounts. However, the conditions required for the formation of ferrous sulphate, namely, a reducing atmosphere and a high firing temperature, are also those necessary to the production of some of the most attractive colours in handmade facing bricks. The same conditions are also used in some kilns firing ordinary bricks from colliery shale. However, the presence of ferrous sulphate is unlikely to be important in so far as rust staining is concerned in the work in which ordinary bricks from colliery shale are likely to be used. When bricks of this type are plastered

with gypsum plasters some staining may appear. (See 'Physical process, 5. Effect of precipitation' later.)

Even relatively low firing temperatures appear to expel sodium chloride (common salt). Consequently this salt is not found among the deposits of soluble salts, even though it may be present (sometimes specifically added to the clay), before firing. Although the decrease in sulphate content is not great enough to warrant its general addition to clay, if sodium chloride is present in the early stages of firing, the sulphate content of the fully fired brick may be less than it would have otherwise been. Butterworth has suggested, however, that addition of sodium chloride is a possibility that might be examined by a brickmaker who is troubled with efflorescence and cannot conveniently raise the firing temperature.

(b) *Sand-lime and concrete bricks and blocks*

In general it is very rare for sand-lime bricks to contain soluble salts. The same is usually true of concrete bricks and blocks. Efflorescence on or within the surface is more likely due to salts derived from external sources.

(c) *Natural stones*

The natural building stones which are of significance here are the sedimentary stones. Despite the fact that it would be expected that these stones should have certain amounts of salts due to their method of formation —originally laid under water, the majority under sea-water—the actual amounts from this source are negligible. Such salts as may have been present have been largely leached out by the action of rainwater.

The traces of chlorides and sulphates found in some specimens of stone are not considered to constitute a common cause of efflorescence in building stones. However, it should be noted that contamination of stone by sea salt may occur, if the stone has at some time been exposed to sea-water. Sometimes this has been accidental, but there is at least one known case (another is suspected) in which a salt was applied in the mistaken belief that salt would serve as a preservative.

Apart from isolated cases, stone 'obtains' its soluble salt content after it has been incorporated in a building as a result of decomposition of calcareous matter in it (see '2. Decomposition' p. 7) or from other external sources (backing materials are often significant).

(d) *Aggregates*

Aggregates, such as sand, clinker, crushed stone and gravels, may be used for mortars, plasters, renders and concretes. Some of these and others such as colliery shale may also be used as hardcore in foundations, under ground-floor slabs or under paving. It is in the

general sense, that is to include all uses, that the term aggregates is being used.

The soluble salt content of the various types of aggregate available is liable to wide variation. In addition to sulphur compounds including sulphates (gypsum is often notable), soluble alkalis may also be present. Coal dust which can have deleterious effects may be present in aggregates from certain districts. In general, however, clean river, pit or crushed natural stone sands, and crushed stone or gravel aggregates are substantially free from soluble salts. The soluble salt content of *crushed brick* aggregate will depend on the soluble content of the brick used, although it is reasonable to assume that in its crushed state the brick is more likely to 'expose' its salt content. However, in general, crushed brick, if clean, is a good aggregate ; if contaminated with old plaster and other rubbish it may be very bad.

There are some aggregates which do require special consideration if they are to be used. These are:

(i) *Sea sand.* It is perhaps all too obvious that sea sand will contain salt in it. Nevertheless there is often a temptation to use unwashed sea sand for mortars or plastering or concrete in districts near the coast or tidal estuaries. In addition to the possibility of causing efflorescence, the presence of sea salt which is hygroscopic and likely to absorb moisture from the atmosphere in humid weather, results in work appearing damp. If sea sand is to be used for building work it should always be *washed*.

(ii) *Ashes and clinker.* Furnace ashes and clinker are sometimes used as mortar aggregates ; clinker may be used for lightweight concrete. They may also be used as hardcore. Both may contain sulphur compounds including sulphates. For mortars and concrete materials of doubtful origin should not be used. Well burnt clinker from large industrial furnaces is, in general, likely to have a reasonably constant composition.

For use as hardcore, the soluble salt content is only of importance in so far as it influences the precautions, usually in terms of d.p.c.'s or d.p.m.'s, which should be taken to prevent water transferred through the hardcore coming into contact with or subsequently being transferred through other porous materials.

(iii) *Colliery shale.* This material, a waste seen in unsightly heaps near coal mines, is often used as a hardcore. Initially the material consisted of shale with a proportion of carbonaceous materials which had burnt slowly and had fired the shale to a varying extent, ranging from well-fired to very under-fired. Consequently the physical condition and the chemical composition of the burnt shale are both very variable, and the material may contain appreciable amounts of soluble salts, particularly sulphates. In the absence of adequate precautions, this material has been known to give rise to severe sulphate attack of concrete ground-floor slabs laid on it.

(e) Cementing agents

Whatever the soluble salt content of the aggregate used, soluble salts may be derived from the cementing agents used. Both lime and Portland cements may be responsible, with their soluble alkali content being important.

(i) *Lime.* Mortars or plasters made with pure high-calcium lime will be practically free from soluble salts. However, limes made by burning limestone containing clay, namely semi-hydraulic and hydraulic lime, usually contain the soluble alkalis of soda and potash. These may appear as efflorescences either as carbonates or sulphates, or a mixture of both. Sulphates will be formed if there is calcium sulphate present. As the amount of soluble alkali increases with the hydraulicity of the lime (roughly proportional to the amount of clay present in the limestone prior to burning), eminently hydraulic limes may contain a maximum of nearly 1·0 per cent of potash and 0·4 per cent of soda, which corresponds to about 2·5 per cent of soluble sulphates.

(ii) *Portland cements.* Although Portland cements contain appreciably less soluble alkali than the maximum found in hydraulic limes, they need special consideration, particularly if the mixing water is allowed to migrate to other building units, from mortar to bricks for example, *before* the cement has set.

In addition to the alkalis of potash and soda Portland cements also contain calcium sulphate which is added in manufacture to control the set of the cement. On being mixed with water, the potash, soda and sulphate go into solution. After a few hours, however, the sulphate is fixed in an insoluble form as calcium sulpho-aluminate, leaving the alkalis as hydroxides, which are gradually converted into carbonates by carbon dioxide in the atmosphere. If the sulphate, however, is removed with the mixing water (usually by capillarity in an adjoining porous building unit), from the environment in which it would normally be rendered insoluble, the quantity of soluble salts in the material into which it has been transferred will be increased.

2. Salts derived from decomposition of a material

Salts derived from this source are usually those which result when a material is exposed after its inclusion in a building and mainly as a result of the effects of a polluted atmosphere. Calcareous sedimentary stones, but mainly the limestones, are the chief sources of salts. Lime leached from concrete may also, under certain conditions (usually implies poor quality concrete) be relevant.

Some of the basic effects of the action of acid gases in the atmosphere (carbon dioxide and sulphur dioxide) on the carbonates of either calcium or magnesium have already been outlined in *Section 3.01,* under 'Weathering, 1. Chemical weathering', Vol. 2, and *Section 3.02* under 'Sulphur dioxide', Vol. 2. For the present purpose, it is considered advisable to discuss, in slightly more detail, the formation of salts which result from the action of carbon dioxide and/or sulphur dioxide in the atmosphere as it applies specifically to calcium and magnesium carbonate in the calcareous sedimentary stones. The chemical reactions described will, in some cases, also be applicable in principle to other materials in which or on which carbonates are present. Concrete is a notable example.

(a) Action of carbon dioxide

Although carbon dioxide is a normal constituent of the atmosphere, the normal proportions may be exceeded particularly in atmospheres polluted as a result of fuel burning. Although only slightly soluble in pure water, calcium carbonate is more readily dissolved in water containing carbon dioxide.

The result of this reaction is the formation of a solution of calcium bicarbonate, which is unstable. Boiling or evaporation of the solution results in calcium carbonate being redeposited. When this happens on the exposed face of a building, the calcareous matter is removed from the stone. Either the calcium carbonate is *carried away* to another part of the building *or* remains behind in the material and will on evaporation of the water, be *deposited* again.

However, it is important to note that, whereas the calcium carbonate in building stones is present in a crystalline form, thus offering a small area to attack, the calcium carbonate redeposited from solution, though probably still crystalline, is usually a finely-divided incoherent powder, thus offering a large area to attack, particularly by sulphur gases. The gradual erosion of stonework by the removal of small quantities of carbonate, as described, cannot normally be regarded as being damaging to the stonework, but the effect of the action of sulphur gases is far more serious.

It may be noted that in the case of concrete, calcium carbonate removed from the surface by the solvent action of carbonic acid, is replaced by diffusion of calcium hydroxide from the interior. Carbon dioxide changes the hydroxide to calcium carbonate. The depth to which the calcium hydroxide is changed depends on the porosity of the concrete, but does not normally exceed 12mm, even for porous concrete.

(b) Action of sulphur dioxide

Sulphur dioxide in the atmosphere may form either sulphurous or sulphuric acid depending on conditions previously described. (See Vol. 2, p. 55). The reaction of sulphurous acid and calcium carbonate results in a relatively insoluble compound, calcium sulphite ($CaSO_3$), which combines with oxygen to form calcium sulphate ($CaSO_4$). Sulphuric acid, being stronger, reacts with the calcium carbonate to form calcium sulphate.

The action of the sulphur gases on the calcium carbonate is, it should be noted, to liberate carbon dioxide, which can react with further quantities of calcium carbonate as already described under (a). In practice it is, of course, difficult to separate the combined effects of both acid gases, as the reactions and processes involved are complex.

When sulphur gases react with *magnesium limestones,* both magnesium and calcium sulphate are formed. Magnesium sulphate, as already noted, in addition to being aggressive is easily dissolved in water and hence readily washed away; calcium sulphate though basically less aggressive, is not as soluble.

3. Salts derived from external sources

In this class some external sources may be difficult to define. In practice each circumstance must be considered on its merits. For the present purposes, external sources are deemed to imply those other than the particular material under consideration. Thus in brickwork, for example, the brick is regarded as the particular material under consideration, so that jointing becomes an external source. There may, of course, be other external sources. Mortar in stonework would also be an external source, although if a backing of brickwork were used, both the bricks and the mortar would constitute an external source, relative to the stone.

External sources may, therefore, be grouped as follows:

(a) jointing materials, (b) backing materials, (c) decomposed materials, (d) the soil and including any hardcore used under paving and ground-floor slabs, (e) the atmosphere, (f) user requirements, and (g) cleansing and other maintenance methods.

(a) Jointing materials

The basic sources of salts in either the aggregate or the cementing agents have already been outlined under '1. Salts originally present in materials, (d) and (e)'. It only remains to discuss the contribution of mortars in *brickwork.* As regards stonework, in which the mortar joint is, in ashlar work at any rate, extremely narrow, the principles are somewhat the same, although staining by the mortar is more usual (see *Section 3.06* later). For convenience a note on 'plasticisers' is added.

In *brickwork* three points arise. *First,* the relative volume of mortar as against that of the bricks, *second,* the contribution of lime as compared to Portland cement and, *third,* the transfer of the mixing water from the mortar to the bricks.

The mortar is usually about one-sixth of the brickwork, while the cementing agents form only one-third

Some examples of soluble salts derived from external sources are given on these pages. In practice, external sources must be considered, at the design stage, in relation to particular circumstances—see text. It should be noted that all the examples are not necessarily conclusive evidence of a particular external source, but are included if only as an analogy of the external source described

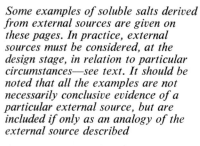

Above right, jointing materials—both lime and Portland cement, particularly the latter, can contribute significantly
Above, backing materials—'It is with stonework that backing materials are chiefly an external source of

soluble salts'. However, soluble salts may manifest themselves on other materials in different ways (below)

In the photograph, below right, it will be seen that the drip cannot cope with water seeping behind the cladding

to one-quarter of the mortar. Taken in isolation, and as described previously, the percentages of soluble alkalies in hydraulic limes and cements are much higher than those usually found in bricks. However, taking the smaller volume of mortar into account, the actual quantity of the more soluble salts introduced into the brickwork by the cementing agents may not, in practice, therefore, greatly exceed that contributed by clay bricks.

In general, limes do not appear to contribute as much to soluble salt content as do the Portland cements. This is probably due to the wide variations in the soluble alkali content of limes in general with non-hydraulic limes in particular rarely contributing to soluble salt content. However, there does seem to have been an increase in efflorescence since the increased use of cement for mortars. In support of this, research in recent years has shown that the amount of efflorescence in brickwork built with any given brick, tends to increase as the proportion of Portland cement increases. This, among other things, further supports the case for using cement : lime : sand mixes that are no stronger than necessary.

Finally, the transfer of mixing water to the bricks by which the sulphate is extracted from its setting environment. This will occur if the bricks are very dry at the time of laying. However, excessive wetting of the bricks prior to laying not only increases the risk of greater efflorescence on drying out but also increases the risk of loss of adhesion between the bricks and the mortar. The right balance must, therefore, be sought. (See *3.04 Exclusion* under 'Joint Design', Vol. 2.)

When considering the use of either sand-lime or concrete bricks (including blocks), the mortar will naturally contribute far more to soluble salt content, as these bricks, particularly sand-limes, do not normally contain any significant amounts of salts themselves.

As mortar *plasticisers* are now often used in Portland cement mortars, it may be noted that there has, as yet, been no evidence to suggest that these contribute significantly to efflorescence. This is probably due to the fact that they are added in such small quantities. As regards undercoats to plaster, it has been found that a plasticised mortar undercoat is more effective than a cement : lime : sand undercoat in preventing salts in the body of the wall from reaching the surface. Although domestic detergents may be effective as mortar plasticisers, they should not be used, as many of them contain sodium sulphate which could contribute to efflorescence.

(b) Backing materials

It is with *stonework* that backing materials are chiefly an external source of soluble salts. In developments of ashlar work, it has become common practice to fix rather thin slabs of stone to either a brick or concrete background, as previously illustrated in

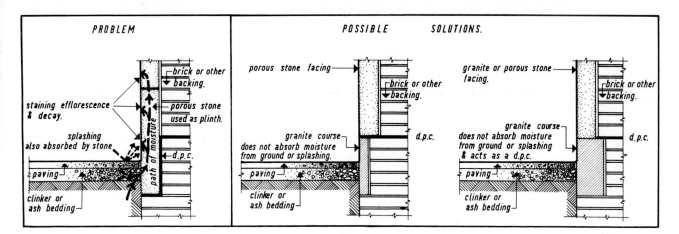

D.3.05/1
Sections through the head of window illustrating the derivation of soluble salts from the concrete lintel

stone facing

cement fillet (cracked)

path of moisture

concrete lintel

efflorescence & decay

efflorescence & dampness

efflorescence & decay

D.3.05/2
Moisture rise and subsequent efflorescence, staining and decay to stone plinth due to soluble salts derived from the soil—see D.3.04/16 under d.p.c.'s (Vol. 2, p. 123)

PROBLEM

POSSIBLE SOLUTIONS.

staining efflorescence & decay.

splashing also absorbed by stone

paving

clinker or ash bedding

brick or other backing.

porous stone used as plinth.

path of moisture

d.p.c.

porous stone facing

granite course does not absorb moisture from ground or splashing.

paving

clinker or ash bedding

brick or other backing.

d.p.c.

granite or porous stone facing.

granite course does not absorb moisture from ground or splashing & acts as a d.p.c.

paving

clinker or ash bedding

brick or other backing.

d.p.c.

principle in diagram D.3.04/6 (Vol. 2). For convenience a section through the head of a window (diagram D.3.05/1) indicating decay by soluble salts derived from a concrete lintel is included here. The possibility of the transference of soluble salts from the backing to the stone is likely when the porous sedimentary stones are used as the facing. With the more impervious types of stone, such as granite, marble or slate, the joints, subject to their composition and porosity, may be affected.

Although the sedimentary stones appear to be the materials most commonly affected by the soluble salt content of backing materials, other porous materials (bricks or tiles or concrete) and some paint films or adhesives may also be affected. In all cases the soluble salt content of the backing can vary between wide limits.

(c) *Decomposed materials*

Decomposition of materials exposed to weathering as described in '2' earlier, can, if the decomposed matter is transferred by rainwater to other materials in the same construction, provide an external source of soluble salts. In brickwork (many Victorian examples are notable) limestone dressings can be significant. Nowadays, lime leached from concrete may also be included.

(d) *The soil*

The reasons for the soluble salt content to be found in soils and in ground water have already been given both in *Section 3.01,* particularly under 'Weathering' (Vol. 2) and *Section 3.02,* under 'Pollution, 2. Ground' (Vol. 2). Suffice it to emphasise here that, in general, the soil provides one of the most prolific external sources of salts, which, among other things, can almost be regarded as perpetual.

Hardcore used under pavings or ground-floor slabs should, if it consists of such materials as ashes, clinker, or colliery shale, be regarded in the same way as soils, particularly in so far as precautions that may be taken to prevent the transference of the soluble salts.

The principles outlined previously in *3.04 Exclusion,* and illustrated in D.3.04/16 (Vol. 2) are applicable. For convenience, another example illustrating moisture rise and subsequent efflorescence, staining or decay as related to stone plinths is included here in diagram D.3.05/2.

(e) *The atmosphere*

Account has already been taken of the effects of the two main acid gases, namely carbon dioxide and sulphur

dioxide, in the atmosphere on calcareous material (see '2' earlier) and the products which result from the action. In addition to these, chlorides and other salts either derived from fuel burning or from sea spray may be significant. It is necessary to note that chlorides have often been found in considerable amounts in areas well away from the sea. Some indication of the distribution of chlorides in country areas well away from large towns, for example, is given in the map in D.3.02/5(4) (Vol. 2), while concentrations in various types of districts are given in the comparative chart, C.3.02/7, Vol. 2). Local measurements or experience may often repay investigation in particular cases, although it may be taken as axiomatic that façades exposed directly to sea spray are potentially vulnerable.

(f) *User requirements*

Many industrial processes may be potential sources of salts which could be transferred to porous materials in solution or with the water vapour in the atmosphere. As regards the latter, there would appear to be greater risk, if there is a possibility of the polluted water vapour condensing within the thickness of a construction. Industrial processes which are likely to become potential sources of soluble salts are

Decomposed material: limestone dressings often decompose when exposed to the weather; the decomposed matter may then be transferred to other adjacent materials. Decomposed matter, as lime from cement-based materials, may be similarly transferred.

The photographs above show decomposed matter from limestone dressings causing disfiguration. Below left, disfiguration and decay of brickwork from decomposed matter from limestone dressings. Below, lime washing from new reconstructed stone coping. The

two bottom pictures show lime washing from cement-based products. Both were taken within one year after completion of respective buildings

Right, user requirements. Wastes provide potential sources of soluble salts which usually manifest themselves when leaks occur

both numerous and variable. It is, therefore, important that each case is considered on its merits. In addition to industrial processes the chemical nature of any materials which may be stored in buildings of any kind should be taken into account. Fertilizers, among other materials, are potential sources of soluble salts.

A rather fortuitous, yet in certain cases, a rather significant source of soluble salts, applicable to *all types of buildings,* is leakage from waste pipes, particularly those from kitchen sinks. Leakage from services was also discussed in *3.02 Exposure,* 'Sources, 6. Faulty services' (Vol. 2) and 'Pollution, 5. Processes and cleansing agents' (Vol. 2).

The soil: the examples given above and below show the results of the failure to provide an impervious stone in contact with the ground (see Vol. 2, diagram D.3.04/16). In the bottom picture some decay of the limestone has taken place (decay first observed about three years after completion)

(g) *Cleansing and other maintenance methods*
Certain chemical compositions used for daily or regular cleansing of buildings or during maintenance may constitute accidental sources of soluble salts. In the case of stone, the BRS has drawn attention to 'even purposeful (though misguided) contamination of stone' through the use of certain detergents for cleaning or 'preservatives' for preservation.

Right, the results of 'soil' collecting around a rainwater drain

Among cleansing agents which should be regarded as potential sources of soluble salts or decay are caustic soda, washing soda, soda ash, household scouring powders and some of the modern organic detergents. The latter contain a high proportion of sodium sulphate. However, it may be noted that there are also some detergents which consist solely of organic compounds and are free from sodium sulphate or other inorganic salt. Although there is no reason to suppose that these will have any detrimental effect, there is reason to believe that, in the case of stonework, organic detergents may not assist in the cleaning process very materially.

Two examples of efflorescences which have only occurred below the surface (of a limestone in both cases) and are visible because the surface layers of the stone have exfoliated

physical processes

The formation of efflorescence depends on a number of physical processes involving both the salts and water transfer in and out of the porous materials concerned. Specific conditions may dictate the extent to which any of the many processes involved may take place. Thus efflorescence can be a baffling phenomenon. However, an understanding of the various physical processes involved should help to overcome most of the apparent anomalies.

Some of the basic characteristics of solutions and salts have been outlined in *Sections 1.06* and *1.10* (Vol. 1), while the relevant outline of water transfer was discussed in *3.03 Moisture content* (Vol. 2). The nature and sources of salts have been included in previous parts of this section. The aim here is, therefore, to bring together, so to speak, all the various aspects previously discussed in general terms, and apply these specifically to the physical processes involved in the formation of efflorescence. Chemical effects are dealt with in detail in *Section 3.06*.

As a point of departure, brickwork is used as the porous material. The principles applicable to brickwork can generally be applied to other porous materials—some detailed differences may, however, be significant. In order to aid understanding, some basic characteristics, such as pore size and distribution for example, are related to other porous materials.

For the purposes of explanation the effects of the different factors involved are dealt with separately. In practice, of course, these are interrelated to

some extent, thus creating a rather complex 'mechanism'.

1. The effects of solubility

A solution of a soluble salt in water is an example of a solution of a solid in a liquid. Saturation of the solution occurs when no more salt can be dissolved in the water. Factors which limit the weight of a given salt that can be dissolved in a fixed weight of water are the properties of the salt (variable) and temperature (variable). Although there are exceptions, warm water will usually dissolve more of a salt than cold water. As an example consider sodium sulphate. One hundred parts of water will dissolve nine parts of sodium sulphate crystals at 10°C and 19·4 parts at 20°C. Once saturated, cooling of a given solution will result in some of the salt separating out in solid form. On the other hand, without any change in temperature, loss of water through evaporation will result in some of the salt being deposited.

Whether or not a porous material is likely to have salts deposited when it *begins* to dry out will depend on whether the salts it contains are either saturated or near to saturation before drying out commences. For example, if a brick, containing only a fraction of 1 per cent of sodium sulphate, absorbs say 25 per cent of water, the relationship between the amount of sodium sulphate and water is insufficient to cause a saturated solution. In effect, there is too much water present and consequently there is no reason why any salt should come out as an efflorescence when the bricks start to dry. (Some salt could eventually be deposited if water continued to evaporate from the solution after saturation had been reached.) On the other hand, if a second brick, containing the same amount of salt as the first, only absorbs 2 per cent of water, the solution would be nearer saturation and efflorescence would be more likely to appear on drying out. In the last case, efflorescence may also appear if, instead of drying out, there is a drop of a few degrees in temperature. In this, the difference in temperature as between summer and winter is notable.

2. The effects of pore structure

The pore structure of the porous material containing a saturated solution will influence drying out and the position in which salts may be deposited on evaporation of the water. Evaporation of water can only take place when a free water surface is presented to an environment in which evaporation can take place.

For purposes of explanation two distinctly different types of pore structure, namely, fine-pored and coarse-pored, are considered. In the case of the fine-pored structure (close-textured brick), capillary forces will tend to draw the solution so that the free water surfaces in the pores are near the face exposed to the evaporating environment. Visible deposits of salt

crystals will take place as evaporation, and thus crystallisation, will tend to occur at the exposed face. With a coarse-pored structure (open-textured brick), the larger dimensions of the pores will cause the free water surfaces to fall below the exposed surface. Nevertheless evaporation by diffusion and by pore ventilation could take place, resulting in crystallisation occurring below the exposed surface, i.e. crypto-florescence. Although the pore structure of a material as a whole will influence the rate of water transfer (fast with fine pores and slower with coarse pores) the pore structure at the surface is particularly significant as regards the position in which salts will be deposited. Some apparent anomalies may now be explained. Efflorescence tends to appear more readily on many dense bricks (facings are notable) than on common bricks, mainly because the former are fine-pored and the latter coarse-pored. Sometimes, however, efflorescence may only appear on certain areas of materials. This may be explained by the fact that these areas are probably finer-pored than the remainder in the material. Thus, in addition to the factors already outlined, the salt solution would be drawn to the finer-pored areas, due to the stronger capillary action which they are capable of exerting. *Distempers* give a very fine-pored surface which promotes efflorescence. It is sometimes found that, if interior brickwork is partly distempered and partly left bare, efflorescence forms on the distempered surface only.

The manner in which pore structure may be distributed in various parts of the same unit of material, different units of the same material or different materials used in a composite construction, will also influence, other things being equal, the position in which salts may be deposited. Mortar and bricks provide a good example for explanation. If either the *mortar* or the *pointing* (the latter is extremely significant as it represents the drying surface) is dense, drying out at the mortar joints will either be prevented or restricted. Drying out of the wall, therefore, takes place mostly through the bricks. Consequently soluble salts will tend to concentrate on the bricks. The lessons to be learnt from this are two-fold. *First,* pointing should not be denser than the mortar and, *second,* the mortar should, ideally, match the porosity of the units it is joining. This is yet another reason for avoiding, wherever possible, the use of mortars which are stronger than the units being joined. It should be noted that, where the building unit is impermeable, salts may be deposited on the mortar joint if this is porous and permeable.

3. The effect of crystal form of the salts

The readiness with which efflorescence forms depends on the shape of the crystals of the salt or mixture of salts that is deposited from solution. If the first small crystals that form in the surface pores are deposited in such a pattern that still finer capillary passages are left between them through which solution can be drawn, then new crystals can form on top of the old. Salts will, however, be discouraged from growing outwards, if the angles between the faces of the salt crystals are such that adjacent crystals fit together and leave no spaces.

Although this complex and difficult field has not been fully explored, it is known that sodium sulphate forms efflorescences much more readily than potassium sulphate. The latter may be more readily formed in the presence of other salts, while even small amounts of sodium sulphate will effloresce readily. Magnesium sulphate also effloresces almost as readily as sodium sulphate.

4. The effect of hygroscopicity of salts

The alkalis (sodium hydroxide and potassium hydroxide) left in solution when Portland cement is mixed with water are not so likely to form efflorescence because they are hygroscopic. Their greater affinity for water means that they can pick up water from the air. Consequently they are unlikely to be dried to the point of appearing as efflorescence at normal outdoor temperature. However, after carbonation, sodium carbonate may appear in efflorescences, but even this is generally unlikely, as it is usually mixed with potassium carbonate which is also hygroscopic.

5. Effect of precipitation

Although slightly outside the scope of the present discussion, it may be noted here that staining on plaster caused by soluble iron salts in the bricks does not take place if the iron is precipitated. Undercoats containing lime and/or Portland cement precipitate the iron and do not allow it to pass through to the surface with any water there may be in the wall as the latter dries. The same is not, however, true of gypsum plasters, as these do not have alkaline constituents capable of precipitating the iron. In addition the pore structure of gypsum plasters favours the passage of salts to the surface.

6. The effect of the distribution of salts in a material

Analyses of salt content are more commonly, though not entirely, carried out on bricks rather than other porous materials. Such analyses usually report on the amount of salt present in an average sample of powder obtained by taking drillings from a number of bricks, or by crushing pieces cut from them. Such analyses are adequate for most purposes, particularly as with most, though not all, bricks, the salts are fairly uniformly distributed. Nevertheless it is the exceptions which prove the rule, and sometimes salts may be concentrated close to the surface. In cases such as these, an average analysis would not show the quantity of salts that is *readily* available to form efflorescences.

Bricks likely to have high concen-trations of salts near the surface are usually those made from a white—or yellow—burning calcareous clay. Even with bricks made from this type of clay only those (usually only a few anyway) fired near the grates or charging shafts of a kiln, where they may absorb sulphur gases from the burning coal, are likely to be affected.

7. The effects of the transfer of water in a material

Although pore structure, including the manner in which the pores are distributed in a material, influence the manner in which, or the rate at which, water is transferred in and out of a porous material, a discussion of some of the basic principles of the transfer of water without referring to the precise pore structure, can explain the reasons why efflorescence is so common in new work and also why it may recur. Account must, of course, also be taken of the other factors which have already been outlined. For the present purposes a brick wall is considered, but reference is also made, for convenience to 'special' effects of the wetting and drying cycle on roofing tiles and sandstones.

(a) *Absorption during laying*

Efflorescence which forms round the edges of bricks, suggests that, during laying, the brick has absorbed water from a mortar containing Portland cement, thus also absorbing alkali sulphates before they can be converted into insoluble compounds as previously explained (see 'Sources of salts, 1 (b) (ii) Portland cement', p. 7).

(b) *Exposure to rainwater*

Assuming there has been no absorption of water from a Portland cement-based mortar by the bricks during actual laying, the alkali sulphates may still be transferred to the bricks, if an unfinished wall is left uncovered during heavy rain. Rain water filtering down through the top of the wall will effect the transfer. 'Evidence' of heavy rain on an unprotected wall may be recognised, many weeks later, by a band of efflorescence on the affected courses.

(c) *Construction water*

Apart from local saturation as described in (b) above, sufficient water may be introduced during construction (see particularly *3.02 Exposure,* 'Sources of water, 3. During construction', Vol. 2) to bring out an efflorescence. Initially the water is uniformly distributed through the wall. Drying out, however, takes place mainly through the most favourably exposed face. (This is usually the external face, but it may, sometimes, be the internal face.) Consequently there is a general movement of water, carrying in solution (not necessarily saturated) any salts that may be present, towards the exposed face of the wall. This explains why efflorescence is most likely to occur during the early life of a building.

Variations in the pore-structure of materials (*individual units, the jointing medium or an element as a whole*) often accounts for the rather 'haphazard' distribution of efflorescence as suggested in these three examples. The appearance of efflorescence on certain areas of the surface may be explained by the fact that these areas are probably finer-pored than the remainder of the material

Above, another example of the 'haphazard' distribution of efflorescence

Examples which suggest that the unfinished wall was left uncovered during heavy rain

(d) *Wetting and drying cycles*

The fact that deposits of salts have disappeared from the surface of a wall does not necessarily mean that they have been washed away by rain (some may have been removed by wind), but rather that they have been washed back into the wall where they may remain or from which they may be subsequently (usually months after being absorbed by the wall) 'extracted' to reappear as efflorescence.

Rain falling on a wall covered with efflorescence soon dissolves the soluble salts which will be reabsorbed into the wall. The dissolved salts will continue to penetrate further into the wall as long as the rain persists. However, whereas the initial solution of dissolved salts will be highly concentrated, subsequent solutions which are absorbed by the wall will have progressively lower concentrations of salt. As the rainwater continues to flow over the exposed surface of the wall, there is less salt for it to dissolve. Consequently a stage is reached, probably soon after the initial fall of rain, when the salt solution is followed by 'pure' rainwater. (The term 'pure' is used in a relative sense to differentiate it from the salt solution. It is more conveniently referred to hereafter as water.) In the narrow pores of the bricks, mixing of the salt solution and the water that follows it will be very slow. Once the rain has ceased and the wall commences to dry out, it is quite probable that drying will reach the stage where the surface pores, which contained the water rather than the solution, are empty before any salts have been brought back near the surface. This produces a state of equilibrium in which the washing of salts into the wall by rain normally compensates for any tendency that they may have to come out again in dry weather.

The fact that efflorescence may reappear in the second spring of a building's life may be explained partly by two factors which favour efflorescence, namely the lower temperature and slower evaporation of springtime as compared with summer and partly by a disturbance of the equilibrium already described. Disturbance of the equilibrium can occur during the winter, when the surface of wall may remain wet for long enough to allow any salts previously washed into the wall to diffuse back towards the surface. Fortunately any efflorescence formed during the second spring will be less prominent than the first outbreak. This is due to the fact that the wall will usually be drier, and consequently there is less water in it to move towards the surface carrying salts with it.

Clay roofing tiles present a special problem. In a tiled roof, for example, the tail ends are exposed (wet) while the heads, which are fixed to the roof structure, are sheltered (dry). Consequently there is a tendency for water to creep up the tiles and evaporate at the heads. Salts will gradually be transferred to the heads where they crystallise out.

Some kinds of *sandstones* (occasionally the less durable limestones) develop what has been termed 'contour scaling'—face of the stone breaks away at a depth of maybe 6mm or more, following the contours of the surface, plane or curved, in sills, mouldings and the like. This is attributed to repeated wetting and drying of the stone by rain, known as the 'moisture rhythm' in which soluble matter is transferred from the body of the stone to its surface. During the process the exposed surfaces remain outwardly sound whilst a narrow zone at a more or less uniform distance behind the face becomes soft and friable, until the face eventually breaks off.

This form of weathering is explained as follows: Rainwater falling on the surface penetrates to a limited, but more or less constant depth. A small fraction of the constituents of the stone within the depth of penetration is dissolved by the rainwater. Any soluble matter in solution is deposited at or near the evaporating surfaces as the stone dries out. Repetition of the cycle tends to consolidate the outer zone at the expense of cementitious matter in the underlying zone, which eventually loses cohesion. Although even silica can be dissolved and transported as described, calcium sulphate, which is commonly present in the scales and in the friable zone, also plays a part. The presence of calcium sulphate, even when there are no obvious external sources, underlines the importance of decomposition of materials due to the action of acid gases in the atmosphere.

precautions

As far as efflorescence itself is concerned, it is, in the light of the factors outlined in the preceding parts of this section, foolhardy to suggest that it is possible in practice, even with the greatest care, to prevent the formation of efflorescence completely. The same is true of the chemical actions of some of the soluble salts. However, it is possible to reduce either the amounts of deposit or the effects of soluble salts by taking various precautions. Many of these should in many cases be taken for other reasons. Among the latter are those concerned with movements due to changes in moisture contents (*3.03 Moisture content*); corrosion of metals (*Section 3.07*); frost action (*Section 3.08*); and thermal properties. As in all building work the inter-relationship, perhaps better interaction, of what may appear to be isolated or self-contained aspects cannot normally be overlooked.

At the risk of oversimplification it may be fair to say that, other things being equal, prevention of materials or parts of structure remaining damp for excessively long periods of time is probably the most useful point to bear in mind. However, in the context of the present problem, precautions applicable to porous materials in general may be related to five aspects, namely (1) the selection of material; (2)

details of design; (3) handling, storage and protection of materials (site important); (4) drying out of materials; *and* (5) removal of efflorescence.* Each aspect is considered separately, but, as most of the reasons for the formation of efflorescence and the behaviour of salts have already been outlined in the preceding parts, only the main points which should be taken into account are noted. The relevance of these to specific materials is, however, also noted, as not all the points are necessarily applicable to all materials or forms of construction either in degree or in kind.

1. Selection of materials

Care in the selection of materials regarding either their soluble salt content or their liability to form efflorescence should in the first instance be concerned with all the component parts of a construction. Thus in brickwork, for example, both the bricks and the mortar need consideration; as regards the mortar (plaster, renders or concretes are also relevant) the aggregates, cementing agents and the water must be included.

The choice of suitable materials for a particular condition must take into account conditions of exposure. Once this has been established, either by measurement or experience, the limits of soluble salt content or liability to effloresce may be established. This is particularly true of *clay bricks* which would in any case contain some salts. Under severe conditions of exposure, materials with a high soluble-salts content should be avoided. In this context, the amounts of magnesium sulphate, particularly in some types of clay bricks, are significant.

Most useful information on the performance of particular materials under particular conditions (both are important) may be obtained by careful inquiry. Evidence of quality should be obtained from either manufacturers or suppliers. In the case of bricks and stone their reputation in the district from which they originate or in which they are predominantly used may prove to be useful sources of information. However, account should be taken of any probable effects of changes in environment or methods of use. In the case of clay bricks, Bonnell, D. R. G. and Butterworth, B., *Clay bricks of the United Kingdom*, National Brick Advisory Council Paper Five, HMSO, 1950, is an invaluable reference. Some manufacturers may have a Building Research Station report on their bricks. In some cases it may be necessary to require tests. These should be undertaken in accordance with British Standard procedure. (The

*It is perhaps axiomatic that only those porous materials which are permeable need to be taken into consideration. However, account must be taken of the characteristics of each component making up any particular element. It is also important to remember that materials like dense concrete, for example, although basically impermeable may become permeable in localised zones—cracks through the material are important in this respect.

introduction of the new standard—Reference (1), article 62—may cause a little confusion for a while.)

As regards the *sedimentary stones* it is useful to note that, in general, most of these are unlikely to contain significant, if any, soluble salts. Some types, but particularly some qualities, may be the exception. With *limestones,* their susceptibility to deterioration due to crystallisation of soluble salts is the property which is most important in distinguishing a durable stone.

Specification of *mortar* mixes requires care. Their most important property is that they should be the weakest that conditions allow. In this, account should be taken of the fact that mortars containing high-calcium limes are unlikely to contribute to soluble salt content of a construction. The soluble salt content is, however, likely to rise as the hydraulicity of the lime increases, but more important, Portland cement in the mortar is likely to be the most significant contributor of soluble salts. Similar considerations are required with plaster and renders. Tests of various mortar mixes for their liability to cause efflorescence or staining may often be advisable with stonework.

2. Details of design

Details of design are primarily concerned with methods which aim to exclude as much water as possible (d.p.c.'s and other water excluding features are significant). However, an equally important consideration is the relationship of different materials in the same construction.

As regards exclusion of water, special care is required with those parts which are likely to be more heavily exposed than others. It is important that the body of a construction is prevented from becoming saturated by water percolating through horizontal features. Parapets are notable as points of entry. Accordingly these should incorporate appropriate d.p.c.'s or flashings. Other projecting horizontal surfaces may require weatherings and flashings, while even rainwater outlets require suitable detailing. It is probably axiomatic that care in the design of d.p.c.'s and d.p.m.'s in walls and floors is necessary so as to limit the rise of salts from the soil to a predetermined (i.e. designed) level.

It is always as well to remember the weakness of joints between units. These are as has been illustrated in Vol. 2, *Section 3.01,* General considerations and *3.04 Exclusion* under d.p.c.'s, notorious as entry points for water into the body of a construction. With large masses of materials (concrete is notable) cracks which may develop may become troublesome.

The relationship of different materials in the same construction may occur in basically two different ways, namely when one is used as a backing for the other or where they are combined in the same façade in juxtaposition or at different levels.

15

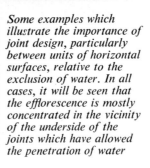

Some examples which illustrate the importance of joint design, particularly between units of horizontal surfaces, relative to the exclusion of water. In all cases, it will be seen that the efflorescence is mostly concentrated in the vicinity of the underside of the joints which have allowed the penetration of water

Problems with backing materials occur mainly, though not entirely, with *sedimentary stones*. A common practice is to coat either the surface of the backing material or the concealed surface of the stone or both with a waterproofing compound. Although generally successful, it should be noted that water and hence salts (or other matter) may penetrate at the joints. A similar consideration needs to be applied to impermeable units having porous, permeable joints. Limestone or cast stone dressings, string courses and the like, used with certain types of clay bricks (usually the soft porous varieties) should be avoided, unless experience has shown that the bricks are resistant to damage from crystallisation. However, it should be noted that changes in appearance, rather than damage as such, from lime washings can also take place on other materials.

3. Handling, storage and protection of materials

Contamination of materials can take place very easily either during handling or storage particularly on a building site, although the works or the yards of manufacturers and builders' merchants cannot be exempt. Care should always be taken to ensure that incompatible materials are not stored in contact with one another, particularly under damp conditions. In general, materials should not be stacked or stored in contact with the ground. Some form of raised platform of d.p.m. material (polythene sheet has proved invaluable for this purpose) should preferably be used.

Materials should be protected from becoming saturated by rainwater while stacked or stored on the site and when they have been incorporated in a construction. Some illustrated examples of protection are given in *3.03 Moisture content* (Vol. 2, pp. 85-89).

4. Drying out

Some applications, such as adhesives and paints, cannot be successfully applied either on damp surfaces or on surfaces which have deposits of soluble salts. The latter should always be removed (see '5. Removal of efflorescence') prior to the use of applications which rely on adhesion (see *Section 1.11*, Vol. 1). Apparently dry surfaces should be checked. (See *3.01* General considerations under 'Dampness', Vol. 2, pp. 14-16). If there is still sufficient water left in the body of the construction, efflorescence may still form. But the salts are likely to be deposited under the adhesive or paint film causing loss of adhesion. On the other hand, salts in solution may attack the film. Some paints, for example, are particularly susceptible to alkaline attack—the alkalis usually derived from damp backgrounds containing Portland cement. Although

some compositions are more resistant than others, the degree of dampness of the background is nevertheless important. (See *Section 3.06 for* detailed discussion.)

It may be noted here that distemper applied to a damp wall may tend to encourage efflorescence in a new building. This is due to the fine-pore structure of the distemper which promotes efflorescence.

5. Removal of efflorescence

In general, it may be assumed that any surface treatments aimed at suppressing evaporation are more likely to force crystallisation to take place below the surface and so cause decay. They may be more harmful than if the surface had not been treated at all. It has been said* that there is no chemical treatment that can be recommended to neutralise or destroy efflorescence. Recently, a spirit-based solution† which penetrates 100–150mm into a structure and is said to neutralise the salts present by vaporising them, has been made available. It is claimed to be 'the only known cure for efflorescence' and does not apparently interrupt the natural migration of moisture. The efficacy of this solution has not yet been 'officially' established.

Unless efflorescence has been derived from external sources (the cure then usually relies on correcting design faults), it is probably unnecessary in most cases (except the application of adhesives, paints, plasters, etc.) to try and remove the deposits of salts. Externally these should eventually disappear as previously described. However, areas sheltered from rain may need special attention. If, in these or any other areas, it is required to remove the efflorescence, then the following basic methods should be adopted: The efflorescence should first be brushed away and then the surface should be washed with *clean* water. The precise procedure followed may vary for individual materials. If efflorescence reappears after this treatment, as it may well do if some of the salts have been driven back into the material, then the brushing‡ and washing procedure should be repeated until the deposits of salts ceases.

The care which should be exercised in the *cleaning of stonework* may be noted here. In addition to the normal soot and grime deposits found on many stone buildings in polluted atmospheres, the sedimentary stones (limestones are usually notable) may have areas of a hard impervious skin (usually forms in sheltered areas). This skin on the stone, particularly when it

*Butterworth, reference 3, p. 4

†'Efforless', Brearly Concrete Units Ltd.

‡Any brushing of the salt deposits should always be undertaken with care, so as to avoid any damage to the surface of the material on which the deposit has occurred.

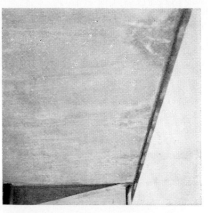

The photograph above shows the soffit of a concrete balcony slab and the efflorescence which has occurred, mainly at the forward edge, at construction joints. Below, the junction of the same slab and a balustrade pipe, at which considerable leakage of water has occurred

is covered with soot or grime (as often happens), increases the difficulties of cleaning and sometimes encourages methods (use of chemicals and detergents notable) which are likely to do more harm than good to the stone after it has been cleaned. As already noted earlier efflorescence or staining may result. However laborious the process may be, the use of clean water either as steam or water spray is still regarded as the most effective method of cleaning stonework. Because of the solubility of the encrusted zones (usually calcium sulphate or calcium carbonate) water soon softens the deposits sufficiently for removal by light brushing. Vigorous brushing of delicate mouldings can be damaging. Effective cleaning of stonework is a specialised job and should, therefore, only be undertaken by established firms who specialise in the cleaning of buildings. Their experience will enable them to use methods which will not be detrimental to the stone. Above all, most experienced firms are prepared to guarantee that no caustic soda, soda ash or other harmful chemical will be used.

C

3.06 chemical attack

In general terms, almost all materials for building may be subjected to chemical action of one kind or another during the life of a building, but as usual in building practice the degree of the action which may take place is always significant. In the present context 'chemical attack' is taken to mean chemical actions which have deleterious effects on materials. The range of what may be termed the sources of attack, together with the concentration of the chemicals involved and associated 'favourable' conditions (the amount of water present is usually significant) are extremely variable, while the resistance which any given material may provide to a given form of attack is also extremely variable. Among other things, variations in the physical and chemical properties of materials of a similar kind, so far as use is concerned, are significant, while the rate of chemical attack may be considerably increased if defects due to physical causes, such as frost action, for example, take place, either before or after the chemical attack. At the same time, a distinction has to be drawn between the common sources of chemicals which may have deleterious effects on buildings in general and between, what may best be termed, specialised sources of chemicals which arise out of particular user requirements. As regards the latter, chemical factories present an extreme case, but other industrial types may be significant, while localised parts of buildings of all kinds may provide sources of chemicals in sufficient quantities to make them potentially aggressive. In cases such as these, materials must be extremely carefully selected with special regard paid to their durability in respect of the particular chemical(s) which may be involved.*

For the present purposes, the special conditions which arise out of particular user requirements are excluded, in so far as detailed considerations are concerned, and emphasis is placed on

the nature and effects of chemical attack which are commonly associated with buildings in general, and more particularly with certain commonly used porous materials. Chemical attack on metals is more conveniently dealt with separately in *3.07 Corrosion of metals,* later.

At this stage it is important to draw a distinction between the *basic* difference in chemical attack of porous materials and non-porous materials. In the case of the latter, chemical attack is confined to the surfaces of the material. Attack may, in due course, proceed into the interior, but the important point is that it commences at the surface. In general terms, this means that only the surfaces of non-porous materials need to be considered particularly in relation to any protective measures which may be taken to prevent attack from taking place. The range of surface ('sacrificial') coatings available for metalwork, for example, may help to illustrate this point. With the porous materials, attack may also take place at the surface, but, subject to the permeability of the material involved, it may, in addition, take place in the interior of the material. Whereas with the non-porous materials the sources of chemicals are external to the material, with porous materials the sources of chemicals may be either external to the material or actually contained within it. As in nearly all cases of chemical attack, and in particular those discussed in this section and *Section 3.07,* the presence of water is necessary, the porous materials may aid chemical attack through the transference of chemicals in solution in and about a construction. Consequently with porous materials prevention of chemical attack does not necessarily imply the use of protective coatings (in some cases they may be invaluable). Instead full account must be taken of the porosity of any given material, including degree of permeability, ease of transference of moisture, and wetting and drying cycles.

In nearly all cases *prolonged* wetting of porous materials accounts for most of the failures which are commonly encountered. Furthermore,

a significant number of failures can be attributed to insufficient regard having been given to the precautions necessary to exclude water, particularly the correct use of d.p.c.'s, as outlined in *3.04 Exclusion* (Vol. 2). It is perhaps axiomatic that under dry conditions actions, and hence chemical attack, cannot take place, However, it is normally impossible to ensure that the exposed parts of the external fabric of a building, for example, are always completely dry. Consequently, cognisance must be taken of the fact that chemical reactions do not necessarily take place instantaneously, while the rate at which reactions proceed is governed (see *1.09 Chemical conventions* under 'Chemical equations', Vol. 1) not only by the concentration of the chemicals involved (their continued 'supply' is significant too) but also by the length of time of contact. In terms of building, chemical reactions having deleterious results, that is, resulting in chemical attack, generally take place comparatively slowly. Thus, other things being equal, relatively short periods of wetness generally have little material effect in so far as chemical attack is concerned.

The porous materials most commonly affected by chemical attack include clay bricks, stones, cement-based products (concrete, plasters, renders, mortars, asbestos-cement, etc.), paint and timber. The types of attack which may take place are not strictly related to one another, while some of the materials mentioned are more susceptible than others. In the case of timber only fungal attack is significant. It is, therefore, more convenient to discuss separately the various types of attack together with the relevant precautionary measures which may be taken to prevent attack. The following general headings are used: (1) unsound materials; (2) acid action; (3) alkali action; (4) sulphate attack; and (5) fungal attack in timber.

unsound materials*

The use of the term 'unsound' in the present context relates specifically to those materials which are unstable

---

*Certain cleansing agents used in maintenance work may have deleterious effects on certain materials. The choice of cleansing agents may, therefore, be important in the maintenance of particular materials.

when exposed to damp or humid atmospheric conditions. The defects which arise when such materials are exposed, and included here, are due to expansion that accompanies the chemical reaction when an expansive particle and moisture combine. The fact that both must be present for a defect to occur is important when considering either prevention or cure. The defects which do occur are mainly, though not entirely, associated with unslaked lime (quicklime, i.e. calcium oxide) used in plaster or mortars or found in some clay bricks. Other materials which may be unsound include sand (may contain certain impurities) but more particularly ashes and clinker used either for mortars or for making clinker concrete which may contain unburnt particles of coal or other impurities. The effects of these impurities, together with others which may be derived from failure to ensure cleanliness of all materials used, are similar to those produced by quicklime.

For convenience, emphasis is being placed here on the delayed hydration of quicklime, as it is probably the more common cause of failures, but brief references, however, made to other factors are relevant. The main headings used are: (1) basic mechanisms (of the delayed hydration of quicklime); (2) plasters and mortars; and (3) bricks.

1. Basic mechanisms

Lime used in building practice is derived essentially from calcium carbonate ($CaCO_3$)—either limestone or chalk may be the raw material—which is calcined to produce calcium oxide (CaO), commonly known as quicklime. During calcination the following chemical reaction takes place:

$$CaCO_3 \rightarrow CaO + CO_2$$

(calcium carbonate) → (calcium oxide) + (carbon
quicklime   dioxide)

Before the quicklime can be used it must first be slaked (a process of hydration) to produce calcium hydroxide ($Ca(OH)_2$) as follows:

$$CaO + H_2O \rightleftharpoons Ca(OH)_2$$

(calcium oxide) + (water) ⇌ (calcium hydroxide)
quicklime

Within the present context the calcium hydroxide is the sound material, while the quicklime the unsound material. During the slaking process, expansion takes place in addition to the evolution of heat.

In use, if slaked lime contains particles of quicklime, and if those particles are able to hydrate in the set or solid material containing them, the resultant expansion may cause defects. Generally speaking, delayed hydration of quicklime in materials in the plastic

*References
(1) *Blowing, Popping or Pitting of Internal Plaster*, BRS Digest (1st Series) No. 26, HMSO, January, 1951. (2) *Some Common Defects in Brickwork*, National Building Studies, Bulletin No. 9, HMSO, 1950. (3) *Sands for Plasters, Mortars and Renderings*, Ministry of Works Advisory Leaflet No. 15, HMSO, 1960. (4) Butterworth, B., *Efflorescence and Staining of Brickwork*. Reprint from *The Brick Bulletin*, amended December, 1962, published by the National Federation of Clay Industries.

state is unlikely to be deleterious, as the expansion can be accommodated before the material sets or hardens. It may be noted here that delayed hydration of quicklime can, and does, take place with moisture absorbed from the atmosphere. This type of slaking is known as 'air-slaking'. Generally, there is greater danger of deleterious effects of expansion caused by air slaking than by immersion.

2. Plasters and mortars

Although the manifestations of defects due to the presence of unsound materials are not the same in plasters and mortars, it is convenient to group them together as they share some of the basic causes of defects, chief of which is the delayed hydration of quicklime.

(a) *Slaking of quicklime*

Quicklime may be run to a putty in a pit or container. This is an operation commonly carried out on a building site. On the other hand, the quicklime may be treated by a steaming process in a factory in which case a dry-hydrated lime is made available ready for use. In general, the latter is less likely to result in defects due to the delayed hydration of quicklime.

Amongst *precautions* which should be taken to minimise the risk of subsequent expansion of quicklime is the avoidance of the use of the bottom layer of material in the pit in which quicklime has been run to a putty. This layer of material contains the larger particles which are most likely to be unsound. When dry-hydrated lime is used it is still recommended that it should be soaked overnight before use. The main object of the soaking treatment is to improve the working properties of the lime, but there is the added advantage that the soaking will reduce the possibility of the expansion of any un-hydrated particles which may be present.

(b) *Impurities in aggregates*

Sand may contain coal dust from soft lignite and some bituminous coals, or iron pyrites, both of which may oxidise. The oxidation results in expansion.

Ashes and clinker may contain unburnt particles or calcium oxide, both of which may lead to expansion when moisture is absorbed. Plaster failures have in some cases been traced to the presence of calcium oxide in the clinker used either in concrete blocks or *in situ* concrete over which the plaster was applied.

Dirt, dust and other impurities which may be present due to failure to ensure cleanliness may also result in expansions large enough to cause failures.

(c) *Manifestations of defects: Plasters*

The terms 'blowing', 'popping' and 'pitting' are used when describing the appearance of a particular type of

defect in an internal plaster finish due to the delayed hydration of quicklime, but see (d) later for the effects of magnesium sulphate. Conical holes usually appear in the finished work, varying in diameter according to the position in which the material responsible for the defect occurs. When the material responsible for the defect is confined to the finishing coat, the individual blemishes are usually not larger than 13mm in diameter, often considerably less, but these may increase to as much as 50–75mm if unsound material occurs in the undercoat. The formation of the conical holes invariably follows the following sequence of events: a bulge first appears on the plaster face, a fine crack tending to be circular in form then develops, the plaster inside the circle lifts, and finally drops out leaving the conical hole.

(d) *Manifestations of defects: Mortars*

Defects may show one or more of the following symptoms:
(i) Small pits, with nodules of friable material at their bases, form in the mortar joint.
(ii) Strong pointing mortars are displaced, and pits develop in the weaker bedding-mortar.
(iii) General expansion occurs, with deformation and consequent cracking of the brickwork, accompanied by disintegration of the mortar. This effect is similar to that caused by sulphate attack.

(e) *Presence of magnesium sulphate*

A type of failure which is associated with lime-based, i.e. alkaline, plasters (neutral or acid plasters, such as calcium sulphate, are not affected) and which, fortunately, does not often occur, is the loss of adhesion of plaster due to the formation of needle-like crystals of magnesium sulphate *below* the surface of the plaster. The formation of the crystals is associated with efflorescence, but the reason why the efflorescence occurs below the surface is attributed to the reaction of magnesium sulphate and the calcium hydroxide in the wet plaster. The explanation for this may be summarised as follows:

Magnesium sulphate in the bricks over which the lime-based plaster is applied dissolves in the water introduced during construction, and reacts chemically with slaked lime (calcium hydroxide) from the plaster, forming a gelatinous deposit of magnesium hydroxide:

$$MgSO_4 + Ca(OH)_2 \rightarrow CaSO_4 + Mg(OH)_2$$

The deposit forms below the surface of the brick because the surface pores of the latter are impregnated with lime during the application of the plaster. In addition, the deposit acts as a semi-permeable membrane, and so water can get through, but not the salts. As the wall dries out, the salt accumulates against the membrane.

Blowing in a finishing coat of plaster (Courtesy: BRS, HMSO: Crown Copyright). Scale: ¾ full size

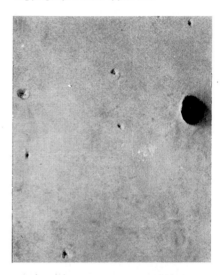

Blowing of plaster caused by unsound material in the background. Below, crystallisation of magnesium sulphate behind plaster (both photographs are Crown Copyright)

The reason why the same type of failure does not occur with neutral or acid plasters, such as gypsum plaster, is because magnesium hydroxide is not precipitated. There is no lime in these plasters and consequently efflorescence forms in the normal way on the surface of the plaster. It follows, therefore, that bricks which are likely to cause loss of adhesion of lime-based plasters, should preferably be plastered with calcium sulphate or other neutral or acid plasters. It may be noted that once the 'disease' has occurred, it is necessary to strip the defective plaster completely, while the wall must be plugged and battened before replastering, that is, the new plaster must not come into contact with the brickwork.

3. Bricks

Bricks made from calcareous clays may contain calcium oxide and have been observed to blow during the erection of brickwork. Experience has shown that hydration of the quicklime will usually occur at this stage rather than at a later stage, and is, therefore, unlikely to be the cause of blowing of plaster after it has been applied. Hydration does more commonly result in splitting of the bricks themselves.

The presence of calcium oxide in bricks occurs as a result of the conversion, during the burning process, of calcium carbonate which is intimately mixed with the clay. Failures, on the other hand, are more commonly associated with the presence of large lumps of calcium oxide which may be derived from limestone pebbles or fossils in the clay. If the lumps of quicklime are allowed to slake by absorbing moisture from the air they are liable to expand and split the brick, as shown in the accompanying photograph.

Solutions aimed at preventing the bricks from splitting include:

(i) Grinding the clay finely prior to the making of the bricks.

(ii) Immersing the bricks in water after burning, so as to slake the quicklime to a plastic mass that cannot exert any pressure on the brick. It should be emphasised that air slaking does not normally slake the quicklime to a plastic mass, and consequently results in splitting.*

(iii) By incorporating a small proportion (¼–1 per cent) of common salt in the clay so as to promote chemical combination of the lime with the clay during burning.

acid action

The extent to which acids may have a deleterious effect on materials varies considerably. This is due not only to

*Bricks known to contain quicklime which may lead to splitting should preferably be immersed as soon as practicable after burning. If, however, this is not done, then it may be necessary to undertake the slaking on site prior to the bricks being incorporated in a construction. This would constitute one of the exceptional cases when complete wetting of bricks may be justified. Nevertheless, it is important that they are allowed to dry out sufficiently before being incorporated in a construction so as to avoid problems associated with shrinkage and loss of adhesion.

the variation in resistance which given materials may offer to attack, but also to the variability of the concentration, and, as important, the sources of acids. It has, therefore, been considered advisable to deal primarily with those materials which are commonly affected by atmospheric gases. The materials so affected are stone, brick and cement-based products. These are considered separately. In the case of cement-based products some consideration is given to the presence of certain acids which arise out of industrial processes. The main headings used are: (1) acid gases and stonework; (2) acid gases and bricks; and (3) acids and cement-based products.

1. Acid gases and stonework*

The basic effects of the two more important acid gases, carbon dioxide and sulphur dioxide, on the carbonates present in the calcareous sedimentary stones (limestones and some sandstones are relevant), are outlined in *3.05 Efflorescence*, under 'Salts derived from decomposition of a material' (p. 7). In this part the significance of these effects as it applies to the more commonly used sedimentary stones is discussed, while a note on the weathering of slate, a metamorphic stone, is also included, as calcite, one of the minerals which occurs in slate, is readily attacked by atmospheric acids.

(a) Solubility

In principle, the fact that limestones are slightly soluble in water, and even more soluble in water containing carbon dioxide and sulphur, means that the surface of the stone, particularly in polluted atmospheres, is kept clean, because the surface is *gradually* eroded, and so unsightly effects produced by sulphur fumes are washed away while soot is unable to gain a foothold. The washing effects are, therefore, *basically* beneficial. However, in practice such washing effects only take place on surfaces which are freely exposed to rain. (See *3.02 Exposure* under 'A portrait of a building: exposure to driving rain' Vol. 2.) This, in addition to the variations which may be encountered in the physical structure of the stone, the non-uniformity of the surface and the effects of building design on the flow of water, results in the erosion being far from uniform (see *3.01 General considerations* under 'Flow', Vol. 2), and contributes to the 'Soot and Whitewash' effects commonly seen in towns and cities.

The basic effect of solubility on the fine-textured limestones with a uniform structure is for the surface to remain smooth; on the coarse-textured limestones the fossil fragments, which are

*References
(1) Schaffer, R., *The Weathering of Natural Building Stones*, Building Research Special Report No. 18, HMSO, 1932. (2) *The Weathering, Preservation and Maintenance of Natural Stone (Part 1)*, BRS Digest (1st Series) No. 20, HMSO, July, 1950 (revised March, 1965).

more resistant to erosive effects than the surrounding material, stand out in low relief after a time, as a result of the differential erosion. The latter may also result in the exposure of the bedding of the stone, if the stone has hard and soft beds; this only happens occasionally. Carvings and sculpture, unless of good, frost-resistant limestone, tend in time to lose their finer detail and may assume a weather-torn appearance.

In sheltered positions where rainwater is unable to erode the surface of the stone, sooty material not only accumulates on the surface but is also firmly bound to the surface with calcium sulphate and calcium carbonate (see '(b) Skin formation' below). Consequently a marked contrast develops between the washed and unwashed areas—'the soot and whitewash' effect. However, in addition, hard black encrustations may form on the surface. Water flowing over the surface of the stone contains calcium carbonate and calcium sulphate in solution with sooty material in suspension; on evaporation of the water, these are deposited as the hard black encrustations.

It may be noted here that although stones which are insoluble, or virtually insoluble in water, such as granites and some of the sandstones (constituent grains of the latter bonded with siliceous or ferruginous matter), also tend to collect surface deposits, these are usually much harder and more insoluble than those which collect on limestones, and are therefore much more difficult to remove. Consequently a more or less continuous black film collects on the insoluble stones with little differentiation in weathering between sheltered and exposed surfaces.* The deposits on limestone, though hard and intractable in the dry condition, can be softened and removed with water.

(b) *Skin formation*
The beneficial effect of the gradual erosion of the surface of limestones only occurs on those areas which are freely washed by rainwater. In sheltered areas, on the other hand, calcium sulphate, one of the products of the action of the acid atmospheric gases, and particularly sulphur dioxide, tends to form a hard, glassy and impermeable surface skin which is harmful rather than protective, as it tends to blister and exfoliate. The fact that this skin formation is found in sheltered areas is mainly due to the relative insolubility of calcium sulphate. Although the skin may form on relatively new stone, it does later on become obscured with soot and dirt.

The reasons why the sulphate skin is harmful have not yet been fully understood. Among other things, the impermeable nature of the skin may result in the formation of cryptoflorescence which may tend to push

*The general rule given does not necessarily apply to polished granite, the surface of which is glass-like and so does not collect surface deposits as readily as unpolished and rough cut surfaces.

Above, bursting of brick caused by unhydrated lime particles in the brick (Crown Copyright). Left and below, some examples of the effects of solubility of limestone. Left, 'the soot and whitewash' effect, commonly seen in towns and cities, is due to non-uniformity of erosion of the surface of the stone

Above, fossil fragments, which are more resistant to erosive effects than the surrounding material, stand out in low relief after a time as a result of the differential erosion. This is characteristic of the coarse-textured limestones. 'Carvings and sculpture, unless of good,

frost-resistant limestone, tend in time to lose their finer detail and may assume a "weather-torn" appearance'. A similar weather-torn appearance may occur even in plain sections, as can be seen in this sill, particularly the right-hand side

Another example showing a 'weather-torn' appearance and general loss of detail

Hard black encrustations are deposited when water evaporates from a solution of calcium carbonate and calcium sulphate with sooty material in suspension

off the skin plus any stone to which the skin may be adhering. On the other hand, the skin has different properties from those of the surface of the stone. Differences in moisture and thermal movements, for example, are significant, and could account for cracking or exfoliation. The deleterious effects of exfoliation are generally more severe when the sulphate skin forms on layers of friable stone, as these layers are weak and thus comparatively easily pulled away from the remainder of the stone with the skin. Finally, the actual crystallisation of the calcium sulphate on the surface may cause blistering.

Some stones, it may be noted, are more susceptible to the deleterious effects of sulphate skins than others. In fact, some varieties of stone offer very good resistance. Although limestones have been referred to in particular, it should be noted that some of the calcareous sandstones may also suffer damage from sulphate skins.

The manifestations of the formation of sulphate skins may be summarised as follows: spontaneous blistering and scaling of the surfaces; cracks develop at the arrises and active centres of decay make themselves apparent where the surfaces are broken; hard surfaces may be found to overlie friable layers of stone, and sometimes scabby protuberances appear, even on well-exposed surfaces.

Some manifestations of the formation of sulphate skins. Above, blistering and scaling of the surfaces with cracks at the arrises and active centres of decay where the surfaces are broken. Above right, sometimes scabby protuberances appear even on well washed surfaces

Below, some examples of the 'cavernous' type of decay which develops in some types of magnesium limestone. (In fairness, it should be stated that these examples are all of a magnesium limestone which has been in service for about 600 years)

(c) Erosion

Some types of magnesium limestone develop a 'cavernous' type of decay in which deep holes are eaten into the stone due to the presence of magnesium sulphate. This is caused by the detachment of successive scales behind which crystals of the active salt (magnesium sulphate) are usually apparent. The effects of this type of decay caused by the aggressive magnesium sulphate, one of the products of the action of an acid atmosphere on magnesium limestones (calcium sulphate is also produced, as previously explained in *3.05 Efflorescence*) which is extremely soluble and hence readily washed away, is more commonly found in the shelter of projecting features, with a very marked contrast in the condition of sheltered and exposed surfaces. However, the decay may also be found in an otherwise well-exposed surface, as the harmful effects of magnesium sulphate will continue after it has managed to gain a foothold in small depressions. Such depressions may be due to the surface characteristics of the stone or due to accidental damage (bomb splinters, for example, have been seen to initiate this type of decay).

(d) Adjacent stone

The soluble products derived from limestones may cause the development of an unsightly type of decay—usually a form of blistering or scaling, probably due to the calcium sulphate crystallising—on some sandstones. Although the latter vary in their resistance to this type of decay, it is gener-

ally wise to avoid the association of both sandstone and limestone in the same façade. The deleterious effects of the washings from limestone buildings can often be seen in sandstone steps and paving.

(e) *Weathering of slates*

Such weathering of slates that does take place is largely due to the action of atmospheric gases. Slate is a metamorphic rock and its mineral complexity and degree of crystallinity are governed by the conditions to which the original material (usually, but not always, clay) was exposed. However, of the minerals which occur in slate, only calcite is readily attacked by the acids commonly found in the atmosphere. Consequently only slates which contain significant amounts of calcite are likely to prove of poor weathering quality. On the other hand, atmospheric sulphation is not necessarily the sole cause of slate decay, but calcium sulphate can be formed from calcite and pyrite present in the slate by repeated wetting and drying, while the presence of carbonaceous matter aids this reaction.*

In practice, the weathering action often occurs where one slate overlaps another, for it is here that moisture tends to be held by capillarity. The upper exposed surface is usually unaffected as the washing action of rainwater tends to prevent decay.

2. Acid gases and bricks†

In general, bricks are highly resistant to acid gases in the atmosphere. However, when facing bricks are used with limestone dressings, they sometimes undergo a form of decay associated with calcium sulphate that is caused by and characteristic of the weathering of limestone in polluted atmospheres. The formation of blisters is characteristic of the decay, due, it is thought, to the crystallisation of calcium sulphate on the surface of the brick. The blisters are usually sooty in appearance. The calcium sulphate is derived from the limestone, so attack of the bricks only takes place if soluble matter from the limestone is washed over the bricks, as can be seen in the accompanying photographs. Soft bricks, although otherwise resistant, are particularly susceptible to decay from calcium sulphate action.

3. Acids and cement-based products‡

Acids of various kinds may attack concrete and other cement-based products. The various types of acids, and particularly their chief sources, are more conveniently discussed separately.

*The durability of slates can be determined by subjecting samples to the action of sulphuric acid, as required by BS 680, for example. Microscopic examination of thin sections may also be of value.

†Butterworth, B., *Bricks and Modern Research*, Crosby Lockwood, 1948.

‡Lea, F. M., *The Chemistry of Cement and Concrete*, Arnold, Revised edition, 1956.

(a) *Organic acids*

A number of organic acids may come into contact with concrete or other cement-based products mainly in buildings of an industrial nature. Two groups of acids may be identified, namely those of relatively low molecular weight, such as lactic acid and butyric acid (result from souring of milk and butter—dairies significant), acetic acid (vinegar, food pickling and other industries significant), oxalic and tartaric acid (fruit juices significant), and those of relatively high molecular weight, such as oleic, stearic and palmitic acids, encountered as constituents of various oils and fats.

Generally most types of cement are attacked by the acids mentioned, although some types may be more resistant than others with Portland cement usually the least resistant. Special acid resisting cements are available. Depending on the concentrations of acid which may be present, materials which are resistant to acids should be used as linings to protect the concrete. (In some cases acid-resistant paints may be sufficient.) It is also important to note that acid attack may be encouraged if concrete or a cement-based product (mortar in a tiled floor, for example), is damaged by abrasion or weakened by alkaline detergents.

(b) *Sewage*

In general, concrete and concrete pipes are not attacked appreciably by normal sewage, but certain sewage conditions, arising chiefly from industrial processes, may give rise to severe attack. Normal sewage has an alkaline reaction, but effluents arising from industrial processes may sometimes be acid, unless neutralised immediately by discharge into an excess of normal sewage. As the discharge of acidic effluents is hazardous if they are allowed to discharge into concrete pipes, or into any cement-jointed pipe, they (the effluents) should always be neutralised before discharge into the drainage system.

Concrete and mortars have been known to be attacked indirectly by hydrogen sulphide, which under some conditions may be evolved from normal sewage-action of anaerobic bacteria on organic sulphur compounds and on sulphates and other inorganic sulphur compounds. Serious trouble has mainly occurred in other countries (North and South Africa, Australia and the USA, for example).

(c) *Acid gases*

Sulphur dioxide and carbon dioxide are the chief gases which normally attack concrete and cement-based products, but then usually only under moist conditions. In general, trouble is more commonly associated with the sulphur products of combustion of fuel. Thus chimneys, both industrial and domestic of concrete or of brick with cement mortar, may be attacked, particularly if condensation occurs within the chimney. Attack may, of

Another example of the 'cavernous' type of decay which develops in some types of magnesium limestone (see also examples at the bottom of p. 22). Below, although generally resistant to the effects of acid gases, bricks may blister when soluble material from limestone is washed over the bricks

Material	Alkali resistance (1)	Absorption through paint (porosity)
Alkyd emulsion paints (2)	Poor	High
Gloss paints (water thinned)	Poor	Low
Flat oil paints (pigment flatted)	Usually poor	High
(other types)	Usually poor	Low
Size bound distempers	Moderate	High
Distemper, oil bound	Moderate	High
Cement paint (cement based)	Good	Fairly high
Limewash	Good	Fairly high
Polyvinyl acetate emulsion paints (flat finished)	Good	Variable, often high
Chlorinated rubber paints	Good	Low
Bituminous paints	Good	Low
Cold glazes (3)	Good	Low
Epoxy paints	Good	Low
Anti-condensation (cork filled)	Variable	Variable
Plastics (textured)	Variable	Variable

Table 3.06/1. Alkali resistance and absorption of paints

Notes: (1) Alkali-resistant materials are desirable over surfaces likely to contain Portland cement or lime. If the chosen finish is not alkali-resistant, one or preferably two coats of alkali-resistant primer should be first applied. These make any paint system impermeable to moisture and hence the background must be dry before the primer is applied.
(2) Because the lack of resistance to alkali was too great a handicap, few brands of this type of emulsion are now available.
(3) Term covers a wide variety of materials.
References: (1) *Wall and Ceiling Surfaces and Condensation*, BRS Digest (1st Series) No. 58, HMSO, September, 1953, revised 1962, Table on p. 2. (2) *New Types of Paint*, BRS Digest (2nd, Series) No. 21, HMSO, April, 1962. (3) *Principles of Modern Building*, Vol. I, HMSO, 3rd Ed., 1959.

course, also take place in chemical factories.

With industrial chimneys methods may be devised to limit the amount of sulphur compounds which arise from combustion of fuel, although other protective measures within the flue may also be required. The treatment of domestic chimneys in order to avoid attack is considered under 'Sulphate attack, 6. Domestic chimneys', p. 35.

It may be noted that there are likely to be high concentrations of sulphur dioxide in the atmosphere in the vicinity of large power stations when flue gases are emitted without treatment, and under these conditions Portland cement concrete may suffer surface attack (high alumina cement is usually more resistant).

alkali action

Alkali action is mainly, though not entirely, associated with cement-based products and especially those containing Portland cement. Portland cement particularly (in some cases lime) is the source of the alkali. The action may manifest itself in a number of different ways depending on the materials involved. Those included here are:

(1) The saponification of certain paint films (that is, the conversion of oil to soap which is dissolved in water) applied to surfaces of plaster or renderings containing cement (or, in some cases, lime), asbestos cement sheets and concrete.

(2) Expansion and cracking of concrete as a result of alkali-reactive aggregates.

(3) The staining of new limestone masonry as the result of the reaction of the alkali content of mortars and traces of organic matter present in the stone.

(4) The staining of brickwork due to the action of iron compounds in bricks and alkali in the mortar and of lime leached from concrete.

(5) Effects of alkaline solutions on glass.

All of the above are essentially self-contained problems and are, therefore, dealt with separately. For convenience staining due to causes other than the presence of alkalis are included in (3) and (4). Where relevant, sources of alkali other than cement or lime are noted.

1. Paint films*

There are a number of different paint formulations now available for application to various surfaces, including those of cement-based products, while developments aimed at improving specific properties of paints are constantly taking place. Not all types of paint are, however, attacked by alkalis, and there is a wide variation in the resistance offered by various types as will be seen in Table 3.06/1, which lists the main types and includes the porosity of each type. It may be noted here that the degree of resistance provided by any given brand of paint in any given type may vary from that given in the table. Consequently it is always important to check the degree of resistance of a particular brand which is being considered for use, while taking into account the other relevant factors which are discussed below.

Although emphasis is being placed here on the alkali attack of paint films applied to cement-based products, with Portland cement providing the source of the alkali, it is important to remember that attack of the kind to be described may also result from alkalis contained in strong cleansing agents (soda and caustic soda) or alkaline paint removers. In some cases, lime, particularly hydraulic lime, may be an alkaline source.

*References
(1) *Painting Asbestos Cement*, BRS Digest (1st Series) No. 38, HMSO, January, 1952, revised September, 1963. (2) Lea, F. M., *The Chemistry of Cement and Concrete*, Arnold. Rev. Ed. 1956.

(a) *Basic mechanisms*

Saponification manifests itself as a grey discoloration and breakdown of the film into soapy runs and 'tears', and a softened paint film. It is the *oil medium* of the paint which is attacked by alkalis, linseed oil being particularly vulnerable. The attack can only take place in the presence of moisture, the result of which is the formation of a soap.

Any caustic alkali will saponify the linseed oil base of paints. Other types of oil may also be attacked, but usually to a lesser degree, while synthetic resins are highly resistant. One of the chief caustic alkalis liberated from cement as hydroxide is free lime, calcium hydroxide, which remains as such until it is carbonated, that is combined with atmospheric carbon dioxide—in the present context, the calcium carbonate formed is harmless. However, carbonation of the free lime usually occurs at the surface of a material, being transferred there during the drying-out process. A fully matured and completely dry cement-based product is unlikely to result in alkali attack, as the uncarbonated lime remains inactive.

Any subsequent wetting of the material will, however, enable the free lime to become potentially reactive as, among other things, it can be transferred, due to the presence of the moisture, and thereby come into contact with any paint film previously applied.

The cause of the breakdown of the paint film, its stickiness and softness, is not entirely attributed to the presence of calcium hydroxide, as other water soluble alkalis, such as those of sodium and potassium, which are also liberated from the cement as hydroxides* in small but significant amounts, are also involved. The action of the free calcium hydroxide on linseed oil is the formation of a calcium soap which is insoluble. On coming into contact with the oil film, the *insoluble* calcium soap appears to form a layer which largely acts as a protection for the remainder of the film from further attack. However, solutions of caustic soda and potash readily attack drying oils, but the soaps formed are *soluble* in water. On the other hand, any alkali salt in the presence of calcium hydroxide and moisture forms an alkali hydroxide, and this attacks and quickly destroys any film containing linseed oil with which it comes into contact.

(b) *Precautions*

The precautions which should be taken to minimise the risk of alkali attack are associated with the selection of a suitable type of paint or painting system (primers, undercoats and top or finishing coats, as relevant) as related to given conditions of the background to which the paint is to be applied, such as degree of alkalinity of

*These remain as hydroxides as long as there is uncarbonated lime available.

24

the background, and the presence of moisture in the background either at the time of painting or during service. All these are subject to variation, while in addition there are the variables related to the properties of the paint or painting system, such as its resistance to alkali attack and its porosity. The existence of so many variables makes any clearly defined set of precautions, particularly in relation to the painting of new surfaces, difficult to formulate. Consequently, it is necessary to consider the effects of any of the variables on the likelihood of attack taking place. For convenience these are considered separately.

The presence of moisture. It is perhaps axiomatic that whatever the alkali content of a background, there is no risk of attack even to a non-alkali resistant paint, provided the surface on which the paint is applied is dry at the time of painting, and, as important, remains dry during service. In new work care is needed to ensure that there is insufficient moisture in the interior, although the surface of the background may appear to be dry (See *3.03 Moisture content* under 'General influences, 1. Capillarity', Vol. 2.) On the other hand, the precautions which are necessary to ensure the exclusion of water during service are outlined in *Section 3.04* (Vol. 2), and are, therefore, not repeated here. However, asbestos cement sheeting needs special consideration.

In service, moisture may be transferred through the back, that is the concealed and unpainted surface, of an asbestos cement sheet. Condensation is often an important source of water. Consequently, it is always advisable to paint the back and the edges of the sheet with alkali resistant primer, bitumen paint or a colourless waterproofer, so as to prevent the passage of moisture through the sheet to the exposed paint film. Ideally such treatment should be carried out prior to the fixing of the sheeting—there is always the risk that later access may be difficult.

Degree of alkalinity. The degree of alkalinity in a material is likely to vary considerably. In general, exposure to the atmosphere will reduce the amount at the surface as a result of carbonation. For example, with asbestos cement sheeting, fresh material is often very active, but much of this activity is lost after a few weeks' exposure, even indoors. When exposed out of doors, the alkalis tend to be leached by rainwater.

The period of exposure required so as to render an otherwise active material inactive is difficult to specify as there is the combined effect of the variability of alkali content and exposure conditions. In the case of asbestos cement sheeting, the BRS have suggested that the period should be not less than one month nor so long that the surface becomes powdery or heavy deposits of dirt or algae, etc., are formed. With other cement-based

products it may not always be practicable or convenient to rely on exposure to reduce the alkali content of the surface. Special paint treatment would be the only alternative, other things being equal.

Attempts have been made to neutralise alkalis by using solutions of hydrochloric acid, zinc sulphate or other chemicals. These treatments may not always be effective, and in any case only help to neutralise the alkalis at or near the surface. They must be used sparingly and must be thoroughly washed off. Thus they involve additional work and delay, while they may result in the formation of a powdery deposit on the surface which may interfere with the adhesion of the paint.

Type of paint. Although it is generally recommended that all surfaces likely to contain either Portland cement or lime should be painted with alkali-resistant materials, it is possible, though not always necessarily desirable, to use a finish which is not alkali resistant. In cases such as these it is, however, imperative that one or preferably two coats of alkali-resistant primer should first be applied. These, it should be noted, make any paint system impermeable to moisture, and hence the background must be dry before the primer is applied.

With *asbestos cement sheets* no special precautions, as regards treatment of the sheet, are required when porous paints having a high degree of resistance to alkalis are used. As the porosity of this type of paint decreases, back painting of the sheet may be necessary. In order to decrease the risk of blistering, back painting is desirable if impermeable paints which are highly resistant to alkalis are used. Porous paints which are not highly resistant to alkalis are generally effective without the need for special precautions, provided dry conditions are maintained—back painting may be necessary with the less porous paints. Finally, impermeable paints which are not specially resistant to alkalis, should not be used unless dry conditions can be assured. If this is not the case then two coats of alkali resistant primer must be used, while back painting is essential.

2. Reactive aggregates*

Expansion and cracking of concrete has in some cases been attributed to a reaction between sodium and potassium hydroxides released from the cement and a reactive form of silica in the aggregates. For the reaction to take place a relatively high content of alkali in the cement and the presence of particular reactive constituents in the aggregate are necessary. The reaction, it may be noted, does not take place when high alkali cements are used with other aggregates, or when reactive agents are used with cements of sufficiently low alkali content. In general, the problem of alkali attack of concrete has been restricted

*Lea, F. M., *The Chemistry of Cement and Concrete*, Arnold. Rev. Ed., 1956.

Cracks in concrete caused by alkali-aggregate reaction. (Courtesy: Dr. W. Lerch, of the Portland Cement Association, USA)

to some of the aggregates found in America, Australia and New Zealand. Although it appears that a survey of common British aggregates, as quoted by Lea, has failed to reveal any containing alkali-reactive constituents, care is needed when using aggregates of geological types which might contain such constituents, and of which no previous experience is available.

Finally it may be noted that, although alkali-aggregate reaction can be responsible for deterioration of large mass concrete structures, the effects of the reaction may be accentuated by frost action, or by thermal or moisture changes in thin members.

3. Staining of limestone*

Disfiguring brownish or yellowish stains which are unsightly, often develop on the surface of limestone masonry, usually near the joints, soon after it has been incorporated in a building. In sheltered positions the stains may persist for years, but generally they soon disappear or are masked by superficial deposits. Sometimes brownish stains also develop on newly cleaned limestone previously covered with soot. The stains which occur on new limestone are attributable to a reaction between the alkali compounds of a mortar and organic matter in the stone; those that occur on newly cleaned limestone are attributable to soluble matter absorbed from soot deposits into the stone and brought to the surface as the stone dries out after cleaning.

*References
(1) Schaffer, R., *The Weathering of Natural Building Stone*, Building Research Special Report No. 18, HMSO, 1932. (2) *The Weathering, Preservation and Maintenance of Natural Stone* (Parts I and II), BRS Digests (1st Series) Nos. 20 and 21, HMSO, July, 1950 (revised March, 1965) and August, 1950, respectively. (3) *The Principles of Modern Building*, Volume I, HMSO, 3rd Ed., 1959.

Rusty stains on mortar joints due to iron salts (Crown Copyright). Below, disfiguring brownish or yellowish stains often develop on the surface of limestone masonry as a result of a reaction between the alkali compounds of a mortar and organic compounds in the stone. The stains develop soon after the incorporation of the stone in a building, and although they may persist for several years in sheltered positions, they usually disappear after a comparatively short period of exposure

(a) *New limestone*

The mechanism involved in the staining of new limestone is similar to that involved in the production of soluble salts from mortars—see *3.05 Efflorescence.* Alkali compounds are leached from the mortar as hydroxides and carbonates into the stone and there react with organic matter which is present in most limestones to form a soluble organic salt which is deposited on the surface of the stone and appears as the stain. Mortar used for both jointing and grouting may 'supply' the alkali compounds. Both the presence and availability of the alkalis may vary. Waterproofing the back of the stone does in some measure help to reduce the transference of the alkali compounds from the grout behind the stone; the limitations (mainly the weakness at the joint) of this treatment, which may be used for reasons other than staining, are outlined in *3.04 Exclusion* under 'Ashlar', Vol. 2, p. 102.

Other treatments, such as applying a lime slurry to the back of the stone, are reported to have given satisfactory results, even when the stone was backed with concrete.

If the risk of staining is to be minimised, even if it is only from the jointing, then it is probably better to test different mortars in respect of their staining potential.

A simple test for the production of the stain has been devised.* A cube of stone is allowed to stand on a cube of mortar with a layer of clean washed blotting paper between them. The cube of mortar is placed in a shallow dish or tray containing distilled water, and the water rises by capillarity through the mortar and into the stone, where it evaporates at the surface. Thus the relative tendency for staining of any particular combinations of stone and mortar can be observed. No rule can be laid down as to the relative merits of different mortars in respect of staining, for the effect depends not only on the amount of alkali present, but also on its availability. For example, bad stains on Portland stone have been caused by both ordinary and rapid hardening Portland cement (the grey cements) in this type of test, while there has been considerably less staining when a white cement has been used. The least amount of staining has been produced by a specially prepared alkali-free cement. From the tests which have been carried out, it would seem that mortars of high-calcium (fat) limes and similar limes gauged with a moderate amount of cement (preferably white cement) will cause less staining than straight cement mortars.

(b) *Newly cleaned limestone*

The brownish stains mentioned before which sometimes occur on newly cleaned limestone are generally fortuitous and are not the fault of the operator. Their development depends to some extent on prevailing weather conditions. Slow drying would encourage staining; rapid drying discourages it. The stains often disappear quite quickly; sometimes they may persist for a considerable time. Although not always effective, repeated rinsing with water is helpful.

4. Staining of brickwork†

Two types of staining are included here, namely rusty stains from iron compounds in either the bricks or mortar, and white stains from concrete. However, it may be noted that stains may also result from embedded ironwork, copper and bronze (see *3.07 Corrosion of metals*) and from vegetation.

Principles of Modern Building, Volume I, HMSO, 3rd Ed., p. 244, 1959.

†Butterworth, B., *Efflorescence and Staining of Brickwork.* Article reprinted from *The Brick Bulletin* and amended December, 1962.

(a) *Rusty stains*

Rusty stains on mortar joints are usually due to iron salts, especially ferrous sulphate, which form efflorescences when they first come to the surface. However, they react chemically with the lime in the mortar and are subsequently washed over the mortar joints by rain.* If bricks known to give rusty stains owing to the presence of iron salts are to be used, it is wise to allow the stain to develop harmlessly on the bed joints and then to cover it by pointing after the work is complete. It is unlikely that the staining will recur. On the other hand, if this method cannot be adopted, the amount of staining can be considerably reduced, if, as Butterworth advises, the unfinished walls are kept covered so as to prevent rain percolating through the brickwork, until the mortar has aged for at least a week.

Mortar sands that contain particles of ironstone may result in rusty stains, which generally flow from particular grains in the surface of the mortar. Repointing is the only cure.

(b) *White stains*

White stains which do not disappear when the brickwork is washed by rainwater, and thus distinguishable from efflorescence, may be caused by water percolating through poor quality concrete, in adjoining elements such as lintels, copings, etc., particularly when the requisite d.p.c.'s have been omitted. The stains consist of calcium carbonate which is formed when atmospheric carbon dioxide reacts with the free lime, calcium hydroxide leached from the concrete, and may, under favourable conditions build up to an appreciable thickness of stalactite-like material.

Removal of these stains can be carried out as follows: The brickwork must first be well wetted, and then brushed over with *diluted* hydrochloric acid (spirits of salts) to dissolve the deposits. Finally the work must be thoroughly washed down with clean water. In order to avoid a recurrence, attention should be given to taking the necessary steps to prevent further percolation of water.

5. Glass

The durability of glass used in buildings is generally excellent under ordinary conditions, but all glasses are subject to deterioration by the action of water, particularly if the latter contains alkalis. In other words attack is more rapid with alkalis.

Alkaline solutions such as alkaline paint removers that are allowed to encroach on the glass and that are not properly cleaned off may cause trouble.

Rainwater running off new concrete or cement rendered wall faces may contain enough alkali to damage the glass.

*The staining which may occur on plasters of gypsum applied over bricks which contain iron salts is discussed in *3.05 Efflorescence* under 'Physical processes, 5. Effect of pecipitation' (p. 13).

sulphate attack

The term 'sulphate attack' is generally used to refer to the results of the chemical reaction (in many cases a series of reactions but more conveniently referred to here as 'reaction') that takes place between sulphates in solution and certain constituents of cement and hydraulic lime. The reaction is accompanied by considerable expansion, causing gradual softening and possible disintegration, together with loss of strength of the material in which it takes place. The materials most commonly affected are all those which are cement-based, such as concrete, mortars, renders, etc., and these are included here. Generally the attack is more often associated with cement-based products in which ordinary Portland cement has been used, although other types of cement (including other types of Portland) may be attacked, while the attack is more likely to be found in constructions where dampness is persistent.

These generalisations must, in a great many cases, be strictly qualified. This may be attributed to two reasons. First, there are many variables involved, which are likely to influence the rate of attack. Second, the nature of the reactions or the compound involved, although now better understood than they were twenty years ago, are still being investigated.

This part is in a sense an extension of *Section 3.05* in which the sources and transmission of soluble salts are included, and aims to outline those factors which are common to sulphate attack in all cement-based products, the mechanisms involved, and to consider the detailed implications of sulphate attack including the relevant precautions which should be taken, in three types of cement-based products, namely, concrete, brickwork and rendering. Accordingly, the following general headings are used: (1) general considerations; (2) basic mechanisms; (3) concrete; (4) brickwork; (5) rendering; and (6) domestic chimneys.

1. General considerations

Although there are likely to be detailed and important variations with given cement-based products under given conditions, it is possible to identify the existence of some fundamental criteria common in all cases of sulphate attack. Apart from the basic mechanisms involved which can conveniently be considered separately, these are associated with the nature and derivation of the soluble salts likely to cause attack, the constituents of the cement which are involved, and the significance of the characteristics of the materials in which the attack takes place together with the effects of exposure to water.

(a) *Basic requirements*

Three things are basically necessary for sulphate attack to take place. These are: (i) sulphates; (ii) tricalcium aluminate* (a normal constituent of cements); and (iii) water.

(b) *Sulphates*

The sulphates which most commonly attack *set* cements are those of sodium, potassium, calcium and magnesium. It is important to note that it is in fact the set cement which is attacked. In general, mortars and concretes attacked by calcium or sodium sulphate become eventually reduced to a soft mush, but when magnesium sulphate, which is by far the most aggressive, is the main destructive agent, the mortar or concrete remains hard though it becomes much expanded and the disrupted mass usually consists of hard granular particles.

The nature, behaviour and sources of sulphates are included, in detail, in *3.05 Efflorescence*, and are, therefore, not repeated here, apart from emphasising the importance of solubility. In general, two sulphates commonly encountered, those of sodium and magnesium are highly soluble, and their presence is, therefore, far more significant than that of calcium sulphate which is, by comparison, less soluble. An aspect not previously covered in detail, namely the variability of soluble salt content of soils. is included. for convenience, in '3. Concrete', p. 29.

(c) *Rate of attack*

The rate at which sulphate attack may proceed is governed by a number of interrelated factors, which may be summarised as follows:

(i) The quantity and type of sulphate present. Generally magnesium sulphate has the most far-reaching effects.

(ii) The quantity of tricalcium aluminate present in the cement used. With Portland cements, those with a low tricalcium aluminate content are more resistant to sulphate attack than those with high tricalcium aluminate contents.

(iii) The permeability of the cement-based product. This is one of the factors governing the extent to which water may 'bring together' the soluble sulphates and tricalcium aluminate (or other relevant constituent in the cement used—see '2. Basic mechanisms' for the exceptions) so that the requisite chemical reaction may proceed. In general, highly impermeable products will only suffer surface attack, and then usually by sulphates from external sources; with highly permeable products, attack may proceed simultaneously throughout the mass of the product and by sulphates either present in the material or from external sources, or both.

Permeability of cement-based products, which is dependent on mix

*This compound has been included in the basic requirements as it appears to be generally regarded as the most significant in sulphate attack, particularly when Portland cements are involved, and secondary to free lime (calcium hydroxide) which may also react with sulphates. The significance of these reactions together with basic reasons for the particularly high resistance to attack provided by high alumina cement (rich in aluminates, an apparent paradox) are noted in '2. Basic mechanisms' later.

design and control of quality on site or in factory, plays an extremely important part in the resistance which a product will offer to sulphate attack. Thus in the case of concrete, for example, precast units are likely to be more resistant than concrete cast *in situ*. The latter also suffer the added disadvantage of being more susceptible to attack if exposed to sulphate sources during their 'green' state.

(iv) The permeability of materials (including soils) adjacent to and in contact with the cement-based product, which may provide possible sources of sulphates. The more impermeable these surrounding materials are, the less likely are sulphates to be transferred to the cement-based product.

(v) The availability and quantity of water. Without water there can be no chemical reaction, while certain minimum quantities of water are necessary for the reaction to proceed. For any given condition, the rate of attack increases as the duration of the presence of water increases. Time, it should be noted, is extremely important.

(vi) Closely associated with the permeability of the cement-based product is whether pressure differences will tend to force a sulphate solution through the material. In this connection it may be noted here, that the most severe condition occurs when a cement-based product, such as a concrete retaining wall, for example, is exposed to water pressure on one side and to air on the other, in which case evaporation is promoted, thus tending to increase the volume of sulphates in solution drawn through the material. In addition, evaporation at the exposed face leaves the sulphate salts behind. This then increases the concentration of those salts in the water in the concrete. The very soluble magnesium and sodium sulphates would constitute a greater danger from this effect than would the more insoluble calcium sulphate. A similar, though less severe, condition occurs in a partly buried concrete mass, when water is drawn up by capillary forces from the portion below ground and evaporates at the exposed surface.

2. Basic mechanisms

The chemistry associated with sulphate attack on set cement is extremely complex, with a number of different compounds involved in what may best be termed a series of reactions, some of which are interrelated. However, tricalcium aluminate appears to be the most important compound in set Portland cement which governs the resistance a given cement will offer to attack, although the reactions of other compounds, such as calcium hydroxide (free lime) must also be taken into account. On the other hand, the type of sulphate involved in any reaction has a marked effect on the rate at which attack may proceed and on the deleterious results in the cement-based product. In this the particularly aggressive nature of magnesium sulphate is significant.

27

TYPE OF CEMENT	BS Nº	RESISTANCE	Low	Medium	High	Very High
MAIN TYPES OF PORTLAND CEMENTS						
Ordinary	12	Low	▬			
Rapid – hardening	12	Low	▬			
Low – heat	1370	Medium	▬▬▬			
Sulphate – resisting	4027	High	▬▬▬▬			
OTHER TYPES OF PORTLAND CEMENT						
Extra – rapid – hardening						
Waterproof and water – repellent		Low	▬			
Hydrophobic						
White						
Coloured						
CEMENTS CONTAINING BLASTFURNACE SLAG						
Portland blastfurnace	146	Medium	▬▬▬			
Super – sulphate	4248	Very high	▬▬▬▬▬▬			
HIGH – ALUMINA CEMENT	915	Very high	▬▬▬▬▬▬			
POZZOLANIC CEMENT	–	High	▬▬▬▬▬			

C.3.06/1

Comparative chart showing the resistance of various types of cement to sulphate (From: 'Materials for Concrete', BRS Digest (2nd Series), No. 5, HMSO, Dec. 1960)

The purpose of this part is mainly to outline, in general terms, the fundamental chemistry involved in sulphate attack; to note the effects of magnesium sulphate; to consider the effects of sea-water; and to compare the resistance of various cements to sulphate attack.

(a) *Fundamental chemistry*

There are *two* basic reactions which account for expansion and disruption of mortars and concrete attack by sulphates.

(i) The formation of calcium sulphate* (gypsum) by the conversion of calcium hydroxide (free lime). Various sulphates, including sodium, potassium, and magnesium may react with calcium hydroxide.

The molecular volume of calcium hydroxide ($Ca(OH)_2$) is 33·2 ml, while that of gypsum ($CaSO_4 . 2H_2O$) is 74·3 ml. Thus the formation of gypsum from the free lime results in more than a doubling of the solid volume.

(ii) The formation of the more insoluble calcium sulphoaluminate from the combination of hydrated tricalcium aluminate and gypsum. This too is accompanied by an increase in solid volume. The increase is rather smaller than that described in (i) above, but nevertheless significant.

*It is extremely important to note that under no circumstances should calcium sulphate be added to Portland cements (or hydraulic limes) in order to alter the setting or other properties of the cement (or lime). In the British Standard Specifications, as in most specifications in other countries, the amount of calcium sulphate which may be present in the finished cement (i.e. *ex* works) is strictly limited to a few per cent, with the amount added during manufacture varying between 1 and 3 per cent. The limited amount of calcium sulphate allowed is valuable in the control it affords of the setting time and in its favourable effect on strength. On the other hand, the presence of large quantities of calcium sulphate leads to slow expansion in the *set* cement, and this accounts for its stringent limitation.

(b) *Effects of magnesium sulphate*

In addition to reacting with the aluminates and calcium hydroxide as do the other sulphates, magnesium sulphate is particularly aggressive because it decomposes the hydrated calcium silicates (usually unaffected by the other bases), and by continued action also decomposes calcium sulphoaluminate.

Initially magnesium sulphate has a similar action to that of the other sulphates on the hydrated calcium aluminates, and calcium sulphoaluminate is formed together with magnesium hydroxide. However, calcium sulphoaluminate is itself unstable in the presence of a magnesium sulphate solution. Continued action of the magnesium solution results in the decomposition of the calcium sulphoaluminate to form gypsum, hydrated alumina and magnesium hydroxide. In this, the length of exposure to the magnesium sulphate solution is significant. Thus, after a fairly long period of action, the external skin of a mortar or concrete is relatively free of calcium sulphoaluminate while gypsum is present in a large amount; but in the interior of the mortar or concrete, where access to the solution has been much slower, both calcium sulphoaluminate and gypsum are found.

Another characteristic of the action of magnesium sulphate on mortars and concrete is the formation of a hard glassy skin on the surface which tends to hinder the penetration of the solution. This skin is formed by the deposition of magnesium hydroxide in the pores of the cement-based product, and accounts for the fact that the disrupted mass of a product attacked by magnesium sulphate more often consists of hard granular particles. This

may be contrasted with attack by either sodium or calcium sulphate when the cement-based product becomes soft and incoherent.

(c) *The effects of sea-water*

Although the predominant constituents of sea-water are the chlorides, there are, nevertheless, significant quantities of sulphates present. The percentage of magnesium sulphate, for example, may be in the region of 5 per cent of the total (see Table 3.01/1, Vol. 2, p. 6) and the chemical action of sea-water on concrete, is, in fact, due to the action of magnesium sulphate. However, and this is important, the presence of chlorides in sea-water retards and inhibits the expansion of concrete by sulphate solutions, although the degree of reaction remains unchanged.

The chemical action of sea-water is better considered as one of a series of reactions proceeding concurrently. Calcium hydroxide and calcium sulphate are considerably more soluble in sea-water than in plain water and the leaching actions which occur (accelerated to some extent by wave motion) remove lime and calcium sulphate from the concrete. At the same time the reaction with magnesium sulphate leads to the formation of calcium sulphoaluminate (as described previously in (b)) which may cause expansion. This then renders the concrete open to further attack and leaching, and so the cycle may be repeated. The relative contribution to deterioration which may be attributed to either expansion or leaching is largely dependent on conditions. The rate of chemical attack is increased by temperature, while both the rate and its effects are influenced by the type of cement.

(d) *Increasing resistance of set cement*
A comparison of the resistance of various types of cement to sulphates is given in comparative chart C.3.06/1. From this chart it will be seen that most types of Portland cement have low resistance, except for low-heat (medium) and sulphate resisting (high). Resistance is increased with other types of cement, notably supersulphate (cement containing blast furnace slag) and high alumina cement.

In order to increase the resistance of Portland cement it is necessary to reduce the tricalcium aluminate content. Consequently *sulphate-resisting Portland cements* differ from the ordinary cement in that they have a low calculated tricalcium aluminate content and a carefully controlled iron oxide to alumina ratio. Sulphate-resisting Portland cements have been manufactured and used in the United Kingdom since 1949. These have conformed to BS 12 for ordinary Portland cement with a composition so adjusted as to give a product containing not more than a few per cent tricalcium aluminate. The recently-published BS 4027 : 1966 limits the amount of tricalcium aluminate to 3·5 per cent, but sets no limit on the ratio of alumina to iron oxide, stating that there is no reason why this should not be reduced below the value of 0·66 specified in BS 12*.

Among reasons which have been offered for the high resistance of *pozzolanic cement* and the very high resistance of both *super-sulphate* and *high-alumina cements* to sulphate attack, including sea-water, is the absence or limitation of calcium hydroxide in the set cement. This has not necessarily been accepted as the only reason, particularly as high-alumina cement, for example, contains a high proportion (a content of approximately 40 per cent) of aluminates.

It would appear that during the setting of these cements a protective film is formed over the more vulnerable compounds. This is seen to be the primary reason for their high resistance, although in some cases increased permeability of the set mass, facilitated in part by the cement, may be relevant.

Steam curing results in various transformations in the set cement and these add to the inherent chemical resistance of the set cement to attack by sulphates. The transformations are favoured by increasing temperature and time of steam curing, while the permeability of a mortar or concrete is also reduced, and this, too, contributes to increased resistance. Among the transformations which occur is the removal of calcium hydroxide which increases resistance to sodium sulphate, although it gives less protection against magnesium sulphate, which

can attack the hydrated calcium silicates as outlined in (b) previously.

3. Concrete*

The main emphasis here is on sulphate attack on concrete in *sulphate-bearing clays and ground waters,* and on the measures which can be taken to prevent serious deterioration of the concrete. It may be noted, however, that sulphate attack of concrete may also occur if it is exposed to certain industrial wastes, as these may contain sulphates. Although this aspect of exposure is not covered here, it should be remembered that when concrete is to be exposed to industrial wastes containing sulphates, then special consideration must be given to the selection of cements or other protective measures. Special measures will also be necessary when both sulphates and acids are present, as may occur, for example, in soils near colliery waste tips.

Shale used as hardcore for concrete floors has given rise to a number of failures. The related precautionary measures are, therefore, dealt with separately at the end.

The factors which influence the *rate of attack* of the sulphates on cement-based products have already been outlined in general terms in '1. General considerations'. These are equally applicable to concrete and are, therefore, not repeated here. However, those aspects which are of particular significance to concrete in sulphate-bearing clays and ground water are outlined in the separate headings set out below.

(a) *Sulphates commonly encountered*
The sulphate salts commonly encountered in sulphate-bearing clays and ground waters are:

(i) *Calcium sulphate* (gypsum or selenite), which is only slightly soluble in water. The maximum amount that can be dissolved is 200 parts calcium sulphate per 100 000; this corresponds to about 120 parts of sulphur trioxide† (SO_3) per 100 000. Clay heavily charged with gypsum may result in the

ground water containing nearly this amount.

(ii) *Magnesium sulphate* (Epsom salt), which is far more soluble than calcium sulphate, and as already noted under '2. Basic mechanisms' is likely to be the most destructive.

(iii) *Sodium sulphate* (Glauber's salt), is also more soluble than calcium sulphate.

As both magnesium and sodium sulphate are highly soluble in water, and so much more soluble than calcium sulphate, the amount of sulphur trioxide in the ground water in which they may be present may be much greater. Also the concentration in ground water of either magnesium or sodium sulphate can vary much more widely than that of calcium sulphate, and for this reason they must be regarded as potentially more dangerous. However, it is to be remembered that in addition to the nature of the sulphate salts involved, their amount is also important.

(b) *'Sulphate-bearing' areas*
Although there does not appear to be any comprehensive information available as to the areas in the United Kingdom in which the three most important salts may occur, it is known that they are found in appreciable quantities in clays in *parts* of the London, Gault, Weald, Lias, Oxford and Kimmeridge formations, while in the Keuper Marl, gypsum is the predominant sulphate. (A map showing sulphate conditions in major areas known chemically and geologically to contain sulphates in the soil and in groundwater is given in *Section 3.02, diagram D.3.02/8*, Vol. 2, p. 62.)

(c) *Variability of sulphate content*
In the United Kingdom the distribution of sulphate salts in a clay is often very irregular and may vary much between points only 15m apart. As a result of constant leaching by rain-water, there is also a considerable variation in sulphate salt distribution with depth, and consequently the top 0·610m or 0·915m of soil are often, though not always, relatively free of sulphate salts. On the other hand, considerable amounts are more usually found at depths from 0·915m to 1·830m, or even more, below the surface.

These factors, but in particular the wide variations in salt content that can occur between points quite close together, are important when making any assessment of the precautionary measures which may be advisable in any given conditions. However, some caution is also necessary when analysing the results of any field tests which may be undertaken to determine the sulphate content of a soil or ground water (i.e. the degree of exposure), because local conditions, such as the weather (at the time of the test), the prevailing wetness or dryness of a soil, and drainage facilities and fluctuations in the water table are extremely significant.

---

*It may be noted that in America specifications such as ASTM C150-59 sets the following limits of T.C.A. (tricalcium aluminate):
For Type V (cement of *high* resistance to sulphate solutions) a maximum of 5 per cent T.C.A.
For Type II (cement of *moderate* resistance to sulphate solutions) a maximum of 8 per cent T.C.A.

*References
(1) Lea, F. M., *The Chemistry of Cement and Concrete*, Arnold, 2nd Rev. Ed., 1956. (2) *Concrete in Sulphate-bearing Clays and Ground Waters*, BRS Digest (1st Series) No. 31, HMSO, June, 1951. *Note* : in view of the revision of this digest (revised edition, 1967) information concerning general principles only has been used in this study. The classification of sulphate soil conditions affecting concrete, and recommended precautionary measures contained in the digest, have not, therefore, been used. Instead a revised classification and related precautionary measures, based on current trade literature and other information, have been included as interim recommendations. (3) *Durability*, BS Code of Practice, CP3 – Chapter IV, 1950. Note for reference (2) applies. (4) *Principles of Modern Building, Volume I*, HMSO, 3rd Ed., 1959. Note for reference (2) applies. (5) van Aardt, H. H. P., *Deterioration of Cement Products in Aggressive Media*. Paper VI–S1 to the Fourth International Symposium on the Chemistry of Cement, Washington, DC 1960. Contribution from the South African Council for Scientific and Industrial Research – CSIR Reference No. RD 17. (6) Current trade literature. See note for reference (2). (7) Eldridge, H. J., *Concrete Floors on Shale Hardcore*, Building Research, Current Papers, Design Series 30, BRS, 1964.

†In analyses of soils and water, sulphates are usually recorded in terms of *equivalent* sulphur trioxide, that is, the part which actually causes attack.

Table 3.06/2. Sulphates in soils and groundwaters—classification and recommendations

This table applies to concrete placed in near-neutral groundwaters of pH 6–9, containing naturally occurring sulphates but not contaminants such as ammonium salts. Concrete prepared from ordinary Portland cement would not be recommended in acidic conditions (pH < 6). Sulphate-resisting Portland cement is slightly more acid-resistant but no experience of large-scale use in these conditions is currently available. High alumina cement can be used down to pH 4·0 and supersulphated cement has given an acceptable life provided that the concrete is dense and prepared with a free water/cement ratio of 0·40 or less, in mineral acids down to pH 3·5.

	Concentration of sulphates in terms of SO₃ content			Recommendations for types of cement to be used in dense, fully compacted concrete, and special protective measures when necessary (see Note 1). Aggregates should comply with BS 882 or BS 1047
	In soil			
Class	Total SO₃	SO₃ in 1:1 water extract	In groundwater	
1	Less than 0·2%		Less than 30 parts/100 000	For structural reinforced concrete work, *Ordinary Portland cement* or *Portland-blastfurnace cement*. Minimum cement content 280kg/m³, maximum free water/cement ratio 0·55 by weight. For plain concrete, less stringent requirements apply
2	0·2–0·5%		30–120 parts/100 000	(See Note 2) (a) *Ordinary Portland cement* or *Portland-blastfurnace cement*. Minimum cement content 330kg/m³. Maximum free water/cement ratio 0·50 by weight (b) *Sulphate-resisting Portland cement*. Minimum cement content 280kg/m³. Maximum free water/cement ratio 0·55 by weight (c) *Supersulphated cement*. Minimum cement content 310kg/m³. Maximum free water/cement ratio 0·50 by weight
3	0·5–1·0%	2·5–5·0 g/litre	120–250 parts/100 000	*Sulphate-resisting Portland cement, supersulphated cement or high alumina cement*. Minimum cement content 330kg/m³. Maximum free water/cement ratio 0·50 by weight
4	1·0–2·0%	5·0–10·0 g/litre	250–500 parts/100 000	(a) *Sulphate-resisting Portland cement* or *supersulphated cement*. Minimum cement content 370kg/m³. Maximum free water/cement ratio 0·45 by weight (b) *High alumina cement*. Minimum cement content 340kg/m³. Maximum free water/cement ratio 0·45 by weight
5	Over 2·0%	Over 10·0g/litre	Over 500 parts/100 000	*Either* cements described in 4 (a) *plus* adequate protective coatings of inert material such as asphalt or bituminous emulsions reinforced with fibreglass membranes *or* high alumina cement with a minimum cement content of 370kg/m³. Maximum free water/cement ratio 0·40 by weight

Notes:

1. For severe conditions, e.g. thin sections, sections under hydrostatic pressure on one side only and sections partly immersed, consideration should be given to a further reduction of water/cement ratio and, if necessary, an increase in cement content to ensure the degree of workability needed for full compaction and thus minimum permeability.

2. The cement contents given in Class 2 are the minima recommended by the manufacturers. For SO₃ contents near the upper limit of Class 2 cement contents above these minima are advised.

Reference: *Concrete in Sulphate-bearing Soils and Groundwaters*, BRS Digest (2nd Series) No. 90, HMSO, Feb., 1968.

Weather conditions at the time of making tests are important, because, in extreme cases, the concentration found in water in *dry weather* may be several times as large as that found in wet weather.

A soil with a relatively high sulphate content but which is dry for long periods, or which is so drained that the solutions formed are removed from the vicinity of the concrete will be *much less* destructive than one with a lower sulphate content and where the physical conditions are more favourable, that is, wet for long periods or inadequately drained. Generally soils in which wetting and drying occur fairly frequently are likely to be particularly destructive. It may also be noted here that the salt content of a soil is only important in so far as it represents the reserve supplies available for maintaining, or increasing, the salt content of the waters contained in it, or draining from it.

The rate with which the sulphates may be replenished under 'service' conditions is dependent on the rate with which water is transferred through the soil, and this is, in turn, dependent on either drainage or fluctuations in the level of the water table. 'Assisted' drainage may occur, for example, when pipe lines are laid at a gradient. The effect of this is to allow the sulphate-bearing waters to flow along the lines. In so doing sulphates may then be transferred from sulphate-bearing clay, at a high level, to non-sulphate-bearing clay at a lower level, thus increasing the severity of exposure of the concrete. The same may also occur, but in a more restricted way, in shorter excavations. In general, foundations and concrete piles do not form channels along which the flow of ground water is likely to occur.

(d) *Precautions*

The factors associated with the attack of concrete in sulphate-bearing groundwaters and clays are, as outlined earlier, extremely variable. Any precautionary measures which may be recommended should, therefore, generally be regarded as guides rather than a set of invariable rules. Furthermore, when there is any doubt about any of the factors involved, it is wise to tend to err on the side of excessive rather than insufficient precautions.

Table 3.06/2 sets out the limits of sulphate content for five classes of site of increasing severity together with recommended precautionary measures for each class. The divisions between the classes are somewhat arbitrarily drawn, according to BRS, while the recommendations are judgements based on present knowledge.* Particular attention should be given to the notes which accompany the table. For convenience, an elaboration of the more important aspects of the information contained in the table is given, under separate headings, below.

(i) *Classification of soil conditions.* The precautions which should be taken, in terms of the type and quality of concrete including the use of specially resistant cements, to minimise the risk of sulphate attack taking place on concrete in sulphate-bearing groundwaters and clays will be dependent on the amount and nature of the sulphate(s) present. Thus it is convenient to classify soils on the basis of their sulphate content in either groundwaters or clay. In this respect, it should be noted that the results of groundwater analyses are preferable as a criterion to those obtained from analyses of the clay. In some cases it may not be possible to obtain groundwater analyses. For example, a clay may not yield any water in a trial excavation or borehole, although later, under other seasonal conditions, or for other reasons, it may become water-bearing. In those cases where the results of groundwater and clay analyses indicate a different classification of the site in terms of suggested limits of sulphate content, it is advisable to adopt the more severe classification. When evaluating the results of analyses in order to establish the classification of a site, it is important to take into account the factors which influence the variability of sulphate content as discussed in 3 (c) above. The latter imply, among other things, that due care is taken in the survey of the site, the weather conditions during the survey, and the execution of the analyses in the laboratory.

The concentrations of groundwater (column 4 of Table 3.06/2) are expressed as parts SO₃ per 100 000 parts of water as is customary. Thus analytical figures expressed in grams of SO₃ per litre must be *multiplied* by 100.

The total sulphate content of the soil obtained by extraction with hot dilute hydrochloric acid and expressed as a percentage of SO₃ (column 2) may result in a site being assessed too severe if the sulphate present in

*It is interesting to note that as a result of increased knowledge and experience, the present precautions tend to be a good deal less conservative than those first published by BRS in the 1950's. For example, in the earlier recommendations only three classes of site were specified while the quality of concrete and the types of cement that could be used were less clearly defined.

the soil is predominantly calcium sulphate which has a low solubility. Thus in cases where the total sulphate exceeds 0·5 per cent it is suggested that the water-soluble sulphate should be determined. The soluble salts can be extracted from the soil using an equal weight of water and expressed as grams SO_3 per litre of water extract as in column 3 of the table.

(ii) *Type and quality of concrete.* Whatever cement may be used, the principal requirement for concrete is that it should be *dense and impermeable,* as the attack of concrete proceeds inwards from the surface, while the rate of attack is dependent on the ease with which water can penetrate into the concrete. In order to achieve dense and impermeable concrete, it is necessary that particular attention be given to those factors which influence the quality of concrete, namely, richness of the mix (ratio of cement to aggregate), water content (water/cement ratio), quality and grading of the aggregate, methods of mixing and placing and curing, and, also the age of the concrete. As regards the latter, the vulnerability of cast *in situ* concrete to attack when it is still in the green state is noteworthy. In some cases, additional protective measures may be required.

The use of *admixtures* needs a special note. Air-entraining or water-reducing agents may give some *limited* improvement in sulphate resistance. Those containing workability aids improve compaction and allow the use of lower water/cement ratios, but those containing calcium chloride are *not* recommended. Admixtures should *not* be used with high alumina cement without consulting the cement manufacturers.

In order to ensure minimum permeability and a hard surface when any type of concrete uses supersulphated cement, it is important to give particular care during the initial curing period.

The recommendations for the type and quality of concrete given in Table 3.06/2 for each class of soil condition specify the *minimum* cement content in kg/m³ of aggregate. This allows for some modification of the ratio of fine to coarse aggregrate. It should be noted that the cement contents quoted are *minima.* In certain cases, additional amounts of cement may be required if workability is high, or aggregates are harsh, or if hand compaction cannot be avoided. As far as the water/cement ratios are concerned, it is important to note that those specified are *maxima* and based on the 'free' water present in the mix, and should, therefore, not be exceeded. 'Free' water, it is important to note, is the total weight of water in the concrete less that absorbed by the aggregate.

(iii) *Form of construction.* The degree of exposure of concrete is, in addition to the sulphate content of the soil, dependent on the form of construction in which it is used. The

recommendations as to the type and quality of concrete given in Table 3.06/2 should, in this respect, be assumed to apply to the least severe condition of exposure. Such a condition is likely to apply to concrete which is *completely buried* under conditions such that the excavation does not form a channel along which a flow of ground water is likely to occur. Foundations to buildings will usually fall under this class.

The most severe condition of exposure is likely to occur when concrete is subjected to one-sided hydrostatic pressure, as in retaining walls, for example (see 1(c) (vi) earlier). A similar, though less severe, condition occurs in a partly buried concrete mass when water is drawn up by capillary forces from the portion below ground and evaporates at the exposed surface. Severe conditions of exposure can also occur with thin sections or sections with thin bars and therefore smaller cover. In all these cases, consideration should be given to a further *reduction* of water/cement ratio, and, if necessary, an *increase* in cement content so as to ensure adequate workability.

(iv) *Protective coatings.* As sulphate attack proceeds from the surface of the concrete inwards, it is possible to provide protection by the surface application of impermeable coatings of bituminous or similar materials. Such protection may be required if, for any reason, it is impracticable to use a more sulphate resistant cement, or if it is required to provide temporary protection for concrete while it is curing. For the latter condition, the use of bituminised paper, hessian or similar materials may be sufficient for the least severe exposure. When, however, a very high degree of durability is required of the coating, then consideration should be given to the use of asphalt or bituminous emulsions reinforced with fibre glass mat (see recommendations for class 5, the alternative). Alternatively, it may be necessary to consider the use of thick asphalt coatings, applied as tanking.

(e) *Concrete floors on shale hardcore*
Reference is made in *Section 3.05* under 'Sources of soluble salts' (1(d) (iii)) that colliery shale may contain an appreciable amount of soluble salts, particularly sulphates. The soluble salt content of colliery shale is liable to wide variations, and some tips (the unsightly heaps of waste material near coal-mines) contain as much as 5 per cent, whereas others contain less than 1 per cent. Shale has been used as hardcore for concrete ground-floor slabs in a similar way to hardcore of other materials, namely by being tipped into the foundation area and compacted, using water as necessary. The concrete floor slab has, in turn, been cast on top of the hardcore without a d.p.m. between the hardcore and the concrete. Following the investigation by the BRS of cases of failures of concrete slabs laid on colliery shale hardcore,

it is clear that certain precautionary measures are necessary. Before outlining these measures, it is considered advisable to outline the nature and causes of the failures which have occurred.

(i) *Failures.* Failures of concrete slabs laid on shale hardcore in houses have taken various forms, but usually the slab lifts and cracks. Considerable cracking of the concrete occurs in the later stages. In extreme cases, on very wet sites, the underside may become mushy. (An example of the severe cracking which may occur is included in *Section 2.03,* Vol. 1, p. 133.)

In some cases the upward movement of the slab has been accompanied by an outward movement, resulting in the outer walls being pushed out of place. In cavity construction, the inner leaf may be pushed towards the outer leaf without necessarily moving the latter. However, if the cavity ties are stiff enough, the movement may be transferred to the outer leaf. When the latter is of brickwork a crack usually forms somewhere near the corner of the building; but with an outer leaf of precast concrete units, there may be a displacement of the units, causing gaps between them.

Two reasons have been advanced for the lifting of the concrete slabs. These are: (1) swelling of the shale as it gets wet, thus pushing up the concrete, and, (2) transference of salts from the shale into the concrete, causing the sulphate attack of the concrete, which is accompanied by expansion. Although the swelling of the shale would appear to be insignificant, the possibility of it occurring, particularly on permanently very wet sites, should be considered with certain types of shale.

The most severe condition of exposure is likely to occur on poorly drained sites, as there will then be sufficient water present to allow transference of salts from the shale to the concrete. The chance of a sufficient quantity of salts being transferred from the shale to the concrete is considerably reduced on well-drained sites and on those where the water table is nearly always low.

(ii) *Precautions.* Sulphate attack is unlikely to occur if the colliery shale to be used has a low content of soluble salts (*less* than 0·5 per cent). However, due to the variability of the soluble salt content which can be expected in shale (even if it is from the same tip), it would be necessary to test several samples. Even this procedure may not necessarily guarantee that all the shale to be used would have a low sulphate content. Consequently it is advisable to prevent the salts from being transferred from the shale to the concrete. This may be done by laying a sheet of polythene or waterproof building paper as a d.p.m. on the hardcore before the concrete is placed. The d.p.m. should be taken up the sides of the brickwork or concrete footings to link up with the wall d.p.c. (see *Section 3.04,* Vol. 2, p. 127).

Some examples of the ways in which sulphate attack of brickwork may manifest itself. Above, expansion of coping. Below, expansion of parapet wall and, bottom picture, serious disintegration of the brickwork caused by deterioration of the mortar (Courtesy: BRS, HMSO, Crown Copyright)

On sites where the ground is permanently very wet, it is wise, if the shale is of a type which is likely to swell, to place an extra polythene layer on the subsoil before placing the hardcore. Care is needed to ensure that the polythene or other material is not unduly perforated by the hardcore.

4. Brickwork*

Sulphate attack of fairfaced brickwork is more commonly associated with clay bricks, and these types are implied throughout. Rendered brickwork is covered under '4. Rendering'.

(a) *Manifestations*

Basically it is the mortar, particularly in the bed joints, in brickwork which suffers as a result of sulphate attack. The mortar affected generally has a whitish appearance; the mortar in close contact with the bricks will often be whiter than in the centre of the joint. The ways in which the attack may manifest itself may be summarised as follows:

(i) Expansion of the mortar, leading to deformation and cracking of the brickwork. In this the mortar in the bed joints, particularly in the early stages of attack, remain rigid, although cracked, with considerable increase in height of the wall taking place. Height increases of as much as 0·2 per cent in the external leaf of a cavity wall to a two-storeyed dwelling have been reported.

(ii) The edges of the individual bricks may spall.

(iii) The mortar deteriorates. Generally the affected mortar cracks along the length of the joint (i.e. laminates) while the surface may fall off. The surface effects are very similar to those caused by frost action. However, frost action usually shows less extensive cracking and more surface spalling. When much water is present the affected mortar may be reduced to a soft mush.

(iv) Serious disintegration of the brickwork generally, which is the ultimate result following the lamination of the mortar joints outlined in (iii) above.

(b) *Causes*

In principle the causes for the attack of the mortar are similar to those already discussed under '1. General considerations' and '2. Basic mechanisms' previously. However, it is necessary to note here the more common source of sulphates and exposure to water.

The chief source of sulphates is the bricks, which are likely to vary considerably in their sulphate content, as

*References

(1) *Some Common Defects in Brickwork*, National Building Studies, Bulletin No. 9, HMSO, 1950. (2) *Sulphate attack on brickwork*, BRS Digest (2nd Series) No. 89, HMSO, January, 1968. (3) BS 3921 : 1965, Bricks and Blocks of Fired Brickearth, Clay or Shale. (4) *The Selection of Clay Building Bricks :* 1 and 2, BRS Digests (2nd Series) Nos. 65 and 66, HMSO, December, 1965, and January, 1966, respectively.

explained in *3.05 Efflorescence* under '1. Salts originally present in a material, (a) Clay bricks'. In general no correlation has been found between sulphate content of bricks* and sulphate expansion. For example, brickwork does not expand if the bricks have a low sulphate content; there is marked expansion with bricks containing a high sulphate content; but with bricks containing intermediate amounts of sulphate, expansion has varied widely. In this, variations in tricalcium aluminate content of the cement used in a mortar and the presence (or absence) of water are significant.

Normally, the vertical surfaces of walls do not remain wet for long enough for attack to take place, although soluble salts in the bricks may have been transferred during the wet period. In some of the wetter parts of the United Kingdom (see *3.02 Exposure*, Vol. 2), this assumption may have to be questioned. Sulphate attack is, therefore, usually, but not always, confined to those areas of walls where water has been allowed to percolate into the body of the brickwork containing sulphates, such as may occur through the joints of copings or sills, for example. Areas which are likely to remain persistently damp or damp for prolonged periods must, however, also be included. Such areas would include: (1) highly exposed parts of a wall, such as parapets; (2) from foundation level to d.p.c. level; (3) completely free standing walls, such as boundary walls; and (4) of earth retaining walls (extra source of sulphates, i.e. the soil or sulphate-bearing ground waters, together with only one evaporating surface are significant). It may also be noted that defective service pipes may also be an important source of water (and sometimes of sulphates as well).

(c) *Precautions*

In general, the precautions which could be taken to minimise the risk of sulphate attack taking place in brickwork (as in other cement-based materials too) involve the control of one of the three variables—sulphates, tricalcium-aluminate or water. So far as the sulphates are concerned, particularly in bricks, BS 3921 : 1965 only requires a fairly low soluble salt content for bricks of special quality, as shown in Table 3.06/3. The standard may have been unnecessarily stringent if it had attempted to specify sulphate contents of all bricks which would be low enough to enable any type of brick to be used whatever the tricalcium-aluminate content of cement used or however much water was allowed to filter into the walls without any deleterious effects. Among other things, many bricks may be used for internal walls where it may be assumed that walls will not normally become wet enough for sulphate attack to occur.

*In earth retaining brick walls or in brickwork below ground level, sulphates may be derived from the soil of sulphate-bearing groundwaters, as discussed under '3. Concrete' previously.

Table 3.06/3. Soluble salt limit for special quality bricks

Soluble salt	Maximum permissible content—per cent
Sulphate	0·30
Calcium	0·10
Magnesium	0·03
Potassium	0·03
Sodium	0·03

Reference: BS 3921 : 1965, *Bricks and Blocks of Fired Brick-earth Clay or Shale.*
Note: It is important to note that BS 3921 : 1965 specifies *a new method* of extracting soluble salts for analysis. The new method has been designed to secure *more accurate* figures for the minor constituents (magnesium, potassium and sodium) than the old method specified in BS 1257 : 1945. Consequently analyses made by the old method should not be used in conjunction with the limits specified in the new Standard.

Despite the limitations of BS 3921, bricks of low sulphate content complying with the requirements of the standard should be used wherever possible. This is not always possible and so extra precautions namely *either* to increase the resistance of the mortars to sulphate attack *or* to limit the extent to which the brickwork becomes and remains wet should be taken. In exceptional cases it may be necessary to employ both methods.

The sulphate resistance of mortars can be increased *either* by specifying richer mixes (for example $1:0-\frac{1}{4}:3$ or $1:\frac{1}{2}:4-4\frac{1}{2}$ or better still $1:5-6$ with plasticiser in place of lime) *or* by using sulphate-resisting, supersulphate or high alumina cements. It is important to note that lime additions should not be used with high alumina cements (ground limestone may be used).

Precautions may be summarised as follows:

(i) Generally ensure that the brickwork is kept dry in service—attention to details at eaves, verges, sills, parapets (including chimneys) and copings to prevent the ingress of water (see *3.04 Exclusion* under 'D.p.c.'s 2. Walls', Vol. 2) is important. Here it may be emphasised that sulphate attack is unlikely to occur if brickwork does not become and remain unduly wet.

(ii) Ideally parapets and free-standing walls should be avoided. Where this is not possible it is essential to:
   (1) Use low-sulphate bricks.
   (2) Design copings with generous overhang and adequate drip with d.p.c.'s under
   (3) Provide d.p.c's at bases of free-standing walls that are above expected soil levels and at roof level in parapets.
   (4) To provide expansion joints not more than 12m apart.
   (5) Specify sulphate-resisting mortar mixes.

(iii) Although it may be generally assumed that no special precautions are necessary in vertical walls between d.p.c. and roof level (in this the height of any parapets are excluded), the use of sulphate-resisting Portland cement is a worthwhile precaution in the wetter parts of the United Kingdom.

Above, another example of sulphate attack of brickwork showing disintegration of the mortar joints to the parapet area (Courtesy: BRS, HMSO, Crown Copyright)
Below, comparison of two identical chimneys, one of which (left-hand side) serves a solid fuel domestic boiler and has been subjected to sulphate attack, while the other (right-hand side) serves an open living room coal fire and has been unaffected. Sulphate attack has resulted in expansion and disintegration of the mortar joints (see picture on right). The chimneys have been in service for about seven years

D

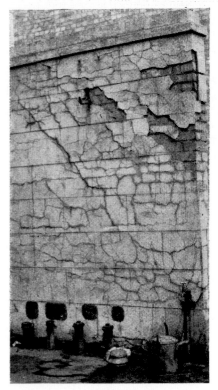

An example of sulphate attack of rendered brickwork showing the 'map' or 'crocodile' pattern of cracking, wide horizontal and vertical cracking, and adhesion failure of the rendering (Courtesy: BRS, HMSO, Crown Copyright)

Curvature or leaning of a chimney stack due to sulphate attack. Note the horizontal cracking at the bed joints (Courtesy: BRS, HMSO, Crown Copyright)

(iv) In retaining walls, manholes, brickwork below d.p.c. level, and in other situations where wet conditions for relatively long periods are likely to be expected, only bricks having a low sulphate content should generally be used. Such bricks should be used in conjunction with sulphate resisting mortar mixes (e.g. $1 : \frac{1}{2} : 4\frac{1}{2}$ or stronger, and preferably containing a sulphate resisting cement). In this an alternative to clay bricks would be sand-lime or concrete bricks as these seldom have sufficient amounts of sulphates—see *3.05 Efflorescence*.

Where however in earth retaining walls it is necessary to use bricks containing appreciable amounts of sulphates, then the retaining wall should be built of *in situ* concrete, without a batter, with the facing brick layer separated from it by a cavity. Adequate copings and expansion joints should be provided as for parapet walls while weep holes at the base of the cavity to ensure drainage but not venting of the cavity should be incorporated.

(v) Brickwork exposed to sea spray or other salt bearing water should preferably be built of dense bricks and cement mortar.

(vi) Gypsum plaster should never be added to mortars containing Portland cement or hydraulic lime.*

5. Rendering†

It is important to note that sulphate attack of rendered brickwork (clay bricks are again implied) is more commonly associated with dense cement renderings (1 : 2 or 1 : 3, cement : sand).

(a) *Manifestations*

With rendered brickwork there are two component parts which may be attacked, namely the mortar joints as previously discussed under '3. Brickwork' and the rendering itself. The amount of expansion vertically may be as much as 2 0 per cent, that is ten times as much as in facing brickwork. The ways in which the attack may manifest itself on rendered brickwork may be summarised as follows:

(i) The 'map' or 'crocodile' pattern of cracking which the rendering may develop as a result of drying out shrinkage of the rendering is accentuated, and may later be followed by horizontal cracks formed along the lines of the mortar joints.

(ii) Wide horizontal and vertical cracks may appear in the renderings, while there may be some outward curling of the rendering at the cracks.

(iii) The adhesion of the rendering to the brickwork may fail, resulting in the rendering falling off, either from individual bricks or in fairly large sheets, depending on the extent to which its under-surface has also been attacked by sulphates. Often the brickwork thus exposed will show white efflorescence.

(b) *Causes*

The causes of sulphate attack are generally the same as those previously outlined under '4. Brickwork'. However, there are some detailed considerations which must be taken into account.

Under similar conditions, the likelihood of the failure, due to sulphate attack, of brickwork rendered with dense cement renders is much greater than that of unrendered brickwork. Two factors are mainly responsible for this. First, there is a much greater surface area on which attack may take place, while in addition there are the mortar joints which may also be attacked. Second, dense renders are more or less impervious, thus encouraging far longer periods of dampness in the brickwork, should water gain access. In this there is the tendency of dense renders to develop cracks, particularly during the drying-out period; these cracks may then provide a further means of ingress for water (that is, in addition to the other common defects which allow water to percolate into brickwork). Once the water has gained entry, it cannot subsequently readily evaporate.

(c) *Precautions*

(i) Particular attention is required to details at eaves, verges, sills, parapets and copings (see *3.04 Exclusion* under 'D.p.c.'s 2. Walls', Vol. 2) to prevent the ingress of water. In parapets it is wise to ensure that one face is left unrendered (the 'roof' face, for example). This then provides one face from which any water that may have gained access may evaporate.

(ii) Dense cement renderings (1 : 2 or 1 : 3, cement : sand) should not be applied to bricks containing large amounts of sulphates, due to the tendency of such renderings to form shrinkage cracks which allow water to enter the brickwork. This water cannot readily evaporate through the dense rendering. Dense renderings may not be required, even if they do not develop cracks, except possibly in the more heavily exposed parts of the United Kingdom. Consequently, consideration should generally, but not exclusively, be given to the use of more porous and hence permeable renderings, containing cement gauged with lime, such as 1 : 1 : 6, cement : lime : sand, which permit evaporation from the brickwork more readily than the dense mixes; they may still afford adequate protection against rain penetration and are less liable to cracking. Thus the permeable renderings are less likely to accentuate sulphate attack.

(iii) In those areas in which sulphate attack is common*, or where exposure

*See footnote to first column, p. 28.

†(1) *Some Common Defects in Brickwork*, National Building Studies, Bulletin No. 9, HMSO. 1950. (2) *Sulphate attack on brickwork*, BRS Digest (2nd Series) No. 89, HMSO, January, 1968.

*Where the risk of sulphate is high it may be far better to avoid renderings completely and to consider alternatives with which the least risk will occur, such as facing brickwork, tile or slate hanging, and weatherboarding.

to driving rain is heavy, and if rendering is essential it is advisable, in addition to choosing bricks with a low sulphate content, to use a cement which is more resistant to sulphate attack than ordinary Portland cement for both the mortar and the rendering. Suitable cements are sulphate-resisting Portland cement, super-sulphated cement or high alumina cement.

(iv) Gypsum plaster should never be added to mortars or renderings containing Portland cement or hydraulic lime.*

6. Domestic chimneys†

Sulphate attack of domestic chimneys mainly occurs when the condensation risk with domestic boilers and slow combustion stoves and cookers has been overlooked. The risk of condensation (see also *4.00 Heat and its effects*) it may be noted here generally increases as the efficiency of the boiler increases, while the flue gases themselves may be destructive. (See also 'Acid action' previously.)

In addition to the signs mentioned previously for brickwork, both unrendered and rendered, sulphate attack in chimney stacks may cause a gradual curvature or leaning of the stack as shown in the accompanying photograph.

In principle, precautions aimed at preventing attack from taking place (that is, in addition to those which should be taken for exposure to rain, as previously described) are concerned with either reducing or eliminating the condensation by increasing the thermal insulation of the chimney, or by introducing relatively dry air into the flue through a ventilator just below the ceiling. Alternatively an impermeable flue lining which prevents any moisture that condenses within the flue from entering the brickwork may be provided. For the modern high efficiency boiler it is, however, advisable, not only to ensure adequate thermal insulation (together with the correct flue size) but also to incorporate a flue lining. The use of a flue lining, together with adequate insulation, particularly when existing flues are to be used, is essential. For convenience flue linings which may be used in both new and existing chimneys are set out below. Insulation requirements are included in *Part 4.00*.

(a) Flue linings

Lining materials suitable for use in both new and existing flues, with spigot and socket or rebated joints, include:

(i) *Impervious clay pipes,* often salt-glazed but may include certain classes of ceramic-glazed and unglazed pipes.

(ii) *Heavy gauge asbestos pipes.* The internal surface should be coated with an acid-resisting compound, for example, one prepared from a vinyl

*See footnote to first column, p. 28.

†(1) *Some Common Defects in Brickwork*, National Building Studies, Bulletin No. 9, HMSO, 1950. (2) *Chimney Design for Domestic Boilers,* BRS Digest (2nd Series) No. 60, HMSO, July, 1965.

acetate polymer or rubber derivative base, if gas appliances are to be used—see CP 331 : 104 : 1963.

(iii) *Dense concrete pipes,* which may require similar surface treatment to that for heavy gauge asbestos pipes (see (ii) above).

For new work, proprietary *precast concrete flue blocks* are available for construction of external flues.

In addition to the above, the following materials are available for use in *existing flues:*

(iv) *Refractory concrete pipes,* made of concrete from crushed fire-brick aggregate and high-alumina cement which is to some extent acid-resisting. The precast sections have rebated joints that should prevent seepage.

(v) *Flexible and jointless metal linings* intended primarily for use with gas and oil-fired boilers, circular in cross section and may be of stainless steel or aluminium, or made with an outer leaf of aluminium separated from an aluminium or lead foil inner leaf by corrugated paper.

(vi) *Lightweight concrete infills,* formed by a method that is basically different from those described above, namely by 'casting' the infill between the existing chimney and an inflated rubber 'core'. Experience with this method is limited, and mainly due to the fact that the flue surface is not impermeable to flue-gases, there appears to be a substantial risk that the gases may diffuse into the voids in the concrete, subsequently condense, and start attacking the cement.

(b) Staining

In the absence of precautions which will reduce the condensation risk in chimneys, the sooty and tarry deposits arising from combustion of fuel may cause ugly stains on ceilings and walls (usually the chimney breast) as shown in the accompanying photograph. These stains are difficult to remove and consequently remedial measures involve the complete removal of plaster or of applying a new lining. Before replastering care must be taken to ensure that the stains have also been removed from the background.

fungal attack in timber*

The rotting of timber, whether of the wet or dry rot type, is a form of chemical attack. Instead of the conventional chemicals, such as those included earlier in this section in connection with the decay of bricks stone, lime and cement-based products, the decaying agencies are fungi.

*References
(1) Desch, H. E., *Timber, Its Structure and Properties* (Macmillan & Co. Ltd.), 4th Ed., 1968. (2) *Dry Rot in Wood,* Forest Products Research, Bulletin No. 1, HMSO, 6th Ed., 1963. (3) *Dry Rot in Buildings,* Forest Products Research, Leaflet No. 6, HMSO, revised 1964. (4) Cartwright & Findlay, *Decay of Timber and its Prevention,* HMSO, 1958. (5) *Preservative Treatments for Constructional Timbers,* BS. CP 98 : 1964. (6) *Design of Timber Floors to Prevent Dry Rot,* BRS Digest (2nd Series), No. 18, HMSO, January, 1962. (7) *Prevention and Decay in Window Joinery,* BRS Digest (2nd Series), No. 73, HMSO, August, 1966. (8) *Painting Woodwork,* BRS Digest 106, HMSO, June, 1969.

Staining of ceiling and walls around a chimney breast by sooty and tarry deposits from the combustion of fuel and condensation in the chimney (Courtesy: BRS, HMSO, Crown Copyright)

Inserting a flexible and jointless metal flue lining (Courtesy: BRS, HMSO, Crown Copyright)

35

Above, strands of Merulius lacrymans, dry rot. The particular characteristics of the strands (see text) make this fungus extremely virulent and often difficult to eradicate. (Courtesy: Rentokil Laboratories Ltd.) Below right, a

portion of a joist attacked by dry rot with two fruit bodies attached. Note the deep cross-cracking, splitting the wood into cubes, and the sheets of mycelium (Crown Copyright)

Above left, a significant characteristic of the cellar fungus (Coniophora cerebella) is that the decay it causes is largely internal, and a thin unbroken layer of more or less sound wood often conceals the rot as can be seen in this example

of a decayed floorboard. Below, a portion of a decayed floorboard caused by cellar fungus showing fine blackish strands and longitudinal cracking (Crown Copyright)

In addition, the decomposition of the wood by the fungi usually causes physical changes such as shrinkage, warping and cracking, while the timber may be reduced to a powder.

In essence, the wood substance, composed chiefly of cellulose and lignin which form the cell walls, provides, under moist conditions, the food supply for the fungi, the cell wall substance being broken down and digested by the fungi. The fungi cannot, however, accomplish the decomposition of the wood substance, if the moisture content of the timber is much *below* fibre-saturation point, that is much below 25–30 per cent of the oven dry weight of the timber. In a well constructed building timber should always be below fibre-saturation point, as thoroughly air-seasoned timber contains 15–18 per cent moisture content,* while in a properly ventilated house this soon falls to 12 or 14 per cent, or even lower if central heating is operational. (See *3.03 Moisture content*, particularly 'Movement in timber', Vol. 2.) It may be noted here that when there is no air present, wood does not rot even when subjected to damp conditions for prolonged periods (completely waterlogged timber does not decay, as exemplified by many historic remains which have been found intact, such as wooden galleys which have been submerged since Roman times, or the timber foundations of lake dwellings). The conditions necessary for fungal growth, as explained later, must always be taken into account.

Basically two types of rot may be identified, namely wet and dry rot. *Wet rot* is characterised by the fact that the timber generally remains in a damp condition after the fungi responsible have attacked the timber; *dry rot*, on the other hand, is characterised by the fact that the timber is left in a dry friable condition after the fungi responsible have attacked the timber. Whereas wet rot usually only takes place in timber with a relatively high moisture content (between 25 and 30 per cent) and ceases when drier conditions prevail, dry rot takes place in timber with a relatively low moisture content (between 20 and 25 per cent). Unlike the wet rot, subsequent lowering of the moisture content of timber infected by dry rot does not necessarily cause the rot to cease. Among other things, the dry rot fungi have water-conducting strands which enables the infection to spread from the wetter to the drier areas of timber, while the fungi are able to spread over other building materials. The dry rot fungi are, therefore, extremely virulent and often difficult to eradicate. Pre-

*It is important to note that the range of 15–18 per cent moisture content quoted is the best obtainable for *thoroughly* air-seasoned timber. In general the range of moisture content for air seasoning in this country is roughly between 17 and 23 per cent (sometimes as high as 25 per cent) depending on conditions. See C.3.03/8, Vol 2. In the present context the range of moisture contents which may be attained in a well ventilated building are particularly significant.

vention of this type of decay is extremely important.

There are a number of different fungi responsible for either wet or dry rot. However, for the present purpose only two types of fungi are considered in detail, namely *Coniophora cerebella,* the *Cellar fungus,* which is characteristic of wet rot, and *Merulius lacrymans,* the dry rot fungus, which is not only characteristic of dry rot, but is also mainly responsible for the majority of serious cases of dry rot found in this country. Other types of fungi which may cause decay have, for convenience, been included in Table 3.06/4. It may be noted that there are other types of fungi such as Blue stain fungi, and mould-like growths which are not injurious in timber, although they may cause changes in appearance of timber.

Although in general terms it is possible to say that timber maintained at or below 20 per cent moisture content will not suffer fungal attack of any kind, account must be taken of the fact that it may not always be practicable to maintain all the timber in a building at or below 20 per cent moisture content (this may be extremely significant during the initial life of a building, when drying out is still taking place), while timbers vary in their resistance to decay. Consequently the precautions which should be taken are likely to vary according to conditions (moisture and the fungi likely to be present) and the timber selected. Thus it is necessary to consider a number of factors related to both the fungi and the timber. For convenience these are discussed under the following general headings.; (1) Nature of fungi; (2) Sources of infection; (3) Conditions necessary for growth; (4) Resistance of timbers; and (5) Precautions.

1. Nature of fungi

(a) *Structure and growth*

The fungi which destroy wood are part of a large family known as Basidiomycetes. The reproductive parts are contained in the fruit bodies. Mushrooms and toadstools, which are included in the same family, are typical and familiar examples of fruit bodies which appear above ground; the fruit bodies in fungi are equivalent to the flowers and fruits of the higher plants.

Exceedingly fine tubes or hollow threads, known as *hyphæ,* make up the vegetative part of a fungus, and grow in length by elongation of the tips. These tubes may be arranged loosely, or bunched closely, to form soft cushions. Dense skins, sheets, lumps or long strings are the manifestation of closely interwoven tubes. The large fruit bodies, which may be shaped like mushrooms, or be flat and plate- or pancake-like, are formed through the interweaving of the threads.

New fungus plants are formed from each (in some cases a pair) of the minute spores (equivalent to the seeds of the higher plants) which are pro-

duced on the fruit bodies. Each fruit body is capable of producing countless numbers of spores. It is important to note that even when dried the spores of the dry rot fungi may remain capable of germinating for several years.

(b) *The dry rot fungus*

The general characteristics of this fungus are included in Table 3.06/4.

It is, however, important to draw attention to the particular characteristics of the strands or strings of the dry rot fungus. The strands or strings, which may vary in thickness from thin threads to hard strands as thick as a pencil lead, are able to pass across inert substances such as bricks or metals. Consequently the fungus can be transported from timber in one area of a building to timber in another.

Table 3.06/4. Diagnosis of fungi causing decay of timber in buildings

Fungus	Effect on the wood	Strings on the surface of the wood	Other growths on the surface of the wood	Fruit bodies
Merulius lacrymans (Dry rot)	Rotted wood shrinks and becomes split up into cubical pieces by deep cross-cracking. Generally occurs in humid, unventilated places where the air is still and the woodwork damp but not saturated. Does not occur unless moisture content of timber over 20 per cent. Once established can affect dry timber	Strings grey, sometimes as thick as a lead pencil, becoming brittle when dried	In damp, dark places, soft white cushions; in drier places, thick silver-grey sheets or skins usually showing patches of lemon yellow and tinges of lilac	Fleshy, soft but rather tough, shaped like pancakes or brackets. Spore bearing surface, yellow to red brown, with wide pores or labyrinthine ridges and furrows. Margin white
Poria vaillantii (and other related species of *Poria*)	Rot similar but less widespread than that produced by *Merulius*. Several species of *Poria* occur in houses, all requiring more moisture than *Merulius*. Only limited power of spreading beyond damp area	Strings white, seldom thicker than stout twine, remaining flexible when dried	White or cream-coloured sheets and growths, never showing coloration	Shaped like sheets or plates, white in colour. Spore bearing surface, white, showing numerous minute pores
Coniophora cerebella (Cellar fungus —wet rot)	Dark brown, cracking along the grain in early stages. Rot sometimes internal leaving apparently sound skin of wood. Cracking across grain occurs when attack is more advanced, but cubes are smaller than with *Merulius*. Requires higher moisture conditions than *Merulius*. Generally associated with leaks or condensation. Fungus does not spread beyond area which is damp	Strings, slender, usually thread-like, at first yellowish, soon becoming deep brown or nearly black	Occasionally very thin skin-like growths	Sheet-like in shape. Fertile surface greenish to olive brown, bearing spores on many minute pimples
Paxillus panuoides	Causes a characteristic yellow discoloration in the attacked wood, which finally becomes red brown	Very slender, yellow but eventually brownish yellow	Rather hairy or woolly, dull yellow, sometimes pale-violet in colour	Fleshy, fan- or shell-shaped, stalkless. Spore bearing surface with radiating ridges (gills), at first yellow, then ochre
Lentinus lepideus	Causes an internal brown cubical rot. This fungus and the attacked wood have a characteristic strong aromatic smell	None	Only present occasionally. Purplish brown felted woolly sheet	Normal form, shaped like a mushroom with radiating gills beneath, tough and woody. Frequently abortive forms occur without a cap and consisting only of cylindrical branching outgrowths
Trametes serialis (*Poria monticola*)	Causes 'dote' in the form of isolated small pockets of brown rot. Eventually may cause general brown cubical rot. Usually found only on timber imported from America	Slender, white, much branched	Only developed under very damp conditions, soft, white, cotton woolly, sometimes with dark brown patches	Seldom seen in houses: consisting of thin plates or broad thin teeth forming wide pores

References: (1) *Dry Rot in Wood,* Forest Products Research; Bulletin No. 1, HMSO, 6th Ed., 1960.
(2) *Preservation Treatments for Constructional Timber,* CP 98 : 1964.

Furthermore, the strands are capable of passing through walls. Thus the fungus can spread from room to room. The strands also contain special hyphæ which are capable of carrying water. The transportation of water from damp to dry areas enables the fungus to attack relatively dry timber. (During active growth the fungus often produces drops of moisture—hence the name *lacrymans,* weeping). In addition, the strands contain a reserve supply of food materials. This means that growth can be renewed after the replacement of infected timber if the surrounding walls have not been sterilised.

A characteristic of the fruit bodies is that they produce rusty red spores in enormous numbers, many millions being shed from a single fruit body. The spores are capable of being blown about with the slightest draught, and can be carried by insects and other vermin. Consequently it is comparatively easy for infection to become widespread.

Thoroughly decayed wood has the appearance of charred wood. It is friable, light and dry, and falls to powder under the fingers. The wood is broken up into more or less cubical pieces due to cracks running both along and across the grain.

(c) The cellar fungus

The general characteristics of this fungus are included in Table 3.06/4. As stated earlier the cellar fungus only attacks timber which is *definitely wet* and is commonly found where leakage of water has occurred, or as the result of condensation. Contact with wet porous materials may also be significant.

The strands of the cellar fungus are not as strong, nor as well developed as those of the dry rot fungus (the strands are never thicker than stout twine), do not carry water and do not spread over inert materials. Consequently growth ceases when dry conditions return in the timber.

The effect of the cellar fungus on wood is to cause it to become much darkened (sometimes coal-black), particularly near the surface. Splitting of the timber results initially with longitudinal cracks; in the advanced state cross cracking occurs, although the cubes are smaller than those of *Merulius.* Another significant characteristic is that the decay is often largely internal, and a thin unbroken layer of more or less sound wood often conceals the rot.

2. Sources of infection

Before considering the sources of infection of the dry rot fungus, it is necessary to emphasise that the dry rot fungus will spread by contagion, that is by the actual growth of the fungus from an infected piece of timber as previously outlined in 1 (b). It may be noted here that under unfavourable conditions (for the user of a building) the fungus can travel several feet in a few months; under very bad conditions it may eventually reach every piece of timber in a house.

Timber yards, unless they are well kept, may provide a source of infection for timber. Contamination may take place either by spores or by contact with decayed wood.

In existing buildings, dry rot fungi may be introduced with timber which has been used to effect some repair or addition to the structure. Firewood, which is not infrequently obtained from houses affected with dry rot, may be stored in a damp cellar or outhouse and there develop active dry rot, which spreads into the rest of the building.

As already noted, spores are produced in their millions, while they are light and small. Thus they may easily be blown everywhere. They may also be introduced with coal. Fortunately, *Merulius lacrymans* is seldom, if ever, found out-of-doors while its spores do not germinate readily. Consequently the dry rot fungi are not so generally dispersed as are those of some other fungi, such as the cellar fungus.

3. Conditions necessary for growth

Assuming the presence of some infection, in the form of spores or *mycelium** which will act as a seed or a germ from which the fungus can develop, *four* conditions are necessary for the growth of fungi. These are:

(a) A supply of food material from which the fungus can derive its nourishment; (b) a suitable temperature; (c) a supply of moisture; and (d) a sufficient amount of oxygen for the respiration of the fungus.

As each of these four conditions must be operative for growth to take place, it follows that the control of rot, particularly the initial attack of the dry rot fungus, involves rendering as many of the conditions as possible unfavourable for the fungus to grow. The significance of each of the conditions necessary for growth are considered separately.

(a) Food material

Although wood is the obvious food material for the wood-destroying fungi, most of them can feed, or at least live for considerable periods, upon other materials having a similar chemical composition, such as paper, straw, etc. Consequently it is advisable to have as little as possible of these other materials with similar chemical composition to wood in contact with the woodwork. It may also be noted that a soil rich in humus can also support many of the wood-destroying fungi.

Timber can be rendered immune from attack if the food material is poisoned. This entails the treatment of the wood with a *wood preservative.†*

**The term *mycelium* is used to denote a mass of fungus growth built of the numerous hyphae.*

†The primary consideration here is the preservation of timber against fungal attack. However, it may be noted that many of the preservatives used may also protect timber from insect attack.

Such treatment would have to be used if it is not possible to render the other conditions unfavourable for fungus growth. For example, it may not be possible or practicable in some circumstances to prevent timber from becoming damp.

The effectiveness of treating timber with a preservative in order to eliminate or reduce the risk of attack will depend upon the thoroughness of the treatment used. This is in turn dependent on the preparation of the timber for treatment; methods of treatment; conditioning after treatment, and, the preservative used.

For timber to be in a suitable *condition for treatment* it must be dry (cells of unseasoned wood may be filled with moisture, making it impossible to force in any more liquid), clean and free of surface moisture, while all necessary cutting and shaping should, wherever possible, be carried out prior to treatment (if this is not possible, a liberal application of preservative should be brushed on to any cut surface). Some timbers, such as Douglas fir and spruce, may require an incising process before treatment in order to overcome their resistance to penetration by preservatives.

Methods commonly used *for treatment* are, in order of their effectiveness, as follows: (1) *Pressure impregnation,* in which the preservative is forced into the timber under pressure, thus allowing the deepest possible penetration of the preservative. (2) *Hot-and-Cold open tank treatment,* in which the timber is placed in a tank of preservative, which is then heated to a temperature of about 80–90°C, maintained at this temperature for a few hours and then allowed to cool. (Protection afforded to sap wood and permeable timbers by this method may be comparable to that given by pressure treatment.) (3) *Steeping,* in which the timber is submerged in cold preservative for varying lengths of time, depending on species and size of timber being treated. (4) *Dipping,* in which the timber is submerged in a bath of preservative for a minimum of 10 seconds. (5) *Brushing and spraying,* are methods used with all types of preservatives and most useful for *in situ* work. Preservatives should always be liberally applied, care being taken to treat cracks and checks. This method should be regarded as one that affords temporary protection only to the timber.

Once treated, it is necessary to open-stack the timber in a well-ventilated space in order to allow the surplus solvent in the preservative to dry out. Re-drying, by kiln if necessary, of timber treated with water-borne preservatives is imperative if dimensional fluctuations are to be controlled (floors, panelling and joinery are significant).

There are basically three *types of preservative* which may be used. These are:

(1) *Tar oil preservatives,* such as creosote, which are useful for the

preservation of all external timber (apart from that to be painted), wall plates, ground-floor joists, etc. Care must be taken to ensure that these preservatives do not bleed through plasterwork or paintwork; that they are not used in rooms where food is stored, as they may cause tainting. The smell is fairly strong and objectionable to some people, but it is not unhealthy.

(2) *Water borne preservatives.* Although most of the simple water soluble preservatives are liable to be washed out if the treated timber is exposed to the action of the weather, there are some proprietary water borne mixtures which become highly fixed in the wood after treatment and are satisfactory for use under leaching conditions. Where the more soluble mixtures are to be used they should be protected from the weather either by being under cover or coated with paint. The advantages of the water borne preservatives over the tar oils may be summarised as follows: Wood treated with a water borne preservative may be painted as soon as it has dried; they are odourless; they do not 'creep' and cause stain in plaster work, and they may be obtained colourless if desired. On the other hand, it is important to note that re-drying of timber treated with this type of preservative is necessary, in order to reduce the effects of dimensional fluctuations (see '5. Precautions').

(3) *Solvent type preservatives.* These consist of a toxic substance, such as pentachlorophenol or copper naphtha, dissolved in an organic solvent such as white spirit or solvent naphtha, so that when the solvent evaporates the toxic substances remain in the wood. This type of preservative is very effective provided the active substance is present in sufficient quantity. Some solvent type preservatives contain water-repellants; these improve the dimensional stability of the wood as well as helping to resist decay. When treated timber is to be painted, it is important to ensure that the water-repellant used in the preservative is compatible with the paint system.

(b) Temperature
The temperatures at which the majority of fungi are able to grow range from freezing point to a little below or above blood heat. These temperatures normally obtain in most buildings and consequently this condition is, in general, difficult to render unfavourable for growth. However, it may be noted that the rate of growth is influenced by temperature. At temperatures just above freezing growth is extremely slow, but increases rapidly as the temperature rises to the optimum, although the rate becomes very slow again as the maximum is reached. In the case of the cellar fungus, for example, growth is four times as fast at 24°C as it is at 10°C.

Sterilisation of timber is possible if a temperature well above the maximum for growth is maintained for long enough. In this, it may be noted that many fungi are extremely resistant to heat, particularly when in a dormant condition in dry wood. Consequently sterilisation by heat is a lengthy process, particularly as the heat must be maintained for long enough to reach the innermost parts of the wood. Six hours at a temperature of 54·4°C in a humid atmosphere should suffice to sterilise even thick timbers infected with the dry rot fungus.

Additional heating is sometimes seen as a cure for timber infected with rot, particularly dry rot in existing buildings. Such measures are unlikely to prove effective unless the timber is allowed to dry out, as the rate of decay will merely increase if the timber is allowed to remain damp. Thus, in addition to extra heating, increased ventilation to the timber is also imperative.

(c) Moisture
Moisture, together with air (see (d) later), are the most important factors to be considered in practice in connection with fungal decay of timber, particularly as the initiation of decay in a building is invariably due to the timber being damp, while the requisite amount of air is usually also available.

Moisture requirements vary with both the type of fungus and the type of timber upon which the fungus is growing. However, in general, attack by the dry rot fungus is liable to take place as soon as timber has a moisture content of 20–25 per cent; attack by most other wood-destroying fungus is liable to take place when timber is at the 'fibre-saturation' point, that is, a moisture content of 25–30 per cent, with an optimum moisture content of about 40 per cent, depending on the type of fungus and type of timber.

An important characteristic of some of the fungi which cause active rotting of timber (the dry rot fungus is again significant) is their ability to actually produce water. This is done by chemically splitting up the carbohydrates in the wood. Thus the timber on which the fungus is growing is made much more moist and this in turn stimulates growth. And so the process goes on. In the case of the dry rot fungi it is, therefore, most important that they do not become established, and in order to prevent this, the moisture content of timber should always be maintained below 20 per cent.

(d) Air
In common with most other organisms, fungi require a certain amount of oxygen for their growth and respiration. Consequently completely saturated timber, that is, when the cell spaces in the wood are completely filled with water, is quite immune from attack because it contains no air. However, it is important to note that complete saturation is necessary. Thus exposure of the face of a piece of otherwise saturated timber to air is sufficient to render it liable to decay.

Butts of posts, for example, embedded in waterlogged soil, or submerged in water, decay where the wood is damp but not water-logged—between 'wind and water'. It may be noted that, whereas the dry rot fungus is unable to attack timber which may become thoroughly wet, such timber may be attacked by other fungi, such as the cellar fungus, because there is usually a large surface area of the timber exposed to the air.

4. Resistance of timbers
It is convenient to include under this heading timber products and other organic building materials.

(a) Timbers
When considering the resistance which any timber may have to fungal attack, account must be taken of the fact that there is no risk of attack while the timber remains *perfectly dry*.

In general, few of the timbers commonly used in this country, particularly those used for constructional work, can be relied upon to resist fungal attack, and dry rot attack in particular. There is an enormous variation in the resistance which timbers will provide to fungal attack. In this not only are the various species of timber significant, but also the structure and rate of growth of a given species. Then there is the difference in resistance as between the sapwood and heartwood of any species.

Some timbers such as poplar and beech, for example, may be reduced to a powder in a few months by fungal decay; others, such as teak and greenheart, can resist attack for many years. When it is necessary to select timbers which are naturally resistant to decay, instead of resorting to some form of preservative treatment, a choice from the following could be considered: Canadian western red cedar, opepe, afzelia, kokrudua, teak, iroko, 'Rhodesian teak', jarrah, or (but somewhat less resistant) well-seasoned oak heartwood. Many of these timbers, it will be noted, are hardwoods.

However, in specifications reference to the particular species of timber is important, and so quotations such as 'all timber to be hardwood' should be avoided when resistance to fungal attack is required. In those cases where a non-durable species must be used, then it is advisable to treat the timber with preservative.

Variation in resistance provided by different samples of the same timber and due to rate of growth and other structural changes may be exemplified by the fact that a slow-grown close-ringed resinous sample of a coniferous timber, such as pine or spruce, will exhibit much greater resistance to fungal attack than a quick-grown sample of the same timber.

The sapwood and heartwood of practically all timbers have markedly different resistances to fungal attack. In general, the sapwood is far less durable than the heartwood. In a great

Rotting of that part of a timber hand-rail to a balcony balustrade in contact with porous material (the brickwork), after being in service for only eight years. Above right, '. . . any timbers built into

walls that might become damp should be given suitable preservative treatment. The ends of joists facing onto cavities of external walls also need to be protected from damp'

many cases the sapwood cannot be economically excluded from timber for building use, including joinery. Thus, all timber, unless naturally resistant to decay, which may contain sapwood should always be treated with a preservative.

(b) Plywood

Two factors influence the durability of plywood to decay. These are: (i) the resistance of the wood to decay, and (ii) the resistance of the adhesive to moisture and to decomposition by micro-organisms.

The exterior grades of plywood do incorporate synthetic adhesives which are resistant to moisture and microbial decomposition. However, the veneers themselves are not usually treated with wood-preservative, and thus the ply-wood as a whole is not immune from dry rot, although it will not delaminate even after prolonged exposure to damp conditions. The resistance to decay of plywood of this type may, therefore, be regarded as similar to that of the wood from which it was made.

Certain caution is required in the use of 'interior' grade plywood. The term 'interior' should *not* be regarded as one which allows plywood of this kind to be used under any internal climate. In fact, this type of plywood should not be used in any situation where it is likely to remain damp for any length of time.

(c) Timber and other organic products

In general, wall boards made from defibrated wood, sugar cane, bagasse, and similar cellulose materials, are readily attacked by dry rot if exposed to persistently damp conditions. How-ever, the incorporation of a preserva-tive in some brands of wall boards renders these resistant to decay (and

attack by white ants). The resistance which hardboards may offer to attack varies with their porosity, although all types will rot under bad conditions — the soft, more porous types, are generally less resistant.

Wood wool slabs though resistant to decay are not impervious to the strands of the dry rot fungus. Satura-tion with water may lead to slow dis-integration as a result of fungal decay. Under the influence of moisture alone, some types of slab incorporating gypsum with the cement may lose their cohesion. Resistance of the slabs to decay is not necessarily increased by preserving the wood wool, it being thought that the cement renders in-active the preservatives used.

5. Precautions

In principle, control of fungal decay in buildings can be achieved by follow-ing two simple rules. First, by using only sound, well-seasoned timber, free from any incipient decay, and, second, by maintaining the timber in a *perfectly dry* state. In the present context, and taking into account that precautions should be related to the worst condition, namely attack by the dry rot fungus, perfectly dry implies a moisture content of not more than 20 per cent. Although the choice of the correct quality of timber should not, in practice, present insurmountable difficulties, the maintenance of the dry state may not be so easy to comply with, and to insist on strict adherence to this rule is, in practical terms, un-realistic, particularly as the resistance of any species of timber including the weaker sapwood, may be adequately increased by the use of preservative treatments (see 3 (a) previously). How-ever, it is still wise to ensure that even the most resistant timbers, or

those made more resistant by treat-ment with preservatives, are not allowed to become unduly damp for prolonged periods. The reason for this is really quite simple. The more resis-tant timbers, or those treated with pre-servatives, are not necessarily com-pletely immune from attack under severe conditions of exposure to moisture.

Because of the additional costs im-plied in the use of either timbers which are more resistant to fungal attack or preservative treatment, a thorough analysis of each condition in which timber is to be used in a building and aimed at establishing the likelihood of dampness occurring, not only during service but also during the drying out period of a building, is of the utmost importance. Conditions which are likely to give rise to damp-ness are covered variously in *3.01 General considerations, 3.02 Exposure,* and, in particular, *3.03 Moisture content* (has special and detailed reference to timber), and are, therefore, not repeated here except in outline as relevant later on. In a great many cases, water, and hence damp-ness, may be excluded by paying proper attention to constructional details (subsequent maintenance is also extremely significant), as covered in detail in *3.04 Exclusion.* It is impor-tant to note that attention to details of construction so as to exclude water from reaching timber is one of the most important precautions to be taken in preventing fungal attack. From the considerations outlined in previous sections it will be seen that, in general, timber which is likely to be subjected to fungal attack is to some degree concealed and/or in contact with other porous materials which may transfer moisture to the timber (moisture 'released' during the drying out of a building is most significant). In the case of constructional work, including roof timbers and decking, the whole of the timber is concealed and part in contact with other (usually, but not always, porous) materials; in the case of floor boards, skirtings and joinery such as frames (windows, doors, cupboards, etc.) only the back or side(s), except for timber floor boards covered with other finishes such as carpet, linoleum, etc., are concealed and usually the concealed face(s) are in contact with other (usually, but not always, porous) materials.

In general, the dry rot safety line, which implies a moisture content of not greater than 20 per cent, can be fairly easily achieved with most air seasoned timber in this country, while in a well ventilated building the service moisture content may drop to as low as 12 or 14 per cent. However, in centrally heated buildings, the moisture content of the timber may fall to 8 or 9 per cent. Moisture contents below 17 per cent cannot be achieved without kiln seasoning. At the same time in order to avoid problems associated with dimensional fluctuations in timber, as outlined in detail in *3.03 Moisture content* under 'Movement in timber' (Vol. 2), it is necessary to ensure that when timber is installed in a building its moisture content is not significantly different from that to be expected in service. The margin between installed moisture content and average moisture content in service is, in general, less critical for timber used for constructional purposes, than for joinery and flooring, mainly because the average service moisture content of constructional timber is generally higher than that for joinery, as can be seen in Table 3.06/5.* Control of dimensional fluctuations in timber is related to fungal attack in so far as the fluctuations may cause joints in joinery, for example, to open up, and in exposed positions, allow the ingress of water which in turn may become trapped and hence may cause sufficient dampness for decay to take place (wet rot usually significant). Thus for a variety of different reasons it is necessary to ensure that adequate precautions are taken which will not allow timber to undergo excessive fluctuations in moisture content. Such precautions have been outlined, but are repeated here again.

Precautions may be divided into those which are necessary in the selection and storage of timber, and those which may be necessary under particular conditions in which timber may be used. It is, therefore, convenient, taking into account all that has been said earlier in this part, to use the following general headings: (a) Selection of timber; (b) Storage of timber; (c) Timber floors; (d) Timber roofs; (e) Timber framing and cladding; and (f) Joinery.

(a) Selection of timber

Only sound, well-seasoned timber should be used, free from any incipient decay. Wherever possible it is wise to ascertain the conditions under which the timber has been stored. No timber which originates from a yard in which careless stacking or unclean conditions are tolerated should be allowed on a building site.

In the case of softwoods for joinery, particularly mass-produced joinery, it may be noted that the species normally used are chosen more for their economy and ease of machining rather than for their resistance to decay. Baltic redwood (also known as red or yellow deal, red pine or fir) is a commonly used softwood; its heartwood being more resistant to decay than its sapwood. The heartwood of Douglas fir is also used. Subject to the conditions of service the timber may have to be preserved. Among hardwoods which have proved acceptable as regards their resistance to decay in highly exposed positions (external sills, for example), are English oak (tradi-

*Since the publication of the conversion chart giving equilibrium moisture content of timber for various uses, C3.03/8, Vol. 2, the BRS, in conjunction with the Forest Products Research Laboratory, have issued (BRS Digest (2nd Series), No. 72, HMSO, July, 1966) values relating installed and average service moisture contents. These have been included in Table 3.06/5.

tional hardwood), teak, utile, gurgun and agba. All these should, as mentioned earlier, be specified by name, as merely specifying 'hardwood' could lead to the use of unsuitable timbers such as abura, beech, obeche and ramin, all of which have poor resistance to decay. If it is required that the perishable sapwood of an otherwise decay-resistant timber should *not* be included, then 'Heartwood only' should be specified.

(b) Storage of timber

Precautions necessary in the storage of timber should be aimed to ensure that, at best, the timber does not undergo significant moisture content fluctuations, or, at worst, does not become damp. Care in storage is not only required at the timber yard, or in the joinery works, but also on the building site. It is perhaps only too axiomatic that care taken at the timber yard or in the joinery works is of little value unless matched by similar care on a building site. Details of the precautions necessary for timber used for constructional purposes and for timber used in joinery are more conveniently considered separately.

(i) *Constructional timber.* All precautions taken in connection with constructional timber should aim to ensure that the moisture content of the timber does not exceed 22 per cent (see Table 3.06/5 and note that in the case of timber for prefabricated buildings the upper limit of moisture content is 17 per cent which means that stricter precautions will be necessary). The precautions set out below are only those which should be taken on a building site.

(1) Timber should preferably be stored within a building. If this cannot be achieved the timber should be stacked on bearers so as to avoid close contact with the ground.

(2) Dry, well-seasoned timber should not be allowed to absorb excessive amounts of atmospheric moisture. To achieve this, the timber should be closely stacked and wholly covered with tarpaulins or polythene sheeting around and under the stack as well as over it. (See Vol. 2, pp. 86-87 for some comparative examples of good and bad practice of protection.)

(3) Timber which arrives on the site in a moist condition due to inadequate seasoning and drying, exposure to rain, or impregnation with water-borne preservatives, should be open-piled in such a way that air can circulate round each piece so as to promote further drying. A top cover only should be given to the open-piled stacks; the sides must be left open so as not to hinder air flow through the stack. If the stacks are left in a building to dry out, the windows should be left open. It should be noted that timber that has been treated with water-borne preservatives will not have been redried in a kiln, unless this was especially ordered. Consequently it is normally necessary for such treated timber to be open-piled and air-dried.

(ii) *Joinery.* Whereas it may be possible to allow timber used for constructional purposes, particularly that which is not prefabricated, to dry out after delivery to the site as outlined in (i) above, the same is not true of joinery. Consequently extra special care is required. Taking into account the importance of the limitation of dimensional fluctuations, precautions for joinery may be summarised as follows:

(1) Careful storage after manufacture.

(2) Protection during delivery to the site, avoiding exposure to the weather.

(3) Careful storage on site, before and after fixing, avoiding conditions of exposure which are materially different from those expected in service. Before use all timber should be adequately protected from exposure to the weather (use of tarpaulins and polythene sheeting as described (see (i) *constructional timber* above)), and stacked clear of the ground.

(4) Where adequate protection of joinery on site cannot be ensured, delay the delivery of the joinery to the site until it is needed.

(5) Timber which is to receive paint may be primed* immediately after manufacture. Single-coated 'pink' shop primers vary in quality and will delay

*The primers may give joinery a uniform appearance. However, after short exposure primers become weak or powdery and unfit to take further coats of paint. Many paint failures can be traced back to poor quality primers.

Table 3.06/5. Moisture content of timber for various positions		
Position of timber in building	*Average moisture content attained in use in a dried-out building (per cent of dry weight)*	*Moisture content which should not be exceeded at time of erection (per cent of dry weight)*
Framing and sheathing of timber buildings (not prefabricated)	16	22
Timber for prefabricated buildings	16	17 for precision work, otherwise 22
Rafters and roof boarding, tiling, battens, etc.	15	22
Ground-floor joists	18	22
Upper-floor joists	15	22
Joinery and flooring		
(a) in buildings slightly or occasionally heated	14	14
(b) in continuously heated buildings	11–12	12
(c) in buildings with a high degree of central heating, e.g. hospitals	10	10
Wood flooring over heating elements	8–9	9

Reference: Home-grown softwoods for Building, BRS Digest (II) No. 72, HMSO, July 1966.

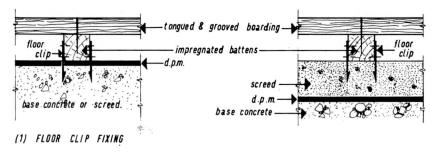

SURFACE D.p.m. (pierced)   SANDWICH D.p.m. (intact)

(1) FLOOR CLIP FIXING

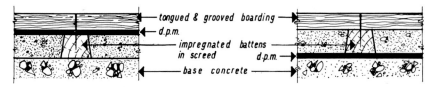

(2) FIXING TO EMBEDDED BATTENS.

D.3.06/1

*Alternative methods of fixing board and
batten flooring to ground floors using
surface or sandwich d.p.m.'s*

the ingress of water for only a comparatively short period of time, and cannot, therefore, be relied upon as a means of protecting timber. Storage under cover is always preferable, but if this is not possible then it is necessary to specify a better quality primer. A water-repellent preservative* plus a good quality primer, or two coats of aluminium primer† would be suitable. In some cases it may be practicable to apply the complete painting system before delivery on site. However, it is important to note that any protective coating must completely envelope all faces of the timber.

(c) *Timber floors*

Timber floors may more conveniently be considered in three separate groups as the risk of fungal attack varies according to the position and construction of the floor. The three groups are: (i) *Unventilated ground floors*, having no air space, or no ventilated air space below them; (ii) *Ventilated ground floors*, with an effective air flow below them; and (iii) *Upper floors*, out of reach of ground moisture.

(i) *Unventilated ground floors*. An important characteristic of floors of this type is that the finish is 'fixed' to a solid concrete base in contact with the ground. Consequently maintaining the timber in a dry state depends on the extent to which, and the positions in which, d.p.c.'s may be necessary. (See *3.04 Exclusion*, Vol. 2.)

*If a water-repellant type of preservative is specified, it should be of a paintable type and the preservative supplier and joinery manufacturer must ensure that it will be compatible with the paint.

†It should be noted that in addition to keeping water out, aluminium primers will also prevent moisture within the timber from getting out. Consequently, before priming, the timber should be correctly seasoned, or the moisture or solvent from preservative treatment allowed to dry out. Failure to do this may allow blistering to occur.

Two types of floors, namely those of wood block and those of board or strip, may be identified, each of which requires different detailed precautions. These are considered separately.

Wood block floors. Table 3.04/3 (Vol. 2) sets out the resistance of floor finishes to ground moisture. Wood blocks laid in *hot-applied* bitumen or pitch adhesives (Group B in the Table) require no further protection against rising damp, although it is important to note that the adhesive in which the blocks are dipped should form a continuous layer and keep them out of contact with the concrete. Blocks laid with cold bitumen adhesives (Group D in the Table) require additional protection from rising damp and this means the inclusion of a d.p.m. as outlined in *3.04 Exclusion* (see diagram D.3.04/20, Vol. 2). If mastic asphalt underlay is used, it is important to ensure that the adhesive used is compatible with the asphalt.

Board or strip flooring. Board and strip flooring may be nailed to battens fixed to the concrete sub-floor either with floor clips or embedded in a screed as shown in diagram D.3.06/1. Floors of this type must be protected by a d.p.m. which may, as shown in the diagram, either be in sandwich form, that is between concrete bed and screed, or on the surface of the screed.* The choice of position for the d.p.m. will depend on circumstances; one important point to be borne in mind is residual moisture which may be in the screed at the time the membrane is laid. A surface membrane will protect

*The types of materials which may be used as d.p.m.'s are included in *3.04 Exclusion*, Vol. 2. Also included in the same chapter is reference to the necessity of ensuring that the d.p.m. and d.p.c. in the walls form a continuous barrier—see diagram D.3.04/20, Vol. 2, p. 127.

the floor not only against rising damp but also against the effects of residual moisture in the screed, although it will be pierced by the legs of the flooring clips or by the flooring nails. A sandwich membrane, on the other hand, need not be pierced, but it is only satisfactory when sufficient time can be allowed to dry the screed above the membrane *before* the boards are fixed in position. In practice, the drying out time may be so long as to make the sandwich method less useful. It must be noted that failure to allow the floor screed to dry out thoroughly before the boards are laid may lead to decay; the risk of decay will be greatly increased if, in addition, the floors are covered prematurely with impervious floor coverings, such as rubber, linoleum, plastics, etc.

The battens, however they are used, should be impregnated with preservative. A recommended additional precaution is the brush application of a preservative to the underside of the boards. The selected preservative should not stain or otherwise disfigure the exposed surface of the timber.

Finally, it is recommended that only tongued and grooved boarding should be used in these floors. This is a precaution aimed to prevent water used for washing, or which may be accidentally spilled, from passing readily through the joints, because any water reaching the underside of the boarding will be slow to evaporate, and dangerous conditions may, therefore, persist for a considerable time.

(ii) *Ventilated ground floors*. Ground floors of timber boarding on joists which are totally suspended have a relatively large air space beneath them and if this air space is efficiently ventilated it is unnecessary to treat the timber with preservative. There is, however, also a need to provide a d.p.c. in all sleeper walls and other supports in actual capillary contact with the ground. Methods by which adequate ventilation may be ensured and the correct use of d.p.c.'s are shown in diagram D.3.04/22 (Vol. 2). The diagram also shows the covering of the ground with dense oversite concrete. For convenience the need for taking these precautions are summarised below.

The dense oversite concrete, which should not be less than 102mm thick, is required in order to minimise the evaporation of water from the ground into the air space below the floor. It is essential that the oversite concrete covers the whole area under the suspended floor. An alternative to the oversite concrete would be a damp-resisting coating to BS 2832 laid on a well-compacted base of hardcore, blinded with ashes to form a level surface free from fissures. The surface of either the concrete or the damp-resisting coating should not be lower than the level of the surrounding ground; where it is not possible to meet this requirement then it is necessary to ensure that the site is suitably drained so that inundation of the area cannot occur. It may be noted here that care should be taken to ensure that there are no shavings, pieces of wood employed during excavation or from wooden forms for concrete work, soil or debris left behind on the surface of the oversite concrete or damp-resisting layer after the floor has been laid. All these should be removed systematically during the course of the work on site.

Ventilation of the underfloor space is necessary so as to ensure that moisture-laden air is replaced with drier air. As explained earlier, it is of the utmost importance that the air in the space below the floor is not allowed to become saturated. In this it should be realised that even when the utmost care has been taken with the oversite concrete or damp-resisting layer, some moisture will probably still find its way to the surface. In order to ensure that adequate and efficient cross-ventilation is maintained it is necessary to comply, as shown in D.3.04/22 (Vol. 2), with the following:

(1) The clear depth between the underside of the joists and the top of the site covering must not be less than 150mm; (2) air bricks in the external walls should be provided so as to give at least 3 200mm² *open area* per metre run of external wall, and should be placed as high as possible on opposite walls, (3) all sleeper walls should be built honey-combed; (4) all cross-walls should be provided with vent holes; (5) care should be taken to avoid unventilated air-pockets such as may occur near bay windows; and (6) ducts should be formed under hearths and solid floors wherever these might interrupt cross-ventilation.

The efficient ventilation of the under floor space* implies a risk of draughts and a reduction in thermal insulation. In order to minimise the risk of objectionable draughts it is advisable to use tongue and grooved boarding rather than plain-edge boarding. An improvement in thermal insulation can be gained by providing a layer of insulating material below the boarding. Provided the floor is properly ventilated, the provision of the insulating layer should not increase the risk of fungal attack.

The importance of the provision of d.p.c.'s in sleeper walls and other supports in capillary contact with the ground need not be repeated here. However, it may be noted that in order

*As a result of experience gained at the Scottish Laboratory of the BRS it is suggested in BRS Digest (II) No. 18 that 'airbricks should not be built into the north walls of buildings which are situated in a frost hollow, particularly if the underbuilding or crawl-space is a deep one; otherwise, there is a risk that in some weather conditions condensation may occur on the underside of the floor near the airbricks. The risk will be greatest below rooms that are unheated or intermittently heated, such as bedrooms. On sloping sites where a deep underbuilding cannot easily be avoided, the need for a second damp-proof course near ground level should be considered. If a terrace around the building is cut into the hillside, it may be desirable to bring the level of the concrete bed or damp-resisting coating at least up to that of the terrace, for in these circumstances drainage of the terrace may not also be able to cope with the volume of rainwater run-off from the hillside. The concrete bed or damp-resisting coating should be stepped so as to coincide approximately with the finished level of the surrounding ground'.

to ensure that there is a clear space (that is, no contact) between the ends of the joists and walls, the former should be cut back.

(iii) *Upper floors.* Upper floors are not exposed to moisture rising from the ground while the air above and below them is usually dry. Consequently the occurrence of fungal attack in these floors is rare.

Suspended timber floors of boarding on joists being essentially a 'dry' construction, do not need special precautions, except, and this is important, that any timbers built into walls that might become damp should be given a suitable preservative treatment.

The types of floors with *boards and battens,* as outlined previously under '(i) Unventilated floors', may, in the case of upper floors, be used on various forms of structural base, as for example *in situ* or precast reinforced concrete, hollow beams, or similar constructions. In these cases the d.p.m. would be omitted. However, the structural base or any screed laid on the base may contain considerable quantities of residual moisture (lightweight screeds are particularly notable in this respect). Consequently the flooring should not be laid until drying-out is well advanced, while the battens should be given protection during the drying-out period. Temporary protection may be obtained by brush application of a preservative; the same treatment may, for safety, also be extended to the underside of the boards. Although pressure impregnation is not essential, it may be considered for the battens, because not only does it give the protection required during drying-out, but it also continues to protect the battens from decay as a result of accidental spillage, etc.

Finally, *wood block* or *parquet flooring* laid on concrete, hollow tile or similar structural upper floors do not require special protection against fungal attack. However, the concrete and screeds should be dry before the timber flooring is laid.

(d) *Timber roofs*

In general, precautions are not normally necessary with most types of pitched roofs as the timber should be free from rain penetration, while there is generally sufficient air circulation around the timbers. An important exception occurs in mansard and similar constructions when the underside of the rafters are covered with plaster or wallboards. In cases such as these it is wise, therefore, to provide a clear air space, freely ventilated, or alternatively to use impregnated timber. When *shingles* are used as the covering it is important that no felt underlay or boarding is used (also noted in *3.04 Exclusion*—see diagram D.3.04/13, Vol. 2). Not only is an underlay or boarding not necessary as the shingles fit closely, but also the inclusion of an underlay or boarding may prove harmful by preventing the circulation of air to the underside of

The photograph shows a void for the collection of water formed by the gap left beneath tenon in joint between lower rail of main frame and the base of the mullion. (Could also occur in joint between stile and sill.) Below, the complexity of joint design in a modern frame and sill means that joints expose a large surface area to the risk of moisture penetration (Courtesy: BRS, Crown Copyright)

the shingles, thus producing conditions favourable to fungal attack.

In the case of flat timber roofs, two unrelated problems may be identified. First, there is dampness which may be associated through incorrect constructional details of parapets. The methods by which the dampness may occur and solutions of the problems involved are outlined in *3.04 Exclusion* under d.p.c.'s (see diagram D.3.04/18, Vol. 2—the concrete shown for the roof structure could equally well be timber). Second, there are the problems associated with 'Entrapped water' as discussed in detail in *3.04 Exclusion* (Vol. 2, p. 156).

(e) *Timber framing and cladding*

Timber may be used as framing for a number of different types of light cladding (see *3.04 Exclusion*). Where the timber is in a dry cavity no special precautions are necessary; in wet cavities it is advisable to impregnate with preservative under pressure, unless the timber is naturally resistant to fungal attack. In those situations where there is no risk of persistent dampness, dip or brush treatment may suffice. Special attention to detail is required, as shown in diagram D.3.04/4 (Vol. 2), when horizontal battens are used with vertical timber boarding so that water can be drained away behind the board.

With timber cladding, rot-resistant timbers such as Western Red cedar need not be painted or otherwise preserved on vertical surfaces. The end grain of the lower edges of timber weatherboarding fixed vertically, is most vulnerable to decay and water must, therefore, drain freely from these edges. If the edges are enclosed in grooves or covered by beads, it is advisable to provide local treatment by dipping in or brushing with colourless preservative. The same type of treatment, but with a possible preference for dipping, is also advisable if the edges, particularly those at the bottom of plywood are to be enclosed in grooves, or covered with beads. Alternatively, plywood, of which the veneers have been impregnated with preservative before manufacture, may be used.

(f) Joinery

Detailed considerations are confined here to external joinery, and windows in particular. Most of the principles outlined are equally applicable to door frames. Apart from those internal environments where there is likely to be a high concentration of moisture, internal joinery may only require temporary protection from fungal attack, during the drying-out stages of a building. In this the effects of residual moisture in wet constructions and with which timber may be in contact are, as outlined earlier, significant. It is also important to remember that there may be significant rises in the moisture content of timber if its exposed surfaces are painted. Unprotected painted skirtings, for example, applied to newly plastered walls have been known to decay in new houses as a result of residual moisture.

The type of decay associated with windows is usually wet rot. In the past such decay has only occurred sporadically, but recent experience has shown that decay has been more widespread, particularly in newly built houses, even when the joinery has complied with current Codes of Practice and Specifications and occurring within five or six years from the time of construction. Cases of decay have been reported from all parts of the country, but, in general, it would seem to take place earlier in the wetter, western areas of the British Isles. Decay has been found to be most pronounced in those windows which are heavily exposed to water. In this connection both the external and internal climates are significant. Thus, externally, it is the ground-floor windows, while internally, it is windows in bathrooms and kitchens, where temperature and humidity conditions are likely to be high (see *4.00 Heat and its effects*), that are particularly susceptible. In addition, it is the lower parts of these windows, that is the sills, the bases of jambs and mullions and the lower rails of opening lights, that are particularly susceptible.

In addition to the precautions that should be taken with the selection and storage of timber, as outlined earlier in (a) and (b), it is necessary to pay particular attention to design and fabrication and to take account of exposure not only to the external climate but also to the internal climate which may, as already noted, be severe in rooms with high temperature and humidity conditions. It is convenient, therefore, to outline the significance of the basic exposure to dampness of frames and the precautions required in design and fabrication.

Reference to diagram D.3.04/17 (Vol. 2), illustrates clearly that, even when d.p.c.'s. have been correctly positioned, either the whole or part of the window frame will be in contact with damp porous materials. This is particularly significant with the jambs and sills.

This means that, in the absence of providing some form of damp-proof barrier between the frame and the porous material, it is imperative to consider the use of naturally resistant timber, or alternatively the preservation of timber of poor resistance to decay.

The precautions which should be taken in design and construction may be summarised as follows:

(i) *Horizontal surfaces.* Horizontal surfaces should be designed to ensure that they shed water (rainwater or condensation) effectively and do not allow water to become entrapped.

(ii) *Joint design.* Joints provide obvious points of entry for water, and so care is required to ensure that fluctuations in moisture content do not stress the joints sufficiently for cross-grain movements to occur. In this it may be noted that modern wedged tenon joints loosen more easily than the old-style mortice-and-tenon joint.

(iii) *Condensation drainage.* Condensation channels and an adequate means of draining them should be provided. In the absence of such provision, water tends to stand on sills against the bottom of the frame, subsequently seeping into the joint between the two.

(iv) *Sills.* Sills present a higher decay risk. This may be overcome by the use of the more durable timbers. However, sills are also required to be of fairly large dimensions. For economic reasons, the trend is to build up sills from two smaller dimension timbers. The two-piece sill implies greater complexity which requires great care in design and manufacture.

(v) *Adhesives.* Care is required in the choice of adhesives. Those, such as animal and casein glues, which are likely to fail under moist conditions, allow joints, particularly in sashes, to open up when these are stressed. The opening up of joints inevitably leads to a broken paint film, thus allowing subsequent penetration of moisture.

(vi) *Size of timbers.* The cross-sectional sizes of timber should be related to the degree of exposure to which the window is to be subjected. Sections of inadequate size are liable to distort, which permits water to enter; there may not be sufficient space for a rebate, while in opening lights the strength may be insufficient to prevent racking and consequent penetration of water at the joints.

(vii) *Painting and maintenance.* The importance of ensuring the correct use of primers has been noted under '(b) Storage'. It may be noted here that end grain and surfaces in contact with porous materials should always receive an extra coat of primer. All putty should be completely painted, including a slight overlap of the paint on the glass—poor quality putties crack and lose adhesion easily, thus allowing water to enter at the bottom rail. Hardwood sills that are to be painted should have the grain filled with a knifing stopper or filler (not a water-mixed type), preferably between two coats of primer.

During service it is important that paint films are not allowed to crack or deteriorate before repainting is undertaken. In many cases it may be advisable to ensure that the paintwork is inspected regularly so that any remedial measures which may be necessary can be taken before water has had the opportunity of gaining entry into the timber.

3.07 corrosion

introduction

Materials such as timber, brick, stone and concrete are more commonly, though by no means exclusively, associated with buildings. Destruction of these materials for building by various agencies is, naturally enough, mostly the concern of a relatively small sector. Metals, on the other hand, although used quite extensively in buildings, have universal application. Destruction of metals by corrosion, which is by and large extensive, is, therefore, virtually everybody's concern. The annual cost of corrosion in countries like the USA and the United Kingdom has been estimated recently* at about £12 per head of population. For the United Kingdom this means a total annual bill of something of the order of £600 million. The annual cost of corrosion to the world has been estimated† to be in the region of £10 000 million. It is, therefore, not surprising that a great deal of study and research has been, and continues to be, devoted to the causes and remedies for corrosion. In building practice there has been an increase in the use of metals due to new techniques (cladding is a notable example) and the greater use of engineering services, for example. An understanding of the problems associated with corrosion is important.

Corrosion of the ferrous metals, that is the rusting of iron and steelwork, is most commonly encountered with the result that the problems of corrosion are often, but mistakenly, associated with this group of metals alone. An extremely important aspect of corrosion, which in simple terms is the chemical interaction of a metal with its surroundings, is that it is inherently inevitable. This means that all metals, and particularly those used in buildings, will, given the right environmental

conditions, corrode. However, whether or not corrosion is deleterious depends on the type of metal and the type of corrosion. In this a distinction has to be drawn between surface films, essentially the product of gaseous corrosion, which are protective (the green patina which develops on copper roofs, for example), and other forms of corrosion which occur in the presence of water, such as rusting of iron, where the corrosion products are not usually protective, thus allowing the metal to be progressively eaten away. In general, it is the non-ferrous metals which develop protective surface films, but even these vary in the degree of protection they may provide. Given the right environmental conditions, the non-ferrous metals will also corrode, sometimes very rapidly. This section is concerned with the deleterious effects of corrosion. One of the environmental factors necessary for attack to take place is the presence of water.

The resistance which any metal, or alloy, will provide to corrosion is, environmental conditions apart, largely dependent on the degree to which the metal, as used, varies from the metal in the natural state. The natural, or original, state represents the more stable condition and, however processed, it is natural for metals to tend to return to the state from which they came. Thus, the noble metals platinum, silver and gold, and the 'near' noble metal copper are found in the metallic state in nature and are very resistant to corrosion. Iron and steel as used, on the other hand, are not found in the metallic state and are correspondingly less resistant to corrosion. With most metals, considerable conversion of the original state, as found in the ores from which metals are extracted, is necessary. At the same time it may be noted that the corrosion products of iron, for example, are all found in the natural state, thus illustrating the tendency of a metal to return to its natural state.

In all considerations of corrosion the relationship between a given metal and given environmental conditions is extremely important. In this it is also important to note that there are a large

number of metals, including alloys, available and these may, in practice, be subjected to a wide range of environmental conditions. Many of the latter when related to given metals may result in intensive attack by corrosion. It is not surprising, therefore, that the problems associated with corrosion are complex.

In terms of building, as in other spheres, the fact that corrosion will take place is not of itself vitally important. The rate of attack and the fact that attack is more commonly localised (uniform attack can be conveniently dealt with in terms of adequate thickness of metal relative to service life), are basically far more important. At the same time the possible effects of corrosion need careful consideration. In general, corrosion is a form of waste. In buildings, such wastage is not necessarily confined to the destruction of the metal, which may have to be replaced, but also the destruction (or at best changes in appearance) of other materials which may be caused during, or as a result of, corrosion. The corrosion of metals in services (pipes, tanks, boilers, radiators, etc.) may lead not only to interruption of the services but also to accidental leakage of water into the fabric of a building (see *3.02 Exposure*, Vol. 2). The corrosion of embedded metal work (the steel in reinforced concrete, for example) may lead to spalling and cracking of the surrounding material.

If the deleterious effects of corrosion are to be minimised, then it is necessary for attention to be paid to three main requirements. These are: (1) care in design, that is avoiding conditions which are likely to give rise to corrosion; (2) care in the selection of metals for given conditions; and (3) care in providing the necessary protection. In the final analysis, the successful use of metals depends on the combined efforts of *manufacturer* (manufacturing details, particularly of components for services important), *architect* (building details important), the *builder* (ensuring work is carried out properly important) and the *user* (ensuring that there is adequate care and maintenance important).

*Uhlig in the USA and Vernon in Great Britain. Quoted in introduction to Butler and Ison, *Corrosion and its Prevention in Waters*, Leonard Hill, London, 1966.

†Hendrik, T. W., *Corrosion and its Pevention*, manual published by Organisation for Economic Co-operation and Development, April, 1964.

The use of metals requires, perhaps more than with other materials, that special consideration is given to the relationship of durability and maintenance. In this, it may be noted that, in a great number of cases, metals are selected for reasons other than their resistance to corrosion. Strength properties, particularly when these can be obtained economically (first cost, that is), are often more important, as is often the case with structural iron or steelwork, for example. Strength may, of course, be applicable to situations other than the main structure of a building (see *2.00 Strength of materials,* Vol. 1). However, in order to maintain 'economical' strength properties, the metal has to be protected from corrosion, and preservation generally implies continual, but periodic, maintenance, the period depending on the durability of the kind of protection employed. Exceptions would include those situations in which the metal may be inaccessible—fixings, steel in concrete, etc. Although it is possible to use metals which have equal, or near equal, strength properties but with higher resistance to corrosion (less maintenance), such metals make first cost high. Strength requirements are subject to such wide variations that it is always advisable, in any given circumstance, to evaluate cost implications (first cost + maintenance cost = final cost) of the possible range of metals. In this it is significant to note the increased use of the more corrosion resistant metals such as stainless steel or copper alloys for a wider range of applications than hitherto. At the same time, there have been notable advances in the development of methods of protection.

As already mentioned, the problems associated with corrosion of metals are complex. In practice, corrosion may take various forms, while there are many variable factors that influence its initiation and rate. In a great many cases the time element is important. For example, corrosion may be initiated because of the existence of one set of conditions, but may subsequently progress because of another. The conditions prevailing at any given time may influence the rate of attack. In buildings, environmental conditions which may result in corrosion are dynamic rather than static. At the same time detailed design may often encourage conditions that will increase the rate of attack.

A better understanding of need for special care in the use of metals can be obtained by an understanding of not only the causes of corrosion but also the remedies for corrosion. In this it seems appropriate to consider first the general principles of corrosion so as to illustrate the interrelationship of the various factors involved. This should help to illustrate the complexities involved and, as important, to underline the necessity for the special care required when metals are used. The general principles (dealt with under 'General considerations') are not specifically related to conditions in buildings, although examples taken from building practice are used wherever possible. After considering the general principles, it is then convenient to consider, in terms of building practice, the effects of corrosion, the exposure conditions under which corrosion is likely to occur, the resistance to corrosion provided by ferrous and non-ferrous metals and alloys commonly used in buildings, the protection which may be provided (including the properties of the various methods now available) and, finally, the precautions which should be taken in order to minimise the risk or effects of corrosion. For convenience all these aspects are covered separately under the following general headings: (1) General considerations; (2) Effects of corrosion; (3) Exposure conditions; (4) Resistance to corrosion; (5) Protection; and (6) Precautions.

general considerations

The main purpose of this part is to outline the basic principles of corrosion generally and to note the more important factors involved, so as to form a background for the parts that follow dealing specifically with the corrosion of metals used in building practice.

Although various theories have been advanced to account for the anomalies of corrosion, it is now generally agreed that there is a relationship between corrosion and electrolysis. This has given rise to the electro-chemical theory, that is that a corroding metal behaves as if it is part of a kind of electric cell or wet battery. It has been shown that corrosion is accompanied by the setting-up of *small* electric currents. Electric currents are produced in a battery, for example, when two different metals are suspended in a chemical solution. When the circuit is completed (the exposed portions of the metals connected by a wire), one metal, known as the *anode,* dissolves, while an electric current flows through the solution from this corroding metal to the other, known as the *cathode* (see diagram D.3.07/1).

In practice, different metals may be in contact with moisture so as to behave like a small battery (galvanic cell as it is often known in corrosion theory). However, currents (and thus corrosion) may also be set up in single metals when one part becomes the anode and another the cathode. In both cases the moisture involved may contain air or other dissolved chemical substances, which conducts electricity.

In some ways the basic principles of corrosion based on the electrochemical theory are fairly straightforward. However, the study, or understanding of corrosion, is complicated by the fact that there are so many variable factors involved that are likely to influence the initiation, course, rate and final result (i.e. form) of corrosion. Some of these factors include the purity of the metal, the composition and interrelation of all the substances with which it comes into contact, the presence of bacteria and the possibility of minute externally-produced electric currents being present. In addition, it is also necessary to remember that the time element may be significant. Corrosion may well be initiated by one set of conditions, but over a period of time other conditions may exist which enable corrosion to proceed. In order to deal with all these factors and the effect they may have, it has been convenient to use the following general headings: (1) Definition (of corrosion); (2) Surface films; (3) Basic mechanisms (of corrosion); (4) Corrosion classification; (5) Initiation of attack; (6) Rate of attack; and (7) Forms of corrosion.

1. Definition

Corrosion may be simply defined as the destructive chemical attack of a metal by agents with which it comes into contact. In fact, destruction occurs as a result of the interaction of a metal with its environment. It is important that a distinction is made between corrosion and erosion. The latter is the destruction of materials by mechanical agencies. However, it may be noted that corrosion and erosion often occur together.

Although the chemical changes of a metal that take place during corrosion (here more conveniently referred to as 'corrosion changes') are generally taken to imply wearing or eating away of the metal, this is not strictly the case as corrosion changes may be divided into two classes, namely, those which produce a solid film and those which do not. The former usually performs a protective function, that is once the film has formed corrosion of the underlying metal is stifled (but see also '2. Surface films', later), whilst in the absence of a film-formation corrosion generally proceeds until a reactant has been exhausted. It is the latter, known as electro-chemical cor-

References

(1) Evans, Ulick R., *An Introduction to Metallic Corrosion,* 2nd Ed., Arnold, 1963. (2) Butler, G., and Ison, H. C. K., *Corrosion and its Prevention in Waters,* Leonard Hill, London, 1966. (3) Hendrick, T. W., *Corrosion and its Prevention,* a manual published by the Organization for Economic Co-operation and Development, April, 1964. (4) *Corrosion of Non-ferrous Metals: I & II,* BRS Digests (1st Series) Nos. 110 and 111, HMSO, May and June, 1958, respectively. (5) *Protection against Corrosion of Reinforcing Steel in Concrete,* BRS Digest (2nd Series) No. 59, HMSO, June, 1965. (6) *Painting Metals in Buildings: 1—Iron and Steel and 2: Non-ferrous Metals and Coatings:* BRS Digests (2nd Series) Nos. 70 and 71, HMSO, May and June, 1966, respectively. (7) *Principles of Modern Building,* Volumes 1 and 2, HMSO, 1959 and 1963 respectively. (8) *Protection of Iron and Steel Structures from Corrosion,* British Standard CP 2008 : 1966. (9) Schikorr, G., *Atmospheric Corrosion Resistance of Zinc* (Zinc Development Association and American Zinc Institute Inc.), 1965. (10) *Aluminium in Building —1 : Properties and Uses and 2 : Finishes.* BRS Digests (2nd Series), Nos. 29 and 30, HMSO, December, 1962. and January, 1963, respectively. (11) Alexander, William, and Street, Arthur, *Metals in the Service of Man* (Penguin Books—A125), 4th Ed., 1962. (12) Various publications by the Copper Development Association, Lead Development Association, Zinc Development Association, Stainless Steel Development Association, British Iron and Steel Research Association (particularly The Corrosion Advice Bureau). (13) *Durability of Metals in Natural Waters,* BRS Digest (2nd Series) No. 98, HMSO, October, 1968.

rosion, that is emphasised in this section.

2. Surface films

The formation of surface films on metals is regarded as gaseous corrosion in which oxidation takes place. The most significant fact about film-forming reactions is that they are usually very rapid in the opening stages, but become increasingly slow as the film thickens, thereby isolating the metal and air from one another. Furthermore, the fact that such reactions often choke themselves is important, as it does help to explain why metals exposed to the atmosphere usually escape destruction, particularly when the atmosphere is dry.

The degree of protection which surface films may give to the underlying metal when exposed to environments other than gases depends not only on the resistance of the film itself but also on the extent to which it adheres to the underlying metal. The poor resistance of the surface film formed on iron exposed to the atmosphere may, therefore, be explained by the fact that the film (iron oxide) is porous and only adheres loosely to the underlying metal. On the other hand, the high resistance of the surface film formed on copper (among other non-ferrous metals) may be attributed to the fact that the film is solid and adheres firmly to the underlying metal. Two other factors which will influence the resistance a surface film will provide to subsequent corrosion is its uniformity and its continuity. Non-uniformity, that is varying thickness, and discontinuity, that is a break in the film, may often account for localised corrosion.

It is also important to note that surface film formation, which is the result of direct oxidation, takes place at the point where the oxidising impinges on the exposed metal. This, as discussed in '3. Basic mechanisms' below, is not generally the case with electrochemical corrosion as the metal goes into solution in *one* place, with oxygen taken up at a *second* place, and with the oxide or hydroxide formed at a *third* place. It is because the solid corrosion product is formed at a distance from the point of attack that it cannot stifle the action. Thus, direct oxidation is generally less dangerous than electro-chemical corrosion.

3. Basic mechanisms

It is now generally held that the corrosion of metals is basically *electrochemical in nature*. Consequently, the attack is basically a chemical reaction accompanied by the passage of an electric current. The flow of electricity occurs between certain areas of a metal surface, known as *anodes* and *cathodes,* through a solution capable of conducting an electric current, known as an *electrolyte*. However, the flow of electricity can only occur when a potential difference exists between the anode and the cathode. During the flow of electricity *destruction of the anode* occurs.

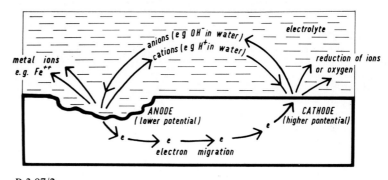

Connecting wire completing the circuit and showing electron flow.*

Dissolution of the anode with the release of metal ions (M+).

Anode & Cathode are Dissimilar Metals

Electrolyte - solution capable of conducting an electric current.

* NOTE: Electrons are current carriers but by convention they flow in the opposite direction to the current.

D.3.07/1
Principle of a simple battery

D.3.07/2
Simple corrosion cell

(a) Electrolyte

An electrolyte is a liquid that contains ions, which are positively or negatively charged atoms or groups of atoms in an aqueous solution. In equilibrium, the negative and positive charges are in electrical balance. Pure water, for example, contains an equal number of hydrogen $(H+)$ and hydroxyl $(OH-)$ ions. Electrical current is conveyed through the solution by ion migration. Thus, electrolytes conduct electricity but are decomposed by it.

Acids, alkalis and many other solutions (those containing salts are significant) are considerably more ionised than water, and therefore act as good electrolytes.

(b) Simple corrosion cell

During corrosion there is a flow of electricity resulting in *simultaneous processes* taking place at the anodes and cathodes. A number of reactions are possible at the cathode, while the formation of corrosion products occurs as a result of the interaction of cathodic and anodic processes. The basic mechanisms involved may be illustrated with a simple corrosion cell.

(i) *Flow of electricity*. A simple corrosion cell consisting of a metal immersed in an electrolyte is illustrated in diagram D.3.07/2. At the anode, which is the region at the lower potential, the atoms dissolve to form ions, leaving behind electrons and giving, in the case of iron, the following reaction:

$$Fe \rightarrow Fe^{++} + 2e \text{ (electrons)}$$

The freed electrons travel through the metal to the cathode, that is that part of the metal at the higher potential, where they are utilised in the reduction of either ions or oxygen. A two-way ionic migration also occurs in the solution in which positively charged cations migrate to the cathode and negatively charged anions to the anode. (Examples of cations and anions in water are $H+$ and $OH-$; in sodium chloride, $Na+$ and $Cl-$; and in sodium sulphate $Na+$ and SO_4^{--}.) Thus a complete circuit is formed by the metal and solution, and the passage of a current through the circuit. The

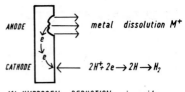

(1) HYDROGEN REDUCTION - in acids.

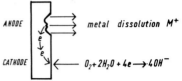

(2) OXYGEN REDUCTION - in natural waters
(i.e. only slightly acidic or alkaline).

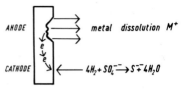

(3) REDUCTION OF SULPHATE (with the aid of bacteria - anaerobic soils notable).

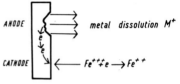

(4) REDUCTION OF METAL IONS - acid waters.

D.3.07/3

The four basic reactions possible at the cathode and the electrolytes in which they occur. In all cases the anodic reaction is the dissociation of the metal

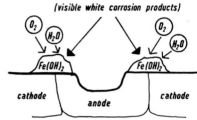

Movement through electrolyte of metal ions (Fe^{++}) from anode and hydroxyl ions ($2OH^-$) from cathode to form FERROUS HYDROXIDE which precipitates

(visible white corrosion products)

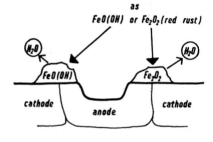

Dissolved oxygen oxidises the ferrous hydroxide and with water forms unstable ferric hydroxide which loses water to form FERRIC OXIDE

as

$FeO(OH)$ or Fe_2O_2 (red rust)

D.3.07/4

The formation of corrosion products on iron. Read from top to bottom

electrons are the current carriers in the metal (it is important to note that by convention they flow in the opposite direction to the current), while in the solution the current is carried by the ions.

(ii) *Cathodic reactions.* The nature of the electrolyte will govern the reactions that will take place at the cathode. However, four basic reactions may be identified, as shown in diagram D.3.07/3 and which may be summarised as follows:

(1) Reduction of hydrogen:

$$2H^+ + 2e \rightarrow 2H \rightarrow H_2$$

This is the main cathodic process in acid solutions, and the metal dissolves with the simultaneous evolution of hydrogen gas (See (4) for an alternative cathodic process in acid waters.)

(2) Reduction of oxygen:

$$O_2 + 2H_2O + 4e \rightarrow 4OH^-$$

This reaction is generally responsible for corrosion of metals in natural waters which have an approximately neutral reaction, that is they are only slightly acidic or alkaline.

(3) Reduction of sulphate (with the aid of bacteria):

$$4H_2 + SO_4^{--} \rightarrow S^{--} + 4H_2O$$

This reaction takes place when there is an absence of oxygen, as may occur in underground conditions for example (see 4(c), p. 50), and requires the presence of adequate dissolved sulphate and the bacteria, *Disulpho-vibrio disulphuricans.* The bacteria use cathodic hydrogen in their living process and bring about the reduction of sulphate to form sulphide. A similar cathodic reaction can also take place in aerated solutions that occur beneath any impervious corrosion product which prevents oxygen from gaining access to the surface of the metal.

(4) Reduction of metal ions:

$$Fe^{+++} + e \rightarrow Fe^{++}$$

This is an alternative cathodic process to that outlined in (1) for acids and occurs with metals which have two valencies, such as copper and iron, and can exist in solution as cupric and cuprous, or ferric and ferrous ions respectively. This type of cathodic

reaction is usually considered to be the cause of the corrosion of iron in acid mine waters, when the ferrous iron formed at the cathode is subsequently oxidised back to the ferric form by dissolved oxygen.

Although the cathodic reactions are quoted separately, this does not preclude the possibility of more than one of the four participating in the overall cathodic process in any given circumstance. In this the time element may be significant. Time apart, reductions of metal ions (reaction (4)) and hydrogen ions (reaction (1)) can occur in acid solutions, while a certain amount of hydrogen is evolved even when oxygen is present in solutions which are only slightly acidic or alkaline. On the other hand, when all oxygen (reaction (2)) has been removed during corrosion in a closed vessel, the sulphate-reducing bacteria (reaction (3)) can take over, thus allowing the corrosion to proceed.

(iii) *Formation of corrosion product.* The formation of the corrosion product, as in the case of rust shown in diagram D.3.07/4, results from the interaction between anodic and cathodic products. The metal ions (Fe^{++}) dissolved from the anode and the hydroxyl ions ($2OH^-$) from the cathodic reactions move in opposite directions through the electrolyte because of their positive and negative charges. When they encounter each other, they react to form ferrous hydroxide which precipitates to form a visible corrosion product:

$$Fe^{++} + 2OH^- \rightarrow Fe(OH)_2$$

The ferrous hydroxide is a white product, but in oxygenated conditions this will rapidly oxidise to form, first, ferric hydroxide:

$$4Fe(OH)_2 + O_2 + 2H_2O \rightarrow 4Fe(OH)_3$$

As the ferric hydroxide is unstable it subsequently loses water to form hydrated ferric oxide, $FeO(OH)$, or Fe_2O_3 (red rust):

$$Fe(OH)_3 \rightarrow FeO(OH) + H_2O$$

It is significant to note that the products of both the cathode and the anode are soluble bodies and will not stifle attack. At the same time the solid substances formed when they meet also cannot stifle further attack of the anode, as the corrosion product forms at a distance from the point of attack.

An important characteristic of most of the solid compounds formed by *corrosion* is that they occupy a *larger volume* than the metal destroyed in producing them. Rust, for example, normally occupies a larger volume than the iron contained in it. This aspect is particularly important when metals are connected or imbedded, as the expansion accompanying corrosion can lead to the development of forces strong enough to cause breakage. In a known case of the failure of a line of rivets holding two steel plates together, the rust which formed between the plates acted in the same way as if a wedge had been driven between them. In

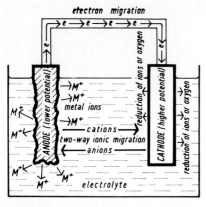

D.3.07/5

Corrosion cell formed by two dissimilar metals

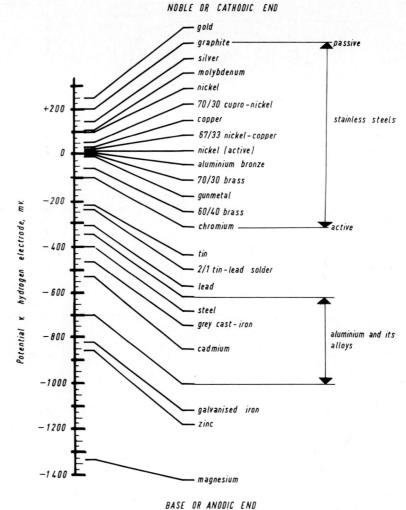

C.3.07/1

Practical galvanic series of metals and alloys. (Based on Butler, G. and Ison, H. C. K., 'Corrosion and its Prevention in Waters', Fig. 4, p. 6, Leonard Hill, London, 1966)

building terms, examples include the cracking of brick, stone or concrete in which embedded iron or steel have corroded.

(c) *Dissimilar metals in contact*

The example of the simple corrosion cell given in (b) (p. 47) is based on a single metal immersed in an electrolyte. Apart from the electrolyte, the factors which give rise to variations in potential between one part and another, and hence the flow of electricity, are variable, but are generally due to some form heterogeneity of the metal. (See '5. Initiation of attack', p. 50.)

When different metals or alloys are immersed in an electrolyte each, after a time, attains a potential which is characteristic for that metal and the electrolyte (for each metal the potentials will vary with the nature of the electrolyte). Thus, if two metals with different potentials (one higher than the other) are connected together, there will be a flow of current from the metal with the *higher* potential to that with the *lower* potential, as shown in diagram D.3.07/5. The metal with the higher potential is said to be *electropositive,* or *cathodic* to the metal with the lower potential. This has given rise to a series known as the *galvanic series*

(sometimes also the electrochemical series) as shown in chart C.3.07/1.

The value of the galvanic series is that it does enable the behaviour of metals when connected together to be predicted. Two common examples found in building practice may help to illustrate this. If copper and zinc are in contact with one another (copper piping and a galvanised steel tank, for example), then the copper will be cathodic to the zinc, and the zinc, being anodic, will corrode. If brass and aluminium are in contact (brass hinges to aluminium window frames, for example), then the brass will be cathodic to the aluminium, and the aluminium, being anodic, will corrode. In addition, the galvanic series enables some prediction to be made of the rate of corrosion of the anodic metal. In this the potential difference between the cathodic and anodic metals is significant. Thus, in the two examples given, and assuming a similar electrolyte, there is likely to be a faster rate of attack of the zinc than of the aluminium—the potential difference between copper and zinc is greater than between brass and aluminium.

4. Corrosion classification

Classification of corrosion depends on

the environment to which a metal is exposed. In general, four classes may be identified, namely gaseous, atmospheric, immersed or underground. Gaseous corrosion is essentially associated with the formation of surface films, as briefly discussed in '2. Surface films' previously and is, therefore, excluded here. An essential feature of the remaining three is that they all require the *presence of water* as the corrosion is electrochemical in nature. It is convenient to discuss these three classes of corrosion under separate headings.

(a) *Atmospheric corrosion*

Metals freely exposed to the atmosphere receive an unlimited supply of oxygen. Attack depends, therefore, on the presence of water and impurities dissolved in it. The dissolved impurities which would commonly include sulphur dioxide (polluted industrial atmospheres) or salt (marine atmospheres) form efficient electrolytes (see *3.02 Exposure,* Vol. 2, but particularly 'Pollution of water'), thus promoting corrosion.

The maintenance of dampness, and hence electrolytes, is often assisted by hygroscopic bodies which adhere to the surface of the metal. Such hygro-

E

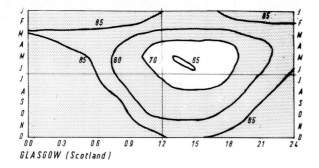

GLASGOW (Scotland)

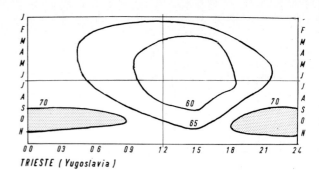

TRIESTE (Yugoslavia)

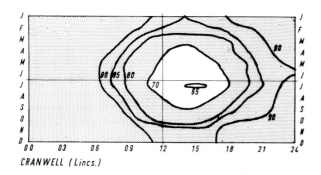

CRANWELL (Lincs.)

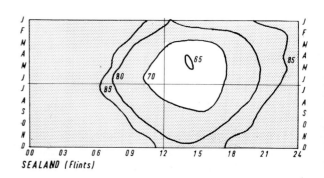

SEALAND (Flints)

D.3.07/6

Annual variations in the relative humidity of some locations in the United Kingdom and, for comparison, Trieste. (References: (1) United Kingdom— 'Averages of humidity for the British Isles', HMSO, 1962. (2) Trieste— 'Atmospheric corrosion resistance of zinc (ZDA and AZ11)', Fig. 13, 1965)

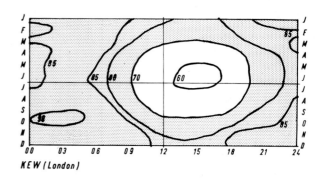

KEW (London)

scopic bodies would include soot, rust and magnesium chloride, the latter originating from marine spray.

In atmospheric corrosion *relative humidity* is a useful guide for predicting both the likelihood and rate of corrosion. It has been shown that there is a sudden rise in the rate of corrosion above a certain *critical humidity*. Above this humidity atmospheric pollution becomes the decisive factor. In general, serious corrosion is unlikely to take place at relative humidities *below* 70 per cent. For convenience, diagram D.3.07/6 illustrates the annual variation in relative humidity for some climates in the United Kingdom. It will be seen that relative humidity only falls below the critical value of 70 per cent for comparatively short periods during the year. When making use of information such as that included in diagram D.3.07/6 it is important to remember that ambient temperature has an effect, although it is the diurnal fluctuations in temperature which determine the incidence and duration of condensation, which are more significant than the average value. In

addition, the presence of deliquescent particles, as already noted, can be highly injurious and corrosion can, therefore, take place below the critical value of 70 per cent relative humidity.

An interesting example of what may best be described as two stage atmospheric corrosion occurs in the formation of the green patina commonly seen on copper roofs. In the early stages the copper darkens. This is due to a dark deposit of sulphide, oxide and soot. The subsequent formation of the final green patina is due partly to the action of sulphuric acid in the soot, and partly to the oxidation of the copper sulphide. The green patina serves to protect the underlying metal from attack. In this example it should be noted that some gaseous corrosion is also involved.

(b) *Immersed corrosion*
Whereas atmospheric corrosion is mainly controlled by moisture, corrosion in totally immersed conditions is controlled mainly by the availability of oxygen. The amount of dissolved oxygen which may occur in waters is

liable to wide variations. However, even when the oxygen supply is severely depleted, corrosion can proceed with the aid of sulphate-reducing bacteria. The composition of the water is important insofar as it affects electrical conductivity. In certain cases, calcareous deposits on metals, formed from hard waters, can have a protective value. The corrosiveness of water is also dependent on temperature. Generally, corrosion proceeds more rapidly as the temperature rises. Finally, under conditions of flow, the rate of water flow often increases the rate of corrosion for two reasons. First, the supply of oxygen is promoted and, second, the adhesion of protective corrosion products may be prevented.

(c) *Underground corrosion*
Corrosion of metals buried underground may take place due to the action of three processes, namely by basic electrochemical action, by sulphate-reducing bacteria, or by stray currents. Although each of these processes do not take place exclusively (in

50

any given circumstance, one or more may be operative—the time element is important), it is more convenient to consider them separately.

(i) *Basic electrochemical action.* Conditions existing in the soil may vary between something comparable to atmospheric exposure and what is almost equivalent to complete immersion. The nature of the soil is an important governing factor. Soils such as sand and chalk, because of their permeable nature, have a plentiful supply of atmospheric oxygen. Such soils are said to be *aerobic*. Consequently, metals buried in open aerobic soils have considerable portions of their surface exposed to oxygen, which is sufficient to ensure that ferric products are formed close to the metal. The rust which may soon appear on the surface once it is wetted, usually stifles further attack. In soils which are completely waterlogged and deficient of free oxygen (known as *anaerobic* soils), corrosion is usually slow, unless sulphate-reducing bacteria are present.

Corrosion is likely to be localised, and intense, when a metal is buried in soils of an intermediate character. In this, the presence of air pockets are significant as differential aeration currents (see 5(b)) may flow, when oxygen is taken up at the air pockets and attack is directed on the places where the soil presses on the metallic surface. Air pockets may be a natural feature of the soil or, as important, may be produced artificially when soil is thrown back into a trench after pipe laying, so that spaces are left between the individual spadefuls. Disturbance of the soil, and hence the subsequent formation of air pockets, can occur not only with trenches dug for pipe or cable laying, but also with holes dug to receive a steel stanchion. It is also important to note that backfilling creates an entirely different environment from that found in undisturbed soil only a few feet away. Such differences, and there are others which may occur naturally (the boundary between horizontal soil-strata, for example), may lead to the formation of a current.

The chemical nature of the soil, and in particular different constituents, may also account for the setting up of corrosion currents. Thus, the acidity or alkalinity of the soil will also affect corrosion. *Made-up ground* containing *ashes and clinker* in which steel pipes have been buried requires special consideration, as under these conditions the steel is rapidly corroded. The reason for this is not due to the acidity of the ashes and clinker (they tend to the alkaline), but to their content of water-soluble matter, which yields electrolytes of low resistivity with the soil water. The presence of any unburnt carbonaceous matter may also promote corrosion, as such matter will act as the cathode of a corrosion cell and, being hygroscopic, will retain moisture in contact with the metal.

(ii) *Corrosion by sulphate-reducing bacteria.* Sulphate-reducing bacteria, previously outlined in 3(b)(ii)—reaction (4)—can flourish only in anaerobic coils such as waterlogged clays, containing sulphates and organic matter. Whereas soils containing no free oxygen are usually non-corrosive, if sterile, similar soils containing the bacteria will be highly corrosive as the organisms present enable sulphates to act as hydrogen-acceptors, with reduction to sulphides. The action of the sulphate-reducing bacteria are even more dangerous than the purely electrochemical types of attack, particularly as the organisms can continue to multiply.

The final corrosion product is a mixture of rust and black iron sulphide. Freshly exposed adjacent soil will be seen to be discoloured and it (or the crust of corrosion product) will evolve hydrogen sulphide when wetted with hydrochloric acid.

(iii) *Corrosion by stray currents.* Metal pipes and structures buried in the soil may act as conductors and pick up stray currents from such sources as tramlines (now generally non-existent in the United Kingdom), power and telephone cables, thus giving rise to serious risk of corrosion by stray currents. Part of the current (up to 15–20 per cent) from the main power line would stray to enter the buried metal and then leave it some distance away to rejoin the main power line. Corrosion generally occurs at the 'loss areas' (diagram D.3.07/7). In the case of steel, attack does occur at the 'loss areas' (the anodes); but with lead sheathings (to cables) attack sometimes occurs at both the 'loss areas' (the anodes) and the 'pick-up areas' (the cathodes), as in the presence of salt the cathodic reaction would produce alkali, which can attack lead. Methods of protecting buried metals from corrosion by stray currents include: insulating the joints, electrical drainage and sacrificial anodes.

Steelwork embedded in concrete and used in chemical works where electrochemical cells are installed in the buildings, requires special consideration, as stray currents from the circuit may occasionally reach the steel, resulting in the production of a voluminous type of rust which, in turn, may cause the concrete to burst, thus exposing the steel. Generally, suitable electrical precautions should prevent this.

5. Initiation of attack

A fundamental concept of the electrochemical theory is that there must, in addition to the presence of an electrolyte, be a potential difference which, in practice, may be either between two dissimilar metals or between areas of a single metal (that is between anodes and cathodes). In the case of the single metal there are a number of factors which may determine the areas which become anodes and cathodes. Emphasis is, therefore, placed on the single metal insofar as initiation of attack is concerned.

As already noted, attack is initiated, and subsequently proceeds, at the anodic areas. Although it is convenient

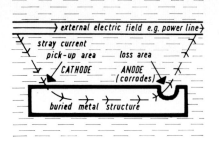

D.3.07/7
Corrosion cell formed by stray currents from an external electric field

to outline separately the main factors involved, it is important to note that the cause of corrosion, in any given circumstance, may be due to one or more of these factors. On the other hand, as corrosion proceeds, the factors responsible for attack may change. The fact that rust, for example, spreads from the original localised area of attack, is due to the formation of concentrated cells beneath the rust.

(a) *Non-uniformity of the metal*
The whole of a metal and in particular its surface will rarely follow the ideal metal lattice, while there may also be differences in the atoms. Boundary conditions between various grains of the metal may exist, giving rise to micro-cells, in which the boundary is usually the anode. Intercrystalline corrosion may occur in a number of alloys (stainless steels and certain aluminium alloys, for example) as a result of precipitation in the grain boundaries. There may be differences in composition from place to place in an alloy, in which case the parts of the alloy which contain a greater concentration of the more noble phase (the component with the more positive potential) will be cathodic to the rest of the surface. The corrosion of aluminium–zinc alloys can be increased under such conditions. In general, departures from the ideal structure of a metal, and hence non-uniformity, are increased by impurities. Thus, pure metals are likely to resist corrosion better than metals containing impurities. For example, pure aluminium resists attack better than a commercial variety.

Electrically conducting materials (metallic or non-metallic) which may be included in a metal or in contact with the surface of a metal do often act as cathodes. The contact of dissimilar metals is an obvious example, but the corrosion of copper tubing as the result of carbon films left during manufacture is another. As regards the latter, it may be noted that BS 659 requires that the internal surfaces of copper tubing shall be free of all deleterious films.

Areas of unequal stress or deformation give rise to different potentials, and are important in the production of galvanic cells with a single metal.

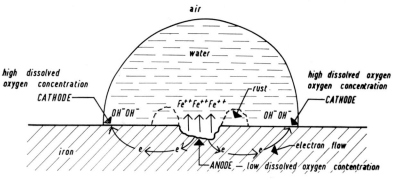

1 DROP OF LIQUID ON THE SURFACE.

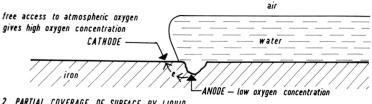

2 PARTIAL COVERAGE OF SURFACE BY LIQUID.

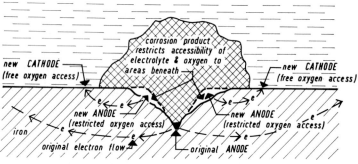

3 PARTIAL COVERAGE OF SURFACE BY SOLIDS.

[Diagram illustrates the way in which the corrosion product may influence the distribution of attack — corrosion is initiated at the original anode but may spread, the attack taking place beneath the product where new anodes are formed, due to restricted oxygen access. In the case of other solids, e.g. dust, paint films, etc. the principle is similar except there is no original anode.]

D.3.07/8

Three basic examples of corrosion cells formed due to differential aeration (see also D.3.07/12)

In general, the more stressed parts are anodic, and corrode more readily. Variations in stress can be caused by many factors, such as strains or external stresses. Some examples of corrosion resulting from unequal stress or deformation include boilers, at bends in iron or steel, heads of rivets and cracking of brass.

An important point for the initiation of attack occurs where there is a breakdown of the protective oxide film on the metal. The breaks in the film cause the underlying metal to be exposed. It is the exposed area which becomes anodic, and hence attacked. Breakdown of the oxide film on aluminium often occurs. In the case of iron or steel discontinuities of the mill-scale are often responsible for intense localised corrosion of the underlying metal.

The phenomenon of rust creeping underneath damaged paint or other similar protective films presents an anomaly because the corrosion is initiated by a breakdown in the film, yet the exposed metal is cathodic, rather than anodic. This can be explained by differential aeration corrosion (see 5(b)). The exposed part of the metal has free access to oxygen, whereas that covered by the paint film has not. The latter, therefore, becomes anodic and corrodes (see diagram D.3.07/8).

(b) *Non-uniformity of the liquid*
Non-uniformity in the composition of the liquid in contact with the metal, or close enough to have an influence on the corrosion process, may lead to the setting up of currents. The requisite non-uniformity may arise due to concentrations of metal ion, salt, hydrogen ion (pH value significant), oxygen or oxidants, as shown in diagram

D.3.07/9. It will be seen in the diagram that, with the exception of the neutral salt, areas of high concentration result in cathodes, and areas of low concentration in anodes.

Some of the conditions under which variations in the liquid are likely to occur are worth noting. With the metal ion, concentration can occur in flowing waters, particularly if there are variations in the rate of flow. In the case of copper, for example, attack takes place at the area from which the copper ions are removed most readily, that is where the flow is fastest. With salts, differences of chloride concentration are likely to occur when fresh and sea water meet (flowing of rivers into the sea).

Variations in oxygen concentration require special consideration, because corrosion currents which arise as a result of the differences of oxygen distribution in the liquid, account for a significant number of corrosion failures in practice (crevice corrosion is notable). Such corrosion is usually known as *differential aeration corrosion*. Cases in which there is likely to be a significant difference in oxygen concentration include partial immersion of a metal, in which only the exposed part has free access to oxygen. As already explained, that part devoid of oxygen becomes anodic, and thus attacked. Similar conditions occur when one part of the surface of a metal is covered with liquid and the other exposed (drops or small areas of liquid on the surface), or when one part is covered by solids (dust, corrosion products, paint and similar protective films, etc.) and the other exposed to the atmosphere. (See also '7. Forms of corrosion'.) Some examples of differential aeration corrosion are included, for convenience, in diagram D.3.07/8.

(c) *Variations in physical conditions*
Variations in physical conditions which may give rise to the setting up of currents include differences in temperature, stray currents and flow of water. The significance of stray currents is outlined in 4(c)(iii).

Differences in temperature usually result in the hotter part becoming anodic, although the nature of the liquid and metal involved is important. Thus, in sulphate, the hot part is the cathode on copper and lead. Differences in temperature can lead to corrosion in boilers and refrigerating equipment.

The flow of water has two effects. First, stimulation of the cathodic process by increasing the concentration of reactants at the metal surface and, second, stimulation of the anodic process by facilitating the removal of corrosion products.

6. Rate of attack
The fact that, in any given circumstance, the basic conditions necessary for corrosion to take place may exist, gives no indication of the rate of attack which may take place. In practice, it is

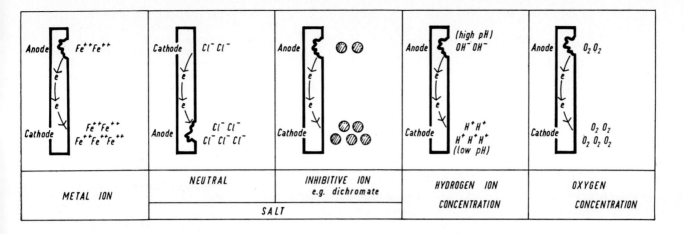

METAL ION	NEUTRAL	INHIBITIVE ION e.g. dichromate	HYDROGEN ION CONCENTRATION	OXYGEN CONCENTRATION
	SALT			

D.3.07/9
Corrosion cells formed by non-uniformity in the composition of the liquid in contact with the metal. Note: apart from the neutral salt, areas of high *concentration result in the formation of the cathode, and those with low concentration the anode*

the rate of attack which is most important. It is perhaps axiomatic that the rate of attack will be dependent on the strength of the electric current in any given galvanic cell. Although it may be possible to predict the strength of the current on the basis of potential differences between the anode and cathode on the open circuit, as given in chart C.3.07/1, there are three other factors, namely polarisation, the conductivity of the electrolyte and the relative areas of the anode and cathode, which must be taken into account. For convenience, the effects of pH value (hydrogen ion concentration) and dissolved matter (collectively referred to as 'composition') are included with conductivity. (Composition of water is also included in *3.02 Exposure, '3. Water supply*', Vol. 2, pp. 63-67).

(a) *Polarisation*
Whatever the potential difference between a given anode and cathode may be on the open-circuit, this difference is modified in an actual galvanic cell by displacement of the potential of the cathode towards the anode and vice versa. The shifts of potential are known as *polarisation*. Thus, the operative potential may be near that of the open-circuit anode or cathode potential, or intermediate between the two. The importance of polarisation lies in the fact that it may, in certain cases, result in extremely small potential differences, even though the potential differences on the open-circuit are large. The precise value of the operative potential will, in turn, depend on whether the corrosion process is controlled by the anode, cathode or a combination of both.

In general, the dissolution of metal ions at the anode is a very fast reaction. The anodic reaction only controls the rate of corrosion with 'near' noble metals, such as copper, or with metals

in the *passive state* (stainless steel notable) as the diffusion of ions through the oxide layer is slow.

Cathodic control is association with the control of the oxygen reduction reaction. Cathodic control, in which oxygen reduction or the effects of polarisation are important, may be illustrated by two examples. On the basis of an open-circuit, the potential difference between copper–aluminium and aluminium–stainless steel are the same. In galvanic cells, the copper is an efficient cathode, with the result that oxygen is readily reduced so that the aluminium is severely attacked. However, because of the passive film on the stainless steel, oxygen is not readily reduced, with the result that the stainless steel will be readily polarised to the aluminium potential so that the galvanic effect will be small or negligible.

(b) *Conductivity and composition*
The conductivity of electrolytes varies widely. However, those which are good conductors not only increase the rate of corrosion in general, but also enable cathodes and anodes which are comparatively far apart from one another to take part in the corrosion process. With those electrolytes of poor conductivity, the flow of current will be limited to the immediate areas of contact between the two areas.

The cathodic protection provided by zinc on galvanised steel when the steel is exposed through breaks in the zinc coating is dependent not only on the area of steel exposed, but also on the conductivity of the electrolyte. When a small area of steel is exposed, the potential of the exposed steel is polarised to a more negative potential at which the ferrous ions can no longer leave the metal. Thus, the steel is cathodically protected, with oxygen reduction taking place on the iron

cathode and an increase in corrosion of the zinc anode. When a large area of steel is exposed, protection is maintained only if the electrolyte has a high conductivity (brackish waters and sea water are notable). If the electrolyte offers a high resistance, then only the steel adjacent to the zinc will be protected.

The *pH value* of solutions is discussed in *3.02 Exposure, '3. Water supply*' (Vol. 2). It is a measure of the acidity or alkalinity of aqueous solutions, in which a scale, ranging from 0 to 14, is used to express the hydrogen ion concentration. On this scale *pure water* has a value of 7·0 (at 25°C), *acid* solutions a value of *less than* 7·0, and *alkaline* solutions a value of *more than* 7·0. The way in which the pH value, that is the hydrogen ion concentration, will influence corrosion rate depends on whether, (1) the metal is noble (noble metals are stable in both acid and alkaline solutions); (2) whether its oxide is soluble in acid or both acid and alkali. Metals such as aluminium, lead, tin and zinc are soluble in both acid and alkaline solutions, their rate of corrosion being parabolic. The minimum rate of corrosion occurs at a pH value of 6·5 for aluminium, 8·0 for lead, 8·5 for tin and 11·5 for zinc. Most metals have oxides which are soluble in acids, but insoluble in alkalis. Generally, the lower the pH value the higher the rate of corrosion. In the case of iron, for example, the critical pH value is 3·0. Below this value the rate of corrosion increases. It is no longer necessary for oxygen to be present as it is possible for hydrogen to be liberated. Between pH 4·0 and 9·0 the rate of corrosion is low and constant, falling to a minimum when a value of pH 12·0 is reached. In alkalis, iron forms a protective film. Above a pH of 12 the rate of corrosion increases. Variation in

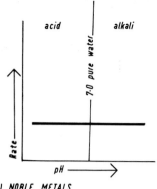

(1) NOBLE METALS
(e.g. gold, platinum)

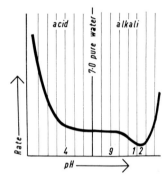

(2) METALS WITH AMPHOTERIC OXIDES
(e.g. aluminium, lead, tin, zinc)

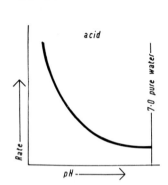

(3) ACID SOLUBLE METALS
(e.g. cadmium, copper, chromium,
manganese, magnesium, nickel)

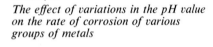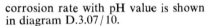

(4) IRON

D.3.07/10
*The effect of variations in the pH value
on the rate of corrosion of various
groups of metals*

corrosion rate with pH value is shown in diagram D.3.07/10.

Dissolved salts may influence corrosion according to their concentration and type. Ions such as chloride, Cl^-, and sulphate, SO_4^{--}, are highly aggressive, capable of breaking down or preventing the formation of protective films, while those such as carbonate and bicarbonate, CO_3^{--} and HCO_3^-, and calcium, Ca^{++}, have inhibiting properties and, therefore, are capable of restraining corrosion. The latter may be exemplified by the formation of a film of calcium carbonate, as occurs in water supply systems carrying hard water. The aggressive or inhibiting properties are, however, dependent on the concentration of the dissolved salts.

Dissolved gases, but principally carbon dioxide and oxygen, may influence corrosion. The effect of carbon dioxide in water is twofold. First, it lowers the pH value, in itself a stimulant to intensive attack. Second, free carbon dioxide makes water aggressive because it reverses the reaction which leads to the formation of carbonate scale, thereby dissolving scale that may be present. Oxygen, on the other hand, acts both as cathodic depolariser and an anodic polariser or passivator.

54

(c) *Relative areas of cathode and anode*

The importance of the relative areas of the anode and cathode, insofar as rate of attack is concerned, depends on the amount of dissolved salts in water, that is the conductivity of the electrolyte. The influence of the latter may be viewed in two different ways:

(1) In waters with a relatively low amount of dissolved salts, the area of the cathode will be unimportant, as the attack on the anode is restricted to the area immediately next to the junction of the anode and cathode (or, in the case of two metals, next to the bimetallic junction), as outlined in 6(b) previously. However, in a highly conductive electrolyte, such as salt water, for example, the attack will be controlled by the relative areas of the anode and cathode. Provided the cathodic reaction is unrestricted by polarisation, the greater the area of the cathode relative to that of the anode, the greater the amount of attack. In fact, the amount of attack at the anode will be proportional to the area of the cathode. For example, an aluminium rivet in copper would suffer intense attack, whereas a copper rivet in aluminium, although undesirable, would suffer less attack.

(2) The strength of the current flow-

ing depends largely on the amount of oxygen reaching the cathode. Consequently, if the cathode is large, the current may be quite strong in relation to the size of the anodic area. In the case of iron or steel, breaks in the mill-scale expose the bare metal which becomes the anode. Attack may, therefore, become very intense when the exposed portion of the iron is small. Intense attack is frequently associated with this combination of large cathode and small anode.

7. Forms of corrosion

Different types of corrosion yield different forms of corrosive attack. The more common forms, most of which are localised, are included below.

(a) *Uniform attack*

This, in a sense, is the ideal form of attack, as there is uniform thinning which can be allowed for in design. Such attack usually takes place in acid solutions, or in strongly alkaline solutions on some metals. It is also likely to take place in solutions with a high content of dissolved salts. Surfaces which have a uniform deposit are more likely to have a reasonably uniform type of attack, while deposits of calcium carbonate will reduce considerably the rate of attack. In practice, it is probably unwise, except in special circumstances, to rely on uniform corrosion taking place, as attack is more commonly localised.

(b) *Grooving*

Grooving is a form of localised attack in which thinning occurs where there has been particular concentration of an electrolyte. In condensers, for example, grooves are initiated where the steam first starts to condense, and consequently indicate the flow path. Such condensates are acid. Local concentrations may also occur from water run-off from roofs or merely from dripping. Grooving of flashings often occurs when the water is acidic.

(c) *Pitting*

Pitting is one of the most dangerous forms of localised attack. It is believed to be associated at its inception with a small anodic area and a large cathodic area, and may be due to variations in the metal, variations in the surface film (metallic or otherwise) or variations in the film solution interface.

Breakdown of mill-scale on iron and steel—a film laid down during manufacture—is a common cause of intense localised attack (see diagram D.3.07/11).

At one time severe pitting occurred with copper cold water pipes in hard waters, due, it is thought, to a film of carbon derived from the lubrication used in the drawing process. Such carbon films are now removed. In fact, BS 659, for copper tubing, requires that the inner surface shall be free from deleterious films. In rare cases pitting may be caused as a result of films by moorland waters.

Some metals, aluminium is notable, may suffer from localised attack by copper-bearing waters. Localised attack is induced if dissolved oxygen, calcium bicarbonate and chloride are present.

Pitting of aluminium which may be due to breakdown in the oxide film or dirt deposits, can usually be minimised by regular cleaning.

Sulphate-reducing bacteria also cause pitting, which may be hemispherical or elongated if individual pits run into one another. Stainless steels may be pitted (usually elongated pits) by salts (particularly chlorides) which break down the passivity of the surface.

(d) Waterline corrosion

Waterline corrosion is commonly associated with water tanks (diagram D.3.07/12), when localised corrosion takes place at the metal/water/air boundary. A similar type of attack can take place at the periphery of a droplet of water on a metal surface. Attack takes place along a line just beneath the level of the miniscus. This is an example of differential aeration corrosion, and as the area above the waterline is cathodic, it is completely unaffected by corrosion.

Susceptibility to waterline attack varies with the metal and the solution. Iron and steel are particularly vulnerable to most waters.

(e) Crevice corrosion

Crevice corrosion usually results from bad design, although it can also occur as the result of deposits of foreign matter on the surface. Invariably the crevices formed are inaccessible and so localised attack is often intense. Attack is more commonly due to differences in oxygen content (differential aeration), although the formation of a concentration cell may be due to differences in salt or hydrogen ion.

One of the main reasons why atmospheric corrosion occurs rapidly in crevices is more likely due to the fact that moisture is retained in them long after moisture has dried up on the surface. Corrosion deposits in crevices can exert considerable forces, which may be sufficient to result in damage to surrounding material (see 3(b)(iii)).

(f) Dezincification

Dezincification is the selective corrosion of brass, in which one of the constituents, usually zinc, is removed, leaving a weak porous residue. Such corrosion occurs more often in moving waters (differential aeration is significant) and so brass taps and valves are commonly affected. Soft waters and sea water are particularly aggressive.

Other copper alloys may be similarly affected. In the case of aluminium bronzes with 8 per cent or more of aluminium, de-aluminification occurs.

(g) Corrosion in rapidly moving water

Corrosion of metals subjected to rapidly moving waters is usually the result of corrosion and mechanical

abrasion (erosion). Attack may be caused by local breakdown of a protective layer by suspended particles (sand for instance), or gas bubbles which impinge on the surface (usually continually in the same place), or by turbulence alone. The form of attack is usually localised, giving rise to pits. The conditions necessary for such attack arise at the entrance to pipes, at sharp bends, near deposits, and where the cross section of the flow stream changes abruptly. Metals most likely to suffer from corrosion/erosion attack are those which form poorly adhering corrosive products.

Changes in the rate of movement of water, resulting in intense local attack, are significant in the case of copper. For local attack to occur, water must pass rapidly over the surface at one point, while the water over the remainder of the surface is relatively stagnant. Under these conditions, copper ions are removed from the point where rapid movement of water occurs, keeping the ionic concentration low, while the ionic concentration will be high elsewhere. The point of low ionic concentration will, therefore, be permanently anodic (see 5(b)).

(h) Stress corrosion

Cracks which may develop in metals are often due to various forms of stress corrosion, in which only a small amount of metal is removed by corrosion. Basically two types of stress corrosion may be identified. One results from the stresses due to applied loads which cause a fracture, with corrosion serving to break down obstructions which would otherwise retard the advance of the crack. The other is essentially steady electrochemical destruction of metal (destruction of the grain boundaries is significant) with stresses due to applied loads serving to concentrate the corrosion on the tip of the crack. Stress corrosion of a kind may occur due to fatigue—this type of corrosion is more correctly known as fatigue corrosion.

The form of cracking or the agents responsible for cracking give rise to various descriptions. Some of these include: (1) Season-cracking, which occurs in brass, and so called because of the resemblance of the cracks to those in seasoned timber; (2) Caustic cracking (sometimes also caustic embrittlement), a type of intercrystalline attack initiated by caustic alkali and found in boilers. The attack occurs in joints, seams or crevices in which water can leak and become sufficiently concentrated with caustic alkali; (3) Nitrate cracking is another example of intergranular attack which takes place on mild steel (not all types of mild steel) at high temperatures in the presence of nitrates.

effects of corrosion

In terms of building practice, the principal effects of corrosion of a metal component may be considered under four headings, namely, (1) Structural

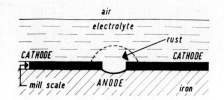

D.3.07/11
Breakdown of mill-scale on iron or steel—a film laid down during manufacture—is a common cause of intense local attack

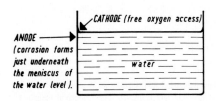

D.3.07/12
Waterline attack (an example of differential aeration corrosion—see also D.3.07/8)

soundness; (2) Distortion or cracking of other building materials; (3) Entry of water into the building; and (4) Changes in appearance.

1. Structural soundness

Corrosion may affect the structural soundness of the component. It may generally be assumed that corrosion will impair the strength of the component. The extent to which a reduction in strength may be significant will depend on circumstances. In the case of uniform attack, the effects of corrosion on strength may be allowed for, as the corrosion will result in uniform reduction of thickness. The same is not necessarily true with the various forms of localised attack, which on the whole are probably more frequent. Other things being equal, localised reduction in strength can, of course, have more serious consequences than uniform reduction.

When considering the effects of corrosion on the structural soundness of a metal component, it is always important to remember that all components are required to be strong enough to perform specific or primary functions, which in a great many cases may not be specifically related to the primary structural stability of a building. A simple example may clarify this important point. The primary function of water pipes is to facilitate the flow of water. In order to do this, the pipes must be strong enough to resist the weight of water, including any pressures involved. A fracture or hole caused or initiated by corrosion would result in leakage of water. Other

55

Corrosion may affect the structural soundness of a metal component

Cracking of glass due to corrosion of steel window frame

Examples of cracking of concrete due to corrosion of steel reinforcing bars are shown in the photographs below and on p. 57 (lower left and bottom right)

examples would include various fixing devices and related components used in pipework, engineering services, panelling or cladding and hinges, etc.

2. Distortion or cracking of other building materials

The products of corrosion are far more voluminous than the metal or alloy from which the products are formed (see 'General considerations 3(b)(iii)'). Apart from special cases, such as some forms of stress corrosion, corrosion is confined to the exposed surface of a metal. Consequently, the growth of corrosion products may cause distortion or cracking of other building materials in which the metal may either be embedded or with which it may be in contact. The failure of other building materials in this way may, in turn, lead to more rapid attack of the metal due to the freer access of water and/or oxygen to the metal and, consequently, 'renewed' damage on the associated building material. And so the cycle may continue, making the deleterious effects of corrosion progressively worse. The fact that the rate of destruction is often increased is also extremely significant.

3. Entry of water into the building

The failure of the component may lead to entry of water into the building, as may occur with metal roof finishes, flashings, d.p.c.'s, gutters, pipes, engineering services, equipment and the like. In this it is important to note that the water which may gain entry is not restricted to rainwater, as outlined in *3.02 Exposure* (Vol. 2).

4. Changes in appearance

The changes in appearance associated with corrosion are generally unsightly.

The surfaces affected may be either the metal or some other building material adjacent but underneath a corroding metal. Examples of the latter include the brown staining from iron and steel, or the green staining from copper and its alloys often seen on concrete, stonework and masonry. Other materials including paint may also be affected. Rainwater, or some other source of water, flowing over the surface of the corroded metal transfers some of the corrosion products on to the adjacent material. Indiscriminate storage of metals (steel reinforcement is often notable) on or near other building materials may cause staining of the latter. In almost all cases, but particularly when porous materials are involved, the staining is extremely difficult to remove.

exposure conditions

The extent to which a metal or alloy may corrode is basically dependent on two interrelated factors: the properties of the metal or alloy, including the effects of deformation *and* the conditions to which the metal or alloy is exposed. In buildings, metals may be exposed to a number of different conditions. In each case *the presence of water is fundamental*, and so all sources of water, including the extent to which the water may be polluted, as discussed in *3.02 Exposure* (Vol. 2), must be considered. A point which needs to be emphasised is that the severity of exposure will be governed by the effects of the specific use of a metal. In this the actual form and exposure condition of a detail are extremely important. Thus, although exposure to the atmosphere, external or internal, does represent a basic condition of exposure, this type of exposure is seldom principally responsible for most cases of corrosion. Although it would be wrong to under-estimate the significance of atmospheric exposure, it is important to note that failure nearly always occurs in some detail and not in general exposure to the atmosphere (even the external atmosphere). In view of the fact that metals are seldom, if ever, used in isolation, it is also necessary to include as a condition of exposure the effects of other building materials, including the juxtaposition of different metals or alloys.

In practice it is important that consideration be given to all types of exposure, with due regard paid to details which may influence the severity of exposure in given circumstances. In general terms, it is possible to identify five types of exposure which may arise. Each of these is considered separately.

1. External atmospheres

The amount of corrosion of metals or alloys exposed to external atmospheres will be primarily dependent on the kind of metal or alloy and the effects of climatic factors. As regards the latter, it is not only the macro-climate which is important, but, more precisely, the

'*The products of corrosion are far more voluminous than the metal or alloy from which the products are formed (see example top right). Consequently, the growth of corrosion products may cause cracking or distortion of other building materials in which the metal may either be embedded or with which it may be in contact.*'

Above, cracking (and staining) of stonework due to an embedded iron post

Below, distortion of top rail due to corrosion of steel bars

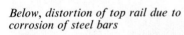

Corrosion may result (generally) in unsightly changes in appearance. Above, staining of reinforced concrete by steel reinforcement during construction.

Below left, green staining on limestone from bronze. Below right, staining due to careless storage on site

Below, perforation of an aluminium rainwater pipe carrying water from a copper roof, the copper, in solution, being deposited on the surface of the aluminium, thus resulting in bimetallic junctions (Crown copyright)

Below, a 'traditional' example of corrosion due to contact, under damp conditions, between two unprotected dissimilar metals; wrought iron railing (corroded) embedded in lead caulking. Note: At present little, if any, wrought iron is made, hence the traditional nature of the example

micro-climate which is influenced to a large extent by the building in general and by details in particular. As previously emphasised, the length of time that moisture may be in contact with the surface of a metal or alloy is an important governing factor so far as the rate of corrosion is concerned. At the same time the aggressive nature of the moisture is significant, insofar as *both* rate *and* intensity of attack is concerned.

Climatic factors which influence conditions of exposure are: humidity, temperature, rainfall, wind and exposure to the prevailing wind and rain. Although it is, in general, unlikely that corrosion will take place when the relative humidity is below 70 per cent (the critical humidity—see 'General considerations' 4(a)), cognisance must be taken of the fact that, under certain temperature/humidity conditions, condensation may take place. Temperature and wind influence significantly the rate at which water is evaporated from surfaces. The effects of seasonal variations are generally important (see *3.01 General considerations* '5. Prevailing wet and dry conditions', Vol. 2), but in the case of metals daily variations may be significant. Rainfall, but particularly exposure to wind-driven rain, will influence which faces will be primarily subjected to water.

The aggressiveness of the water in contact with the surface of a metal, whether derived from atmospheric humidity (condensation notable) or from rain, will be dependent on atmospheric pollution. (See Vol. 2, *3.02 Exposure*, 'Pollution of water' particularly comparative chart C.3.02/3, *'Approximate rates of corrosion of mild steel and zinc coatings on steel in atmospheres of differing pollutions.* Further examples of the effect of pollution in the atmosphere on the rate of corrosion are given under 'Resistance to corrosion' later.)

The extent to which water may be retained on the surface of a metal will be determined by the slope of the surface. In general, horizontal or near horizontal surfaces will have the effect of increasing the severity of exposure, as removal of any retained water will be dependent on evaporation. Retention of water, and hence an increase in the condition of exposure, will occur if water is allowed to enter crevices (see also '4. Contact with conductive water' later).

2. Internal atmospheres

Prevailing conditions of humidity will be of primary importance when considering exposure to internal atmospheres. External humidity conditions only serve as partial guides, as internal humidity, including the degree of pollution, are modified, not only by the nature of the enclosing fabric, but also, more importantly, by conditions in a building. For example, kitchens and bathrooms do, in general, present severe conditions of exposure when compared to, say, living rooms. The effects of different internal environments on the corrosion of zinc are given in comparative chart C.3.07/2.

It should be noted that with the increasing use of heating in buildings, there has been an increase in problems of condensation (see *4.00 Heat and its effects*). Consequently, it is necessary, in practice, to analyse the effects of all forms of atmospheric 'modifiers'. In some cases, as for example when air-conditioning is employed, the severity of exposure conditions may be notably reduced.

Flue gases and smoke from the combustion of various types of fuel create a particularly corrosive 'atmosphere' in buildings. Such an atmosphere has its effect on flue terminals and on flue linings. The aggressive nature of these atmospheres is usually increased if condensation takes place in the flue. (See also *3.06 Chemical attack*, 'Sulphate attack', 5. Domestic chimneys, p. 35.)

3. Other building materials

Metal components may be embedded in or in contact with a variety of building materials. The latter would include mortars, plasters, concrete, floor compositions or wood. The extent to which any of these materials may influence corrosion depends largely on the extent to which water releases, or concentrates, corrosive agents from them. In this, water introduced during construction may be important. For convenience, the corrosive agents which may be derived from building materials and other sources, together with the possible effects of these agents, are included in Table 3.07/1.

Although not strictly a building material, the soil should be regarded basically as an aggressive material in which metals may be embedded or in contact. Conditions of exposure of pipes, and other metalwork buried underground, is covered under 'General considerations', 4(c), pp. 50-51.

4. Contact with conductive water

As mentioned previously in type 1, exposure, there is a greater risk of corrosion if water is retained in crevices between metal surfaces or between a metallic and some other material, than where a metal is simply exposed to the normal action of the weather. Another factor which may equally well increase the condition of exposure is the dripping of rainwater on to the surface of a metal. All these increases in the severity of exposure are, usually inevitably, brought about by details in building construction.

A further increase in the risk of corrosion arises when the water (rainwater or any other source of water) is made more conductive, that is made a more efficient electrolyte, by dissolved acids, alkalis or salts. Such dissolved matter may, in general, be derived from the atmosphere or from material with which the metal comes into contact. There are also those particular cases,

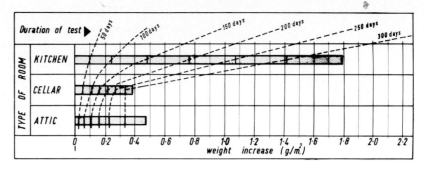

C.3.07/2

Comparative chart of the effects of three different internal atmospheres on the corrosion of zinc (From: Atmospheric corrosion resistance of zinc (ZDA and AZ11)', Fig. 9, 1965)

such as occur in chemical works or other industrial processes, where the water may be highly corrosive. In addition, account must sometimes be taken of the corrosive nature of some materials used during maintenance, including cleaning, or of leaking service pipes and equipment. Finally, supply water may also constitute an increased risk of corrosion.

5. Contact between dissimilar metals

The contact between two unprotected dissimilar metals in the presence of moisture presents a complex condition of exposure. Assessment of the severity of exposure of any given bimetallic junction and, in particular, the risk of corrosion of the less noble metal under given conditions, is made difficult because of the many variable factors involved. The potential difference between two dissimilar metals in contact can give some guidance as to the possible rate of corrosion. The galvanic series, described in 'General considerations', 3(c), from which potential differences between any two metals may be estimated is based on an *open circuit*, whereas, in practice, potential differences result from a *closed circuit*, and these may be significantly different from those in the open circuit. Thus, the galvanic series does not serve as a reliable practical guide. Because of this (and for other reasons), various attempts have been made to formulate, in a simplified way, tables showing the possibility of corrosion when two dissimilar metals are in contact, and based on practical experience. Such tables are usually based on engineering experience, but are, nevertheless, of value in building practice.

Compilers of tables giving the degree of corrosion at bimetallic junctions have, in order to simplify the tables, had to make generalisations. However, the tables are still of value as they do at least give an indication of the basic condition of exposure, *provided* they are not regarded as infallible and *provided* the variables that may alter the basic condition of exposure are taken into account. For convenience,

C.3.07/3 has been prepared from a table produced by the Admiralty, War Office and Ministry of Aviation Interservice Metallurgical Research Council. The original table, based on practical experience, is a useful summary of available information in a simplified form. The value of the table (and C.3.07/3 in this study) lies in the fact that it does show, at a glance, whether there is any danger of the corrosion of one metal being increased by contact with a second metal.* However, when use is made of the chart to assess severity of exposure, account must be taken of the following factors: †

(a) *The electrolyte and its effects*

Corrosion at bimetallic junctions only occurs while a continuous film or body of water joins the different metals so that a small electric current, an essential part of the corrosion process, can pass through this water. The circuit is completed by the metallic contact. The conductivity of the water, in itself dependent on the quantity and nature of electrolyte dissolved in it, will influence the severity of corrosion in a given time. In practice, sea water obviously represents a strong electrolyte, but dissolved fuel combustion products in rainwater also give a water a relatively high conductivity. Intermittent contact through water results in the bimetallic effect being dependent on the total time of contact.

Conditions of exposure are most severe for metals immersed in water. On exposure to atmospheric conditions, corrosion is usually localised in the vicinity of the line of contact. Condensed moisture containing dissolved electrolyte from polluted atmospheres

---

*Evans, Ulick R. and Rance, Vera E., *Corrosion and its Prevention at Bimetallic Contacts*, 3rd. Ed., HMSO, 1963. The main part of this publication is the table setting out the 'Degree of Corrosion at Bimetallic Contacts'. C.3.07/3 is an abridged version of the table insofar as those metals not commonly used in building practice have been omitted, while a different form of presentation has been adopted.

†These factors have been included under 'General considerations' earlier, but are repeated here so that they may be read directly with C.3.07/3.

Table 3.07/1. Effects of corrosive agents on metals

Corrosive Agents			Effects*	
Source	Common occurrence	Type	Metal(s)	Description/Comments
Portland cement	All cement-based products, e.g. mortars, renders, plasters, screeds, concrete	Sodium and potassium hydroxide (alkaline—about pH 12·5)	Aluminium	Generally harmful but degree of attack partly dependent on type of alloy. Protection under damp conditions essential
				Anodising coatings rapidly destroyed
				When embedded, unsightly salt efflorescence can occur above level of embedment. Cracking of the embedding medium may also occur
			Lead Zinc	Harmful. Protection under damp conditions essential
High-alumina cement	All cement-based products	Alkalis (alkalinity less than for Portland cement)	Aluminium Lead Zinc	Generally as for Portland cement, except effects are less marked as high-alumina cement is much less alkaline
High-calcium and magnesium limes	Mortars and plasters		Aluminium	Severely attacked. Protection under damp conditions essential
			Lead Zinc	Relatively slight effect
Salt accelerators	Gypsum plasters (Keene's, Parian anhydrous gypsum plasters)	Acid reaction	All unprotected metals	Some corrosion likely before plaster has dried out, i.e. while it is still damp. Normally corrosion should not be troublesome once the plaster has dried out and provided there are subsequently no prolonged periods of dampness
	Reinforced concrete	Calcium chloride	Mild steel	Calcium chloride added must be evenly distributed (preferably added to mixing water) and must not exceed 2 per cent calculated on the weight of cement
Smoke and flue gases	Flue terminals	Principally sulphur dioxide	Aluminium Copper Zinc (mainly in galvanised steel)	Attack is rapid when metals are directly exposed to smoke and flue gases
Combustion of coal and other fuels, and from sea-spray	Atmosphere Rainwater	Principally sulphur dioxide, carbon dioxide and/or corrosive salts, e.g. sulphates and chlorides	Aluminium	Generally corrosion resistance is fairly high. Sometimes corrosion stifles itself and the corrosion rate falls to a low value, but with a few alloys corrosion may be continuing and severe
			Zinc	Protective film not sufficiently dense and adherent to prevent steady though slow attack
			Iron and steel	Corrosion greatly stimulated. Protection essential
Water supply	Pipes and related components	Principally chlorides and sulphates, but dissolved carbon dioxide also significant	Iron and steel (except stainless steels)	Dissolved carbon dioxide may influence rate of corrosion due to its acidic character, and, indirectly, prevent the formation of protective calcium carbonate
			Aluminium	Generally not recommended for use with ordinary supply waters, but excellent for use in specially treated waters used industrially
			Copper	Corrosion appreciable in soft waters with appreciable dissolved carbon dioxide contents, causing green staining on plumbing fixtures
			Lead	Attack by soft waters sufficient to cause a physiologically dangerous lead concentration—'lead poisoning'
Sea water	Immersed structures and pipe lines	Principally chlorides	Iron and steel	Rate of corrosion increased when compared with fresh water, but this rate is increased by movement of the sea water
			Stainless steels	Local attack and pitting usually marked in stagnant water
Wood	*Softwoods:* Western red cedar and Douglas fir	Mainly organic acids, but also soluble salts	Aluminium Copper Lead Zinc	Corrosion unlikely if timber is well-seasoned, maintained dry or the metal is isolated from the timber
				Copper has been partly affected by acidic rainwater run from cedar roofs
	Hardwoods: Oak and sweet chestnut			Aluminium nails used for cedar shingles or sidings severely attacked if directly exposed to rainwater. No danger of attack if nails are protected by an overlapping shingle
				Zinc valley gutter in contact with hardboard underlay has been known to be attacked within two years
				Aluminium paint can be safely used on wood
Magnesium oxy-chloride cement	Flooring	Salt (hygroscopic)	Aluminium	Severely attacked whether in contact or embedded in flooring. Protection essential
Sulphates	Clay products particularly brickwork	Calcium, magnesium and potassium (soluble salts)	Zinc	Zinc used as flashings, soakers, etc., partly attacked by soluble salts and partly by alkali from mortar
Algae, moss or lichen	Pitched roofs	Organic acids and carbon dioxide	Aluminium Copper Lead, zinc	Attack principally associated with gutters and flashings and where acidic rainwater drips on to the metal
Foaming agents (certain types only)	Foamed cement used for insulation of pipes	Small amounts of ammonia	Copper	Copper containing small amounts of phosphorus affected. In the absence of avoiding the use of ammonia-producing foaming agents, suitably annealed or phosphorus-free copper should be used
Acetic acid fumes	Industrial processes, e.g. breweries, pickle factories and saw-mills	Acid	Lead	Use of lead for glazing bars, flashings, etc., best avoided as complete protection is rarely possible under the particular circumstances
Ashes or clinker	Made-up ground	Water soluble matter, and unburnt carbonaceous matter	Iron and steel	Serious corrosion likely

Note: The effects included in this Table are intended to cover those commonly experienced and taking into account common usage of the various metals in buildings

60

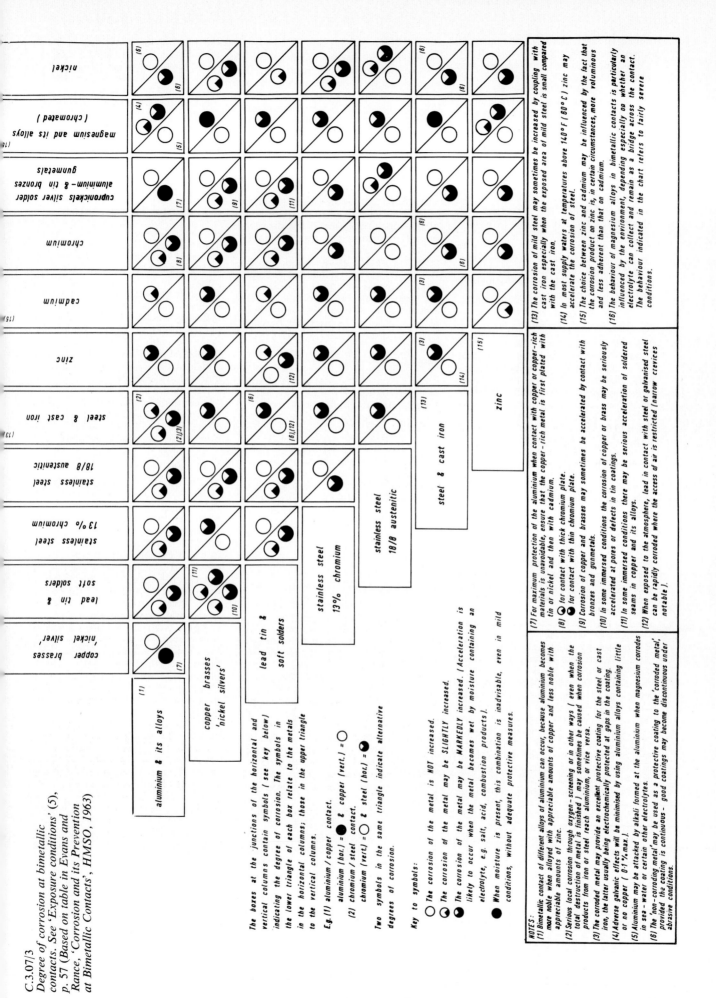

C.3.07/3
Degree of corrosion at bimetallic contacts. See 'Exposure conditions' (5), p. 57 (Based on table in Evans and Rance, 'Corrosion and its Prevention at Bimetallic Contacts', HMSO, 1963)

The boxes at the junctions of the horizontal and vertical columns contain symbols (see key below) indicating the degree of corrosion. The symbols in the lower triangle of each box relate to the metals in the horizontal columns; those in the upper triangle to the vertical columns.

E.g. (1) aluminium / copper contact.
aluminium (hor.) = ● & copper (vert.) = ○
(2) chromium / steel contact.
chromium (vert.) = ○ & steel (hor.) = ●

Two symbols in the same triangle indicate alternative degrees of corrosion.

Key to symbols:
○ The corrosion of the metal is NOT increased.
◔ The corrosion of the metal may be SLIGHTLY increased.
◑ The corrosion of the metal may be MARKEDLY increased. (Acceleration is likely to occur when the metal becomes wet by moisture containing an electrolyte, e.g. salt, acid, combustion products).
● When moisture is present, this combination is inadvisable, even in mild conditions, without adequate protective measures.

NOTES:
(1) Bimetallic contact of different alloys of aluminium can occur, because aluminium becomes more noble when alloyed with appreciable amounts of copper and less noble with appreciable amounts of zinc.
(2) Serious local corrosion through oxygen-screening or in other ways (even when the metal is finished) may sometimes be caused when corrosion products from iron or steel reach aluminium, or vice versa.
(3) The corroded metal may provide an excellent protective coating for the steel or cast iron, the latter usually being electrochemically protected at gaps in the coating.
(4) Adverse galvanic effects will be minimised by using aluminium alloys containing little or no copper (0·1% max.).
(5) Aluminium may be attacked by alkali formed at the aluminium when magnesium corrodes in sea-water or certain other electrolytes.
(6) The non-corroding metal may be used as a protective coating to the 'corroded metal', provided the coating is continuous - good coatings may become discontinuous under abrasive conditions.

(7) For maximum protection of the aluminium when contact with copper or copper-rich materials is unavoidable, ensure that the copper-rich metal is first plated with tin or nickel and then with cadmium.
(8) ◑ for contact with thick chromium plate. ◐ for contact with thin chromium plate.
(9) Corrosion of copper and brasses may sometimes be accelerated by contact with bronzes and gunmetals.
(10) In some immersed conditions the corrosion of copper or brass may be seriously accelerated at pores or defects in tin coatings.
(11) In some immersed conditions there may be serious acceleration of soldered seams in copper and its alloys.
(12) When exposed to the atmosphere, lead in contact with steel or galvanised steel can be rapidly corroded where the access of air is restricted (narrow crevices notable).

(13) The corrosion of mild steel may sometimes be increased by coupling with cast iron especially when the exposed area of mild steel is small compared with the cast iron.
(14) In most supply waters at temperatures above 140°F (60°C) zinc may accelerate the corrosion of steel.
(15) The choice between zinc and cadmium may be influenced by the fact that the corrosion product on zinc is, in certain circumstances, more voluminous and less adherent than that on cadmium.
(16) The behaviour of magnesium alloys in bimetallic contacts is particularly influenced by the environment, depending especially on whether an electrolyte can collect and remain as a bridge across the contact. The behaviour indicated in the chart refers to fairly severe conditions.

(industrial and marine) can cause an appreciable acceleration of corrosion.

Water containing complex ions may alter the data given in the chart. For example, ammonia has no action on iron, but attacks copper (normally a more noble metal) in the presence of air.

At soldered joints certain fluxes, which leave hygroscopic residues and produce moist conditions at the joint, are a source of trouble at bimetallic contacts.

Finally, it should be noted that serious acceleration of corrosion can occur when the two metals concerned are not directly joined together. For example, dissimilar metals, exposed to the sea in the wooden hull of a ship, may be dangerous even though they are connected only remotely by a metallic path through the ship.

(b) Condition of the metal

The chart disregards the fact that different alloys within one group may differ significantly in composition and may, therefore, give rise to bimetallic effects when in contact with each other. In the case of aluminium alloys, for example, bimetallic contact is also dependent on heat treatment conditions.

In the case of stainless steel it may be noted that its more noble character is dependent upon the protective film on the metal and this film is, in turn, maintained only if oxygen is continuously present.

(c) Metallic coatings

Metals such as chromium, nickel and zinc are most commonly used as protective metal coatings on another metal. The electrochemical behaviour of a metallic coating is generally similar to that of the same metal in the passive state, *provided* that it is (1) reasonably thick, and (2) free from pores. Where the coating is thin and contains many pores the electrochemical behaviour of the coated metal may approximate more to that of the basis metal, or to that of a relatively thick non-porous underlay. For example, the electrochemical behaviour of a coated metal with a thin decorative chromium on a good undercoat of nickel on steel or brass may approximate to that of the nickel.

Discontinuities of the coating may set up corrosion cells, with two possible effects. If the coating is more noble, the basis metal may be attacked; if the coating is less noble, the coating may be attacked.

Certain trimetallic contacts may need attention. Consider, for example, galvanised steel (zinc on steel) in contact with a more noble metal aluminium. Contact of the zinc with the aluminium may accelerate the corrosion of the zinc, leaving the steel (the base metal) exposed. In the absence of the zinc, contact between steel and aluminium (now less noble) may accelerate corrosion of the latter.

(d) Relative areas

In general, the danger of corrosion at a bimetallic junction is greatest if the area of the cathode (the nobler metal) is large compared to that of the anode (the less noble metal). Immersed conditions represent more severe exposure than do atmospheric conditions.

(e) Microgalvanic effects

In some cases microscopic bimetallic couples can be formed, resulting in accelerated corrosion (usually pitting) of the baser metal, when small amounts of the more noble metal are dissolved in water. Thus, the two dissimilar metals concerned do not have to be in metallic contact as normally implied. In copper–water systems, for example, small amounts of copper dissolved by the water may be deposited on less noble metals such as zinc, aluminium or ferrous alloys in the same system.

(f) Effects of graphite, coke or a carbonaceous film

These may, if left on a metal after fabrication, act as a noble electrode in a couple and accelerate corrosion.

(g) Other effects

When using the chart account should also be taken of the fact that corrosion may be accelerated due to other types of exposure previously outlined. Thus, for example, corrosion of an identical metal may be accelerated if there are crevices; deposits on the metal surface can cause differential aeration corrosion; certain materials may give off corrosive agents.

Typical examples

Experience has shown that, in building practice, there is serious risk of attack at bimetallic junctions. Consequently, it is convenient to summarise some typical examples of corrosion due to the contact of dissimilar metals which may occur in buildings. In the examples given below it should be noted that it is assumed that no precautions have been taken to isolate the one metal from the other, while no attempt has been made to classify the degree of corrosion. For guidance here reference should be made to C.3.07/3.

(1) Copper flashings in contact with galvanised steel—the galvanised steel corrodes.

(2) Copper parapet capping held in position by steel or galvanised steel nails—the nails corrode.

(3) Aluminium window or door frames with copper or brass hinges and other exposed brass fittings—the aluminium corrodes.

(4) Copper flashings, where the 'run off' is on an aluminium roof—copper will be deposited on the surface of the aluminium, resulting in serious pitting of the aluminium.

(5) Copper pipes in contact with galvanised steel water tanks—corrosion occurs at the point of contact

and often at the water line of the tank as well as on the floor of the tank.

(6) Brass valves in galvanised steel water pipes—corrosion products from the steel blocks the pipes.

(7) Aluminium rainwater goods (particularly pipes) carrying rainwater from copper roofs—copper will be deposited on the surface of the aluminium, resulting in serious localised attack of the aluminium (perforation is usually rapid).

resistance to corrosion

As the resistance to corrosion which a metal or alloy will provide is primarily dependent on its properties and the conditions to which it is exposed, it is more realistic to consider not only the basic composition of the various metals and alloys used in building practice, but also the effects of the different basic conditions of exposure outlined previously under 'Exposure conditions'. The resistances which metals will provide are summarised in Table 3.07/2.

There are two basic groups of metals, namely the *ferrous metals* and the *non-ferrous metals*. The metals and alloys which fall under either of these groups are discussed separately.

1. Ferrous metals

The term ferrous metals is used to include those consisting largely of iron. In engineering and building pig iron from the blast furnace is not used. Instead the pig iron is subjected to refining treatment, including alloying in which carbon is important, although other elements are also used. Consequently, it is the iron alloys which must be considered, and these are basically cast iron, wrought iron, ordinary steels* and stainless steels.

Apart from the stainless steels, ferrous metals are not chosen because of their resistance to corrosion but mainly because of their excellent mechanical properties, ease of fabrication, relative cheapness, wide availability of suitable ores and ease of extraction. In most environments, *iron* has a low resistance to corrosion when compared with other metals. This can be accounted for by the following factors: the ease with which cathodic reactions can proceed on its surface, the readiness with which concentration cells are formed and the poor protection afforded by corrosion products. The basically poor resistance of iron can be increased by alloying and in this the high resistance to corrosion generally offered by the stainless steels, that is alloys of iron containing not less than 12 per cent chromium, may be noted. In general, ferrous metals, apart from stainless steel, need some form of applied protection—the degree of protection depending on the severity of exposure.

---

*As explained later, the term 'ordinary' is used for convenience in order to distinguish mild and low-alloy steels from stainless steels.

Table 3.07/2. Resistance of metals to corrosion

Metal	Resistance to			
	Atmosphere	Other building materials	Conductive water	Other metals (see also C.3.07/3)
Aluminium and its alloys	1. Generally fairly high and dependent on type of alloy and degree of atmospheric pollution 2. Surface corrosion and pitting may take place when atmospheric pollution is high 3. Resistance against direct exposure to flue gases and smoke only fair. In flue terminals the metal cannot be expected to last very long	1. Resistance generally low when in contact with wet cement-based products with either Portland or high-alumina cement. Attack is severe when in contact with wet high-calcium and magnesium limes 2. Resistance low to magnesium oxychloride cement whether in contact or embedded 3. Attack likely by some timbers, e.g. Western Red Cedar, Douglas fir, Oak and Sweet chestnut 4. Some attack likely before gypsum plasters (Keene's, Parian, anhydrous) have dried out. Subsequent attack unlikely unless the plaster becomes damp for prolonged periods	1. Resistance generally good against rainwater—water run-off from copper to be avoided 2. Resistance generally poor against waste water, particularly when water supply is carried in copper or when washing compounds are present in the waste water 3. Excellent resistance when used to carry specially treated waters—not generally recommended for ordinary water supplies 4. Resistance to sea water may be good with some alloys	1. Resistance generally fairly low when in contact with most common metals, including dissimilar alloys in contact 2. Resistance particularly low when in contact with copper and copper alloys—attack of aluminium is rapid 3. Good resistance when in contact with zinc or cadmium 4. Resistance to iron varies according to type of alloy and nature of electrolyte. Attack generally negligible even when in contact with stainless steels
Cast iron	1. Good resistance which is further enhanced if the casting skin on the iron is still intact 2. Corrosion resistance of nodular graphite cast iron is at least as good, if not better, as that of flake graphite cast iron	1. Good resistance relative to those materials with which cast iron normally comes into contact 2. Resistance to soils mainly governed by oxygen content. Resistance generally poor in anaerobic soils, e.g. clays (presence of sulphate-reducing bacteria important). Acid soils usually aggressive 3. Poor resistance in made-up ground containing ashes or clinker (presence of water-soluble and unburnt carbonaceous matter significant)	1. Good resistance in distilled or fresh waters. Rate of attack increased by salt concentration, aeration and temperature 2. Rate of corrosion generally increases in sea water, particularly with increases in movement of water 3. Graphitisation occurs in soft acid waters and sea water 4. Calcareous deposits may help to stifle attack—may be significant when cathodic protection is used	1. Resistance considerably reduced when in contact with cupro nickels, aluminium-bronzes, gunmetals, copper, brasses, lead* and soft solders*, stainless steels and chromium. Accelerated corrosion is likely to occur when highly conductive electrolytes (salt, acid, combustion products) are present 2. Resistance to corrosion may be moderately reduced when in contact with aluminium and its alloys
Copper and its alloys	1. Excellent resistance to most conditions of exposure 2. Flue gases and smoke will attack under severe conditions of exposure	1. Excellent resistance against most building materials except when ammonia is present as in certain types of foamed cement or when organic acids from certain timbers are present 2. Poor resistance when copper tubes are covered with a thin carbonaceous film	1. Generally excellent resistance against most waters. In roofs attack may be caused when water is made acidic by organic matter (algae, lichen or moss) and where this water drips onto the metal 2. Resistance low against soft waters with appreciable amounts of dissolved carbon dioxide	1. Resistance generally excellent when in contact with most common metals, including dissimilar alloys in contact 2. Resistance may be low in some immersed conditions when there are pores or defects in tin coatings to copper or brass
Lead	1. Very high resistance due to formation of basic lead carbonate or sulphate but certain conditions of environment or detail may reduce resistance considerably 2. Resistance poor against acetic acid fumes	1. Resistance fairly low against alkali attack from wet cement-based products 2. Resistance low against contact with certain types of wood 3. Resistance in soils is generally high except sometimes in made-up ground containing ashes and in clay soils containing gypsum and perhaps chloride	1. Resistance against most waters is generally high 2. Resistance against soft waters is sufficiently low to enable a lead concentration to build up that is physiologically dangerous 3. Resistance is considerably lowered when rainwater run-off from roofs is made acidic by organic matter (algae, lichens, moss)	1. In some immersed conditions there may be serious acceleration of soldered seams in copper and its alloys 2. Rapid corrosion where the access of air is restricted (narrow crevices notable) when in contact with steel or galvanised steel and exposed to the atmosphere 3. Varied reduction in resistance when in contact with copper and its alloys, chromium, stainless steels and nickel
Stainless steel (includes a wide range of alloys —as many as 60)	1. Generally excellent, but dependent on composition. (Careful selection for given environment important) 2. Resistance may be lowered considerably, with resultant superficial localised attack, where debris occurs, in crevices or by marine spray	1. Generally excellent, including exposure to most soil conditions	1. Generally excellent to supply, lake or river waters, even when these are relatively highly polluted, irrespective of temperature 2. In sea waters and saline solutions resistance is considerably reduced, depending on the ability of the chloride of breaking down the passive film. Stagnant waters usually result in marked localised attack and pitting 3. Susceptibility to corrosion by strongly reducing mineral acids, but otherwise unaffected by acids and alkalis	1. Generally unaffected by contact with other metals, except in sea water when contact with aluminium alloys, ordinary steel, zinc and sometimes copper may lead to attack, but relative areas of metals involved and movement of water important
Steel (excluding stainless steels)	1. Generally poor but resistance is improved by small additions of copper (e.g. copper-bearing steels) or other alloying elements such as chromium and with relatively high phosphorus and silicon contents (e.g. low-alloy steels)	1. Unaffected by cement- or lime-based products, but resistance seriously reduced if embedded in concrete containing excessive amounts of calcium chloride or if the calcium chloride is not evenly distributed 2. Attack by gypsum plasters, magnesium oxychloride cements and some organic materials (e.g. certain timbers and plastics that exude acids or other corrosive compounds) 3. Resistance to soils mainly governed by oxygen content. Resistance generally poor in anaerobic soils, e.g. clays (presence of sulphate-reducing bacteria important). Acid soils usually aggressive 4. Poor resistance in made-up ground of ashes or clinker (presence of water soluble and unburnt carbonaceous matter significant)	1. Resistance to fresh waters generally low but rate of attack increased by salt concentration, aeration and temperature 2. Rate of corrosion generally increases in sea water particularly with increases in movement of water 3. Rate of corrosion generally increased by soft acidic waters 4. Calcareous deposits may help to stifle attack—may be significant when cathodic protection is used	1. Resistance considerably reduced when in contact with cupro nickels, aluminium-bronzes, gunmetals, copper, brasses, lead* and soft solders,* stainless steels and chromium. Accelerated corrosion is likely to occur when high conductive electrolytes (salt, acid, combustion products) are present 2. In certain soft waters, change of potential occurs at temperatures above 60°C and steel is rapidly corroded by zinc
Zinc	1. Fair resistance as protective film is not dense nor firmly adherent. Resistance considerably reduced by presence of sulphur	1. Resistance fairly low against alkali attack from wet cement-based products, acid attack from acid plasters such as Keene's and salts from brickwork 2. Resistance low against contact with certain types of wood, including hardboard	1. Resistance varies considerably and is largely dependent on the type of dissolved salts and gases. Attack is generally also influenced by temperature—marked increase in attack at high temperatures	1. Resistance generally low to most metals except magnesium. Useful as cathodic protector for iron and steel 2. In certain soft waters, change of potential occurs at temperatures above 60°C and zinc will rapidly corrode iron or steel

*Lead or soft solders may be used as coatings without risk of corrosion, *provided* that continuity of the coating is good.

63

(a) Cast iron

Cast irons are ferrous alloys containing over 1·5 per cent of carbon with significant amounts of phosphorus, silicon and, possibly, deliberate additions of alloying elements. Cast irons include grey iron castings, iron castings in which the graphite is in a spheroidal or nodular form, and malleable iron castings. The familiar grey fracture associated with cast iron is due to the presence of free graphite, which, in the form of flakes, accounts for the brittleness of cast iron while it is the important distinguishing characteristic between cast iron and mild steel.

Small percentages of alloying additions have little effect on the corrosion resistance of cast iron; larger percentages, on the other hand, have been made to develop cast irons of better mechanical and corrosion resistant properties. Special alloys of this kind include the high silicon irons (up to 18 per cent silicon), the high chromium irons (25–30 per cent chromium) and austenitic irons (not less than 15 per cent nickel and 7 per cent copper). In general, these special alloys are not commonly used in buildings.

The presence of a casting skin which may be either white iron, if there has been chilling, or, high in silica if moulded in sand, increases the initial corroding characteristics of cast iron. This skin, it may be noted, adheres more firmly than the mill scale found on mild steel, and thus offers greater protection.

All cast irons have good resistance to atmospheric corrosion. Resistance is also good in distilled or fresh waters, but the rate of attack increases with salt concentration, aeration and temperature. In soft acidic waters and sea water *graphitisation* of the cast iron occurs and, although the appearance and shape of the original iron is largely retained, it is much weaker mechanically (when used underground the corroded component is easily fractured by earth movement). Retention of appearance and shape is due to the fact that graphite is virtually unaffected by most corrosion processes and is often found *in situ* after the iron has been removed by corrosion. Graphitisation results in a porous graphite residue ('graphite corrosion residue') impregnated with insoluble corrosion products (iron phosphide, the phosphorus in cast iron, which is also virtually unaffected by most corrosion processes and silicon which is usually oxidised to silica or silicates, the latter helping to bind the other constituents). It may be noted here that, although the corrosion rates of cast iron and steel are much the same in soft acidic waters and sea water, cast iron appears to behave better due to its normally much thicker section and to the graphitisation which retains the original form and thus enables a pipe, for example, to retain water.

Carbon dioxide dissolved in water influences corrosion for two reasons. First, it can increase the hydrogen evolution type of attack due to its acidic character (carbon dioxide decreases the pH of the solution). Second, and indirectly, concentration of protective calcium carbonate is not formed with increases in carbon dioxide content of water; instead calcium carbonate remains in solution in the form of calcium bicarbonate.

The corrosion resistance of cast iron can be increased if calcareous deposits (hard waters notable) with a favourable type of crystalline structure can develop. Calcareous deposits of some protective value can also develop when cast iron (or steel) is immersed in sea water, particularly when cathodic protection is applied. The protective value of calcareous deposits can be minimised by the presence in sufficient quantities of chloride, which interfere with the deposition of the protective layers. The result is the formation of rust nodules, beneath which intensive attack and pitting can take place. The presence of sulphate ions may also interfere with the formation of protective deposits. It may be noted that only a small amount of saline matter (relatively low concentration) is sufficient to enable corrosion cells to function at or near their maximum efficiency. In sodium chloride solutions, for example, the corrosion rate for iron increases relatively little after the concentration has reached 1000 p.p.m. sodium chloride.

The decomposition and leaching of dead vegetation yields organic acids which, in turn, produce waters with a lower pH value and hence increase the danger of corrosion. The presence of sulphate-reducing bacteria may also increase the risk of corrosion.

(b) Wrought iron

At present little, if any, wrought iron is made. Interest in its behaviour is therefore largely historic, although wrought iron components (pipes, chains, gates, ballustrades and railings, for example) are still in use. When required, wrought iron is often replaced by mild steel and, as service life often favours wrought iron, it is useful to appreciate the reasons for the difference in behaviour.

Wrought iron is an iron alloy of very low carbon content (between 0·02 and 0·03 per cent) and in the case of British wrought irons, with a high slag content (varying between 1·0 and 4·0 per cent but usually about 2·0 per cent) and a characteristic laminated structure. The fundamental differences between wrought iron and steel are due to both processing and composition with the former influencing the latter. In the case of processing, steel is cast into ingots, whereas wrought iron is removed from the furnace in a semi-molten plastic condition and is formed into bars or billets under a steam hammer. As far as composition is concerned, the presence of slag in wrought iron distinguishes it from steel. In addition, wrought iron has less carbon and manganese and usually more phosphorus. Although the silicon content of the two materials is roughly the same (between 0·10 and 0·20 per cent) the state of the silicon is different.

The slag content plays an important, though by no means the only, part in the corrosion resistance of wrought iron. The slag performs a barrier-like action which impedes the penetration by corrosion. The effects of the slag content on the rate of corrosion may be illustrated by comparing the performance of Swedish wrought irons, which are almost slagless, with that of British wrought irons which contain much more slag. The Swedish wrought iron rusts outdoors 25 per cent *more* quickly than mild steel, while the British wrought irons rust about 25 per cent *less* rapidly than mild steel.

In addition to slag content, the existence, in wrought irons, of two types of resistant zones and differences in the nature of the scale and its adhesion to the metal surface (the adhesion is good) account for the reported longer life of wrought iron tubes compared to ones of mild steel.

(c) Ordinary steel

The term 'ordinary' is used here for convenience, in order to differentiate between those steels having a comparatively low percentage of alloying elements, other than carbon, and those, such as the stainless steels, having a high percentage of alloying elements. Two main groups of steel, commonly used, may be identified, namely *mild steel* and *low-alloy* steel. Both of these are classified as low-carbon steels, that is with a carbon content up to 0·25 per cent. The classification of iron–carbon alloys, based on the percentage of carbon present, is usually as follows:

Low-carbon steel	
Low-alloy steel	up to 0·20 per cent
Mild steel	up to 0·25 per cent
Medium carbon steel	0·25 – 0·45 per cent
High-carbon steel	0·45 – 1·50 per cent
Cast iron	2·50 – 4·50 per cent

The role of carbon in steel is important insofar as the hardness and strength of the material is concerned. Neither carbon nor the small quantities of other elements, such as sulphur, phosphorus, silicon and manganese, normally present, have much effect on the general corrosion resistance of steel, particularly in neutral media, as the corrosion rate is controlled primarily by the transport of oxygen. However, the inclusion of small amounts of certain alloying elements such as copper, chromium and nickel, does increase the resistance of iron and steel outdoors.

The primary differences in composition between mild steel and low-alloy steels may be summarised as follows:

(i) *Mild steel* is a steel with no deliberate alloy addition, and with a carbon content not exceeding 0·25 per cent. Although alloying elements are not deliberately included, mild steel

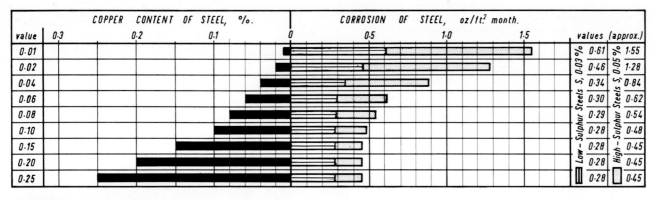

C.3.07/4
Effect of copper content on the corrosion of mild steel outdoors. (Based on: 'Protection of Iron and Steel Structures from Corrosion', CP 2008, Fig. 4, p. 162, 1966)

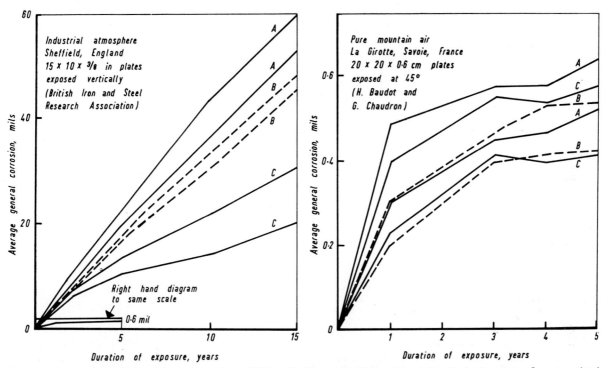

The curves show the limits of results observed by British and French investigators for groups of: A. mild steels; B. copper–bearing steels; C. low–alloy steels containing up to 1·0 per cent chromium and 0·65 per cent copper.

D.3.07/13
Corrosion/time curves for mild steels, copper-bearing steels and low-alloy steels exposed outdoors in an industrial environment (left-hand diagram) and pure mountain air (right-hand diagram). (From: 'Protection of Iron and Steel from Corrosion', CP 2008, Fig. 5, p. 163, 1966)

usually contains small amounts of sulphur, phosphorus, silicon, manganese and copper. Small percentages of these elements are inevitably introduced into steel through the scrap used in its manufacture. Copper contents, for example, of well over 0·03 per cent are common in British steels.

The corrosion resistance of mild steel can be increased by the addition of copper. Such steels are generally known as *copper-bearing steels.* BS 15. *Mild steel for general constructional purposes,* specifies two grades of copper-bearing steel which contain either 0·20–0·35 per cent or 0·035–0·50 per cent copper. The effect of the additional copper is marked, but there is a limit, which is dependent on the sulphur content. However, there is a progressive decrease in corrosion as the copper content is increased until the limit (about 0·1 per cent) is reached. Thereafter, further additions of copper cause little additional improvement. (See comparative chart C.3.07/4.)

(ii) *Low-alloy steel* is a steel, generally with a carbon content not exceeding 0·20 per cent, to which small percentages of alloying elements up to, say, 3·0 per cent in all have been deliberately added. The effect of these additions may be to increase the mechanical properties or corrosion resistance of the steel, or both. Although the low-alloy steels and the copper-bearing steels are more resistant to corrosion than ordinary mild steel, they are not necessarily immune to corrosion and are, therefore, better considered as 'slow-rusting'. For example, steel with 1·0 per cent chromium, 0·6 per cent copper and relatively high phosphorus and silicon contents, corrode in the open atmosphere at one-third, or less, of the rate for ordinary mild steel. The relative performance of some mild steels, copper-bearing steels and low-alloy steels in an industrial atmosphere and in pure mountain air are shown in diagram D.3.07/13 above. Corrosion is most rapid during the first year or so, and the beneficial effects of

F

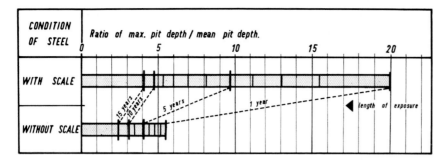

C.3.07/5
*Effect of mill-scale on pitting of steel
in sea water. (Based on Butler, G. and
Ison, H. C. K., 'Corrosion and its
Prevention in Waters', Fig. 19, p. 66,
Leonard Hill, London, 1966)*

low-alloy additions are of greater practical value in the more corrosive atmosphere.

The improved resistance of both copper and low-alloy steels outdoors has been attributed to the influence of alloying elements on the nature of corrosion product. The rust formed on these steels is more compact and less permeable and thus more protective than on ordinary mild steel. However, it may be noted that natural weathering appears to favour this because these alloyed steels show little or no advantage when exposed indoors or when sheltered from the rain.

Another contributing factor to the increased resistance provided by the alloy steels is that their *mill-scale* is more firmly held than on mild steel. If, however, the scale is not removed the danger of localised attack is correspondingly greater than with mild steel. It may be noted that, in general, the presence of mill-scale on the metal surface does not affect the overall corrosion but does increase significantly the localisation of attack, due to breaks in the mill-scale which frequently occur in practice. It has been shown that in sea water the penetration of pitting after one year was four times greater with steel with mill-scale than with steel without mill-scale. Over a period of time this difference decreased, although the effect was still evident after 15 years. See comparative chart C.3.07/5.

Unlike cast iron, steel generally has poor resistance to both fresh water and sea water, although both corrode more rapidly in sea water than in fresh water. The effects of dissolved carbon dioxide, chlorides, sulphate ions, organic acids and calcareous deposits are similar to those described for cast iron. The effects of sulphate-reducing bacteria on steel are severe pitting.

Although *the effect of temperature* on the corrosiveness of a water varies with operating conditions, corrosion reactions do, in general, proceed more rapidly as the temperature rises. In moving waters there is a two-fold increase initially for every rise of 10°C above atmospheric temperature.

At higher temperatures this tendency is reversed, as oxygen becomes less soluble. Thus, in open systems from which liberated gases may escape, there is a maximum corrosion rate at 70° to 80°C followed by a decrease up to the boiling point. On the other hand, in a closed system there is no such maximum rate, as the oxygen is retained within them. However, in such cases corrosion generally ceases when the oxygen supply has become exhausted through the corrosion reaction.

As with most other metals, *water movement* often increases the rate of corrosion by promoting the supply of oxygen to the metal surface, while high speeds may also prevent the adhesion of protective corrosion products or calcareous deposits. There may be a considerable increase in exposure when dissimilar steels are in contact. The scouring effect of sand and detritus may seriously aggravate corrosion in harbour and similar installations.

In general, *the effect of cement mortar and concrete* on iron and steel embedded in or in contact with them is dependent, in addition to the presence of moisture, on a number of factors, chief of which are:

(1) The highly alkaline nature of most cement mortars and concretes (Portland cement mixes have an alkalinity of pH 12·5), is normally sufficient to inhibit rusting. Such inhibition may be reduced if the leachate from the concrete contains appreciable amounts of calcium sulphate (gypsum) in addition to the calcium hydroxide.

(2) Carbonation of the surface layers (the action of carbon dioxide makes these layers less alkaline), which results in an increase in volume of one-sixth, may effectively seal the concrete if it is of good quality; in poor quality concrete such sealing does not occur. Thus with dense concrete and with proper depth of cover to the steel, sufficient uncarbonated material will remain uncarbonated to protect the steel for at least 50 years.

(3) The quality of concrete in which steel is embedded and the depth of cover are important if cracks, and thus

the entry of water, is to be prevented. Entry of water will promote corrosion. In certain cases it may be necessary to prevent the occurrence of large shrinkage cracks (small hair cracks are normally insignificant).

(4) The presence of large amounts of chlorides, either through the use of salt-containing aggregates or as additives to accelerate hardening, will promote corrosion. In general, the amount of chloride used in reinforced concrete should not exceed 2·0 per cent, calculated on the weight of cement.

All types of low alloy and straight carbon steels can be used together without danger of increased attack. Such steels are, however, anodic to the stainless steels containing large amounts of chromium and nickel. In sea water there is a risk of corrosion when mild steel is in contact with copper or stainless steel. Rate of movement of this type of water will influence the rate of attack—generally the faster the flow the faster the rate of corrosion. When considering protective metal coatings the relative position in the galvanic series with regard to iron is extremely important. *Anodic* coatings, such as zinc, provide good protection provided the area of exposed iron is not extensive (see 'General considerations', 6(b)). When cathodic coatings, nickel or chromium for example, are used, pitting may result at pores, cracks or areas of damage. As rivets are the sites of poor paint adhesion, they are frequently heavily corroded. Increased resistance may be provided if the rivets are alloyed with small additions of nickel and copper. Similarly, a weld of 2·0 per cent nickel-steel suffers less corrosion than a carbon-steel weld, while corrosion or pitting of the mild steel plate is not accelerated.

(d) Stainless steel

Stainless steel may be defined as a steel containing sufficient chromium, or chromium and nickel, to render it highly resistant to corrosion. The amount of chromium basically controls corrosion resistance, with a minimum of about 12 per cent required; nickel is added to improve ductility. Increased resistance to corrosion is provided if molybdenum is included.

Although stainless steels have a high resistance to corrosion, they are by no means completely immune from attack, and under certain conditions their resistance is far from good. In this, it is to be remembered that stainless steel does not imply a single alloy but a group of alloys consisting of something like 60 varieties. Consequently, the term 'stainless' should not be taken too literally, while care in selection of the correct type is important.

Stainless steels commonly used in building applications include those containing 17 per cent chromium (known as 17 per cent stainless steel); 18 per cent chromium and 8 per cent nickel (known as 18/8 stainless steel); and 18 per cent chromium, 10 per cent nickel and 3 per cent molybdenum (known as 18/10/3 stainless steel).

The high resistance to corrosion provided by stainless steel is due to the presence of a thin protective oxide film, which reforms and heals itself spontaneously if the surface is damaged. With the protective oxide film the stainless steel is in the passive state, but passivation (for which a 11·5 per cent chromium content is required) occurs readily only in oxygenated environments. Consequently, stainless steel will be in active state, and thus lose its corrosion resistance, in non-oxidising environments, which cannot repair the oxide film. When repair of the film is prevented by lack of oxygen access, severe corrosion can take place at a rate comparable with that of mild steel. Such conditions are likely to occur beneath debris, including sticky particles of sulphur or iron-bearing compounds and suspended salt particles, or in crevices. Adequate cleaning of the surface will minimise the deleterious effects of the debris (superficial local breakdown resulting in disfigurement by rust-staining), and careful design those effects associated with crevices. In this, it is important to note that the particular quality of stainless steel is important. In general, the more corrosion resistant molybdenum-bearing quality provides good resistance to most industrial corrosive atmospheres.

When corrosion of stainless steel does occur it is usually localised. The presence of chlorides increases the susceptibility to attack. The corrosion resistance of stainless steel in sea water or when exposed to marine atmospheres is generally not high. Under these conditions the behaviour of the stainless steel is dependent on the ability of the chloride to break down the passive film. In sea water stainless steel may be attacked when in contact with aluminium alloys, ordinary steel and zinc; sometimes attack may also take place when it is in contact with copper. In this, the relative areas of the metals involved and the movement of water are important.

Stainless steel normally has a high resistance to corrosion when exposed to a wide range of supply, lake and river waters, even when pollution is relatively high, and irrespective of whether the water is hot or cold. Resistance to building materials is also high, although corrosion can take place when stainless steel is exposed to strongly reducing mineral acids.

2. Non-ferrous metals

As a class the non-ferrous metals (only aluminium, copper, lead and zinc are considered in detail here) offer greater resistance to corrosion than do the ferrous metals. This is due *either* to their self-passivation, as in aluminium, *or* to the formation of restraining films, as in zinc, *or* to their inherent nobility, as in copper. However, non-ferrous metals may be corroded, sometimes extensively or rapidly, when exposed to certain acids and alkalis, many of which

may be derived from other building materials in contact with the metal or at bimetallic junctions.

Although non-ferrous metals may be preferred for a number of conditions of exposure because of their high resistance to corrosion, it is not always possible to use them due either to their inadequate mechanical properties or their high cost. In some instances, as in galvanised steel or chromium plating, non-ferrous metals may be used as protective coatings to the less resistant ferrous metals. In this, it should be noted that the efficacy of the non-ferrous metal coating is to a large extent dependent on the thickness of the coating, while breaks in the coating may lead to bimetallic corrosion. As regards the latter, and depending on the metals involved, either the base metal or the 'coating' metal may suffer attack.

(a) *Aluminium and its alloys*

A wide variety of aluminium alloys are available but, apart from some special alloys, are generally known simply as aluminium. As pure aluminium offers the greatest resistance to corrosion, while the presence of impurities, alloying elements, the nature of the surface and heat-treatments tend to lower, sometimes significantly, resistance to corrosion, the selection of a given aluminium alloy for a given condition of exposure is extremely important.

The high resistance to attack offered by aluminium and its alloys depends on the formation of a tightly adherent and protective surface film. *Passivation* of aluminium, that is the formation of the protective surface film, is produced both by the reaction of the metal with oxygen in the air or dissolved in water and by direct reaction with the water itself. If removed, the film immediately reforms.* It may be noted that in the absence of its protective surface film, aluminium is a very reactive chemical element. The film formed on aluminium is generally stable in the pH range 4·5–8·5. However, outside this range the aluminium becomes active. Aluminium dissolves particularly easily in alkalis, but corrosion resistance above pH 8·5 is dependent on the source of the alkali, so that aluminium is stable in many alkaline waters. Thicker oxide films with greater resistance to corrosion and abrasion may be formed by anodic treatment—anodising.

The resistance of aluminium and certain of its alloys is high to normal atmospheric exposure. In clean, dry air the appearance of the aluminium will remain unaltered for a long time. However, when exposed to normal outdoor conditions in this country, surface corrosion does occur to a varying extent and should be taken into account. Surface corrosion, together with the

deposition of dirt, tends to make the aluminium, unless specially finished, become duller and darker, and eventually roughened. Washing, either artificially or by rain, is beneficial as it removes dirt and other debris that accelerate corrosion. Although dulling of aluminium does indicate that corrosion has taken place, it does not imply that the metal is becoming progressively thinner, although some pitting of the surface may occur, particularly in sheltered areas. Corrosion is generally greatest with those aluminium alloys containing copper, and unless these are coated with pure aluminium, they will also suffer severe loss of strength. Susceptibility to corrosion can also be reduced by extended heat-treatment. From experience, both in this country and in America, it would seem that most of the aluminium alloys likely to be used as building elements are, in general, capable of withstanding normal atmospheric conditions without serious deterioration. It may, however, be noted that although the structurally important alloys are slightly more susceptible to corrosion than the purer aluminium used in sheet form, the greater thickness of the former compensates for this. However, in heavily polluted industrial and marine atmospheres corrosion of the structural alloys is accelerated and protection of the metal —usually by painting—is required.

Highly corrosive conditions of exposure are likely to occur in poorly ventilated industrial buildings, particularly those with uninsulated single-skin roofs. Acid vapours condensing on the underside of the aluminium roof sheets will attack the protective film and thus hasten corrosion of the surface. The use of open fires for space heating without adequate ventilation has, in certain cases, led to severe corrosion of the under-surface of aluminium roofing.

Waters contaminated with substances from neighbouring materials, or those present in industrial and marine atmospheres, may become highly corrosive. Pools of water remaining static for long periods on the surface of aluminium can lead to corrosion by limiting the oxygen supply. Small amounts of metallic salts present in domestic water supplies are liable to 'plate out' on the surface of aluminium supply lines and lead to corrosion. However, industrially, in specially treated waters, aluminium tubing, etc., is highly resistant to corrosion.

In rainwater installations alloys of the same type should be used throughout (except for brackets, etc.) as cast and wrought alloys have different surface appearance and corrosion characteristics.

Kitchen and bathroom wastes are liable to harm aluminium. Contact between aluminium and copper leads to corrosion of the aluminium. Thus, in plumbing, aluminium should not be used in any system containing copper, or copper-based materials, or in any

*It is perhaps axiomatic, but worthwhile noting, that a continuing cycle of removal and reforming of the protective film leads to thinning of the aluminium component.

Perforation of copper sheet by acid rainwater dripping from roof (Crown copyright)

Channelling and perforation of lead valley gutters by acid rainwater from roof: upper portion had been covered by the slates (Crown copyright). Below, pitting of an aluminium alloy in a sheltered area which has not been kept clean either artificially or by rain

situation where water passes over a copper surface *before* reaching the aluminium.*

Under damp conditions, cement-based products may give rise to corrosion, the degree of attack depending on the composition of the alloy (anodising coatings are rapidly destroyed) and the richness of the cement (the richer the cement the more intense the attack). Corrosion of embedded metal can lead to cracking of the embedding medium and unsightly salt efflorescence above the level of embedment. Chlorides, used as workability aids, contained in the mix may accelerate corrosion. Lime mortars affect aluminium in the same way as cement, but less severely. All types of gypsum plaster are liable to cause some corrosion either while they are still damp in the early stages, or if prolonged dampness occurs after the gypsum has dried out. Magnesium chloride in magnesium oxychloride flooring is corrosive and, in addition, also absorbs water, thus intensifying attack.

Although generally resistant to organic acids found in most timbers, aluminium may be corroded, under wet conditions, by acids from western red cedar, Douglas fir, oak and sweet chestnut. However, aluminium nails may be used with cedar shingles, *provided* the heads of the nails are covered by the overlapping shingle. It is important to note that aluminium may be corroded when in contact with or adjacent to wood treated with a copper preservative.

Aluminium is likely to be corroded by direct contact with soil. Aluminium flue terminals are often rapidly corroded.

Corrosion of aluminium occurs when in contact with copper, brass or bronze, iron or mild steel. In heavily polluted industrial or marine atmospheres contact with lead or stainless steel also leads to corrosion of the aluminium.

(b) Copper and its alloys

Pure copper has a high chemical stability in many corrosive media. Resistance to corrosion is due to the fact that copper is a relatively noble metal. On exposure it forms relatively thin adherent protective films of corrosion products. Because it has only a weak tendency to passivation, the effect of unequal aeration is very slight. In moving water differential ion concentration may result in corrosion as discussed under 'General considerations' (5(b), p. 52).

Several grades of copper are available. The purest, with 99·9 per cent copper, has high conductivity and is

*Two examples reported by the BRS (in 1958) in which rapid and severe corrosion of aluminium associated with copper in plumbing are worthwhile noting. (1) An aluminium waste pipe (of H10 alloy) used in a cloakroom corroded extensively in three years. The supply water was carried to the basins in copper pipes. Traces of dissolved copper appear to have accentuated corrosion caused by the soapy wastes. (2) Severe corrosion of aluminium sinks (alloy NS3) after three and a half years occurred in three places: (a) the aluminium in contact with the plated brass fitting; (b) under the drip of the tap; (c) below the bowl standing in the sink.

important in electrical work (wires, switches, busbars, generators, etc., etc.). Copper commonly used for building purposes may contain small percentages of other elements such as phosphorus. These, although not as resistant to corrosion as pure copper, have, nevertheless, excellent resistance in most environments. The exceptions are important.

Copper may be severely attacked by acids, particularly if these drip persistently on to the copper. In tiled roofing covered with algae, for example, rainwater run-off is made acidic, and where this drips on to copper, between the joints in the tiles, perforation of the copper has taken place. Acid leached from cedarwood shingles may also lead to perforation.

The usually high corrosion resistance of copper tubing to water may be substantially reduced, with resultant pitting or stress corrosion cracking, if thin carbonaceous films (derived during manufacture but now generally removed) are present. In some rare cases, pitting has been caused by the formation of films by moorland waters.

In soft waters, particularly those containing appreciable amounts of free carbon dioxide, and in carbonated waters in general, corrosion of copper does occur but this is insignificant so far as durability and health risk is concerned. The formation of green stains on plumbing fixtures often implies that such waters may be corrosive enough to pick up sufficient copper to cause the stain. Hard waters are seldom corrosive to copper because of the rapid formation of a protective film of calcium compounds. Softening of waters with an appreciable temporary hardness can lead to corrosion, particularly if the water is heated above 140°C, and the calcium compounds necessary to form the protective film are absent, while sodium bicarbonate breaks down with the release of carbon dioxide.

Copper is highly resistant to sea water, although resistance may be significantly reduced in rapidly flowing sea water.

Copper, particularly if it contains phosphorus, is liable to corrode if ammonia is present. Small amounts of ammonia are released when a foaming agent is mixed with Portland cement to make foamed concrete.

Brasses and bronzes are among the most important alloys of copper used in building. There are also copper–nickel alloys. *Brasses* are essentially alloys of copper with zinc (between 10 and 15 per cent zinc), but often include other components such as tin, iron, manganese, aluminium and lead. *Bronzes,* on the other hand, are generally the copper–tin series of alloys, although other components may be included. Corrosion behaviour of the alloys, although in many ways similar to copper, is largely dependent on their composition. Brass may suffer from a special form of corrosion, dezincification. (See 'General considerations' 7(f), p. 55.)

(c) Lead

The solubility and the physical properties of the lead compounds formed during exposure largely determine the corrosion resistance of lead. If the products are soluble, corrosion can proceed unhindered, but if the products are insoluble the metal surface has highly protective films. Exposure to slightly acidic conditions in the presence of carbon dioxide and organic acids, such as acetic acid, results in the formation of a whitish basic lead carbonate. Exposure to alkaline conditions (lime and cement mortars are notable) results in the formation of a red-coloured lead oxide. Both of these corrosion products allow corrosion to proceed unhindered.

Lead is highly resistant to corrosion when exposed to the atmosphere, due to the formation of a protective film of basic lead carbonate or sulphate. However, certain conditions of exposure or detail may lead to a breakdown of the film or, as important, the formation of a non-protective film.

Occasionally corrosion of lead gutters and weatherings occurs when these are associated with roofs covered with algae, moss or lichen. These produce organic acids and carbon dioxide and thus increase the acidity of rainwater. Attack is generally slow, producing thinning, grooving and finally perforation, and so it can eventually be severe. Retention of moisture at the junction of lead and roof slates can produce corrosion at the edge, probably a form of crevice corrosion.

Lead is relatively easily corroded by acetic acid fumes (factories such as breweries, pickling factories and saw mills significant), even when the fumes are greatly diluted. Acids from timbers such as oak and deal are corrosive. The resistance to corrosion of lead to alkalis is relatively poor, particularly under damp conditions.

Although generally resistant to most soil conditions, corrosion may occur in made-up ground containing ashes, and in clay containing gypsum and perhaps chloride.

The resistance of lead to corrosion in sea water is generally high. Soft waters generally attack lead significantly and in some cases sufficient quantities of a lead concentration (in excess of $0.1 \mu g/cm^3$) to be physiologically harmful ('lead poisoning') can build up. However, lead is stable in soft waters containing calcium sulphate, calcium carbonate or silicic acid. Provided the water is not too soft, both carbonate and sulphate share in the formation of a protective layer.

Among important lead alloys are *soft solders,* lead-tin alloys of varying composition. Many of the failures which result from soldered joints (usually the metal being soldered) can be attributed to the action of the flux residues. Thus the choice of flux is important.

(d) Zinc

When considering zinc it is important to remember that the metal is not only

Above, stress-corrosion cracking of copper water pipes in foamed cement (Crown Copyright) (Courtesy: BRS, HMSO). Right, internal corrosion of extruded aluminium alloy (H10) pipe carrying kitchen wastes (after two years) (Crown Copyright) (Courtesy: BRS, HMSO)

Below, corrosion of lead by contact with wood. (Crown Copyright) (Courtesy: BRS, HMSO). Below right, corrosion of zinc soaker in contact with brickwork. (Crown Copyright) (Courtesy: BRS, HMSO)

used as building components, but also as a protective coating to steel. Thus exposure of galvanised steel is primarily the exposure of zinc, although corrosion of a bimetallic junction must be taken into account at breaks in the zinc coating. The corrosion resistance of zinc is dependent on the formation of protective films, although these are generally not sufficiently dense and adherent to prevent a *steady,* though *slow,* attack on the metal, particularly when exposed to the atmosphere. The corrosion of zinc in various environments at different seasons of the year is shown in comparative chart C.3.07/6, while a comparison of the corrosion of zinc and iron in various environments is shown in comparative chart C.3.07/7. When

exposed to simple atmospheric conditions, the life of zinc is much less than the other non-ferrous metals. For example, 14 gauge (0.812mm) zinc is usually given a life of about 40 years. This life expectancy may, as in the case of the other non-ferrous metals, be considerably reduced by special conditions of exposure or details.

Being amphoteric, zinc corrodes in both acid and alkaline solutions. Normal impurities in zinc include lead, cadmium and iron. A small iron content increases the resistance to attack.

Acid water from roofs has a similar effect on zinc as it does on copper or lead.

Zinc, like lead, is also attacked by alkalis released from lime or cement. In addition, under damp conditions,

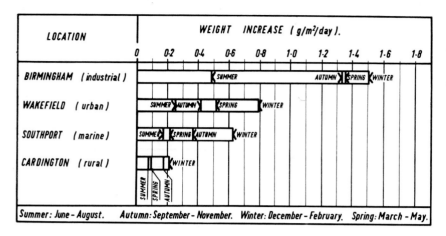

C.3.07/6
Corrosion of zinc during different seasons at sites in Great Britain (Hudson 1929). (Based on: Schikorr, G., 'Atmospheric Corrosion Resistance of Zinc', Fig. 12, ZDA and AZI, 1965)

PLACE COUNTRY AND TYPE OF ATMOSPHERE		INGOT IRON value	ZINC value
DRY INLAND	BASRA, Iraq	10·2	0·7
	KHARTOUM, Sudan	0·7	0·6
HUMID INLAND	ARO, Nigeria	8·6	1·4
RURAL	ABISKO, Sweden	4·0	0·9
	LLANWRTYD WELLS	48·0	3·0
MARINE	APAPA, Nigeria	16·6	1·0
	CALSHOT, U.K.	53·4	3·1
	SINGAPORE, Malaya	13·1	1·2
INDUSTRIAL	MOTHERWELL, U.K.	79·7	4·6
	SHEFFIELD, U.K.	98·6	14·6
	WOOLWICH, U.K.	88·2	3·7

Corrosion in one year expressed in micrometre (µm).

C.3.07/7
Comparison of corrosion rates of iron and zinc in different environments. (Based on: Evans, U. R., 'An Intro-duction to Metallic Corrosion', 2nd Ed., Table VIII, p. 88, Arnold, 1963)

zinc is liable to corrode when in contact with or embedded in acid plasters such as Keene's. Contact with brickwork can also be harmful, due to both salt from the bricks and alkalis from the mortar.

Whereas zinc is normally anodic to iron, a reversal of the potential of the zinc, making it cathodic to the iron, can occur in certain waters, particularly soft waters with an appreciable bicarbonate content, when the temperature of the water is above 60°C.

protection

Although the corrosion resistance of a metal may be increased by modifications in its composition, this is, in a great many cases in practice, only a partial solution to the problem of reducing corrosion. Consequently, some form of protection is often required, particularly in the case of the ferrous metals generally (stainless steels are possible exceptions). It should be emphasised, however, that, although methods of protection are more commonly associated with the ferrous metals generally, occasions do arise in the use of non-ferrous metals (bimetallic contacts or highly corrosive conditions of exposure caused by acids, alkalis and salts, for example) when some form of protection is advisable.

Methods of protection may be divided into *four* groups, namely: (1) Treatment of the environment; (2) Protective coatings; (3) Concrete; and (4) Cathodic protection. Each of these methods is more conveniently discussed separately.

1. Treatment of the environment

As discussed earlier under 'General considerations, 4. Corrosion classification', three classes of environment, namely, atmospheric, immersed and underground, may influence the corrosion of a metal. In general, treatment of the environment is, when compared to other forms of protection, relatively restrictive.

(a) *Atmospheric environment*

Treatment of the atmosphere is necessarily limited to enclosed spaces. Corrosion in such spaces is often due to condensation formed on the metal surface caused by rapid changes in temperature, or by carrying out wet processes within a building (see *4.00 Heat and its effects*). Consequently

remedial measures include lagging the metalwork, space-heating and the installation of air-conditioning plant. The importance of the latter lies chiefly in the fact that *either* the relative humidity *or* the atmospheric pollution, *or both,* may be considerably reduced. In general, the relative humidity should preferably be reduced to 50 per cent (particularly to prevent rusting of iron and steel) and should never be allowed to rise above 70 per cent. Reduction of relative humidity in enclosed spaces, where air changes are infrequent, may be obtained by the use of desiccants.

In a specialised way volatile corrosion inhibitors which create a thin protective film on the metal can also be helpful. (Volatile corrosion inhibitors are dealt with in BS 1133 *Packaging code,* Section 6, *Temporary prevention of corrosion of metal surfaces (during transportation and storage).*)

(b) *Immersed environment*

The extent to which the immersed environment may be treated depends on the quantity of water involved, as it is the water which has to be treated and when large quantities are involved treatment is usually impracticable on economic grounds. It follows, therefore, that much can be done to reduce corrosion by water treatment in *enclosed* water systems.

Water-treatment generally consists of the deliberate addition of chemicals to change or adjust its composition. In this, a distinction should be drawn between treatments which are specifically aimed to reduce or prevent corrosion and those such as filtration, chlorination, softening or distillation, which may either increase or decrease the corrosiveness of water. The important point with these forms of treatment is that they are not necessarily used in connection with specific corrosion problems, but rather for health, convenience or specific industrial use.

Additives used in connection with corrosion may either *restrain* corrosion, that is some corrosion may occur before protection is obtained, or *inhibit* corrosion, that is reduce or prevent attack at the outset. Most of the work on inhibitors has, it may be noted, been carried out with ferrous metals. The results of this work are also applicable to other common structural metals.

An important restrainer is a calcareous film deposited on the surface of a metal. The addition of lime to water enables such a film to be deposited. Although a high oxygen content and a certain bicarbonate hardness facilitates the formation of the calcareous film, it is generally desirable to remove dissolved gases from the water. When large quantities of water are involved it is often possible to effect partial de-aeration for water conveyed in pipelines. De-aeration is effected by physical and thermal processes, which are supplemented by chemical treatments (lime to remove carbon dioxide and sodium sulphite or hydrazine to remove residual oxygen).

Chemicals added to water so as to inhibit corrosion require special care in selection and use. An inhibitor slows down the anodic and cathodic reactions or, in many cases, both. Most inhibitors affect both anodic and cathodic processes, but for convenience they are classified as anodic, cathodic or mixed, according to the processes which they primarily affect. Inhibitors useful for the protection of iron and steel include alkali chromates, nitrites, phosphates, benzoates, carbonates, borates, silicates and hydroxides.

The need for expert advice in the choice and concentration of a suitable inhibitor for a given circumstance is important for a number of different reasons. An inhibitor may prevent corrosion in one environment and increase it in another. The efficiency of inhibitors is effected by the composition of the water (pH value notable); temperature; the rate of flow; the presence of internal or applied stresses; the composition of the metal; and the presence of dissimilar metals. In addition, account must also be taken of loose scale, debris, crevices, etc. Finally, some inhibitors are toxic and precautions should be taken in their use.

(c) *Underground environment*

In the case of steel structures buried in highly corrosive soils, attempts have been made to reduce the attack on the steel by using special backfills. Pipelines, for example, have been surrounded by 150mm or more of alkaline material such as chalk, limestone or calcareous sand. This procedure, by providing good drainage, temporarily converts anaerobic into aerobic soil conditions, but it is uncertain and has been known to increase corrosion.

2. Protective coatings

The covering used to protect a metal may consist of another metal or, as is probably more common, formed of compounds, organic or inorganic, or aggregates of such compounds. There is, in fact, a bewildering variety of coatings, while each type of coating may be produced in more than one way. For convenience, it is possible to identify five broad categories of coatings, namely, (a) metal coatings; (b) anodising aluminium; (c) paint coatings; (d) vitreous enamelling; and (e) plastics coatings. Before considering each of these separately, it is important to note those aspects common to all.

Although the inherent resistance to corrosion provided by coatings is liable to wide variation, the efficacy of any coating is primarily dependent on the fact that it *must adhere well* to the basis metal, while it should be free of pores or cracks and have acceptable mechanical properties.

The requirements of good adhesion (*Section 1.11,* Vol. 1) cannot be over-emphasised if a protected coating is to give its maximum performance, particularly as many failures of protective coatings can be attributed to inadequate adhesion. The application of the most resistant coating to a poorly prepared surface can only ensure mediocre performance of the coating, and any departure from the best practice can only result in a loss of both time and money (and this can be annoying). *Cleanliness* is one most important requirement, if the maintenance of good adhesion is to be assured. In the case of metals to be protected, this means the proper removal of grease, dirt and oxide layers, including manufacturing scales. Pretreatment of metal surfaces in order to remove any undesirable matter that may affect adhesion may be undertaken by various methods, sometimes a combination of methods being required.

Pretreatment methods may be classified as weathering, mechanical treatment, pickling and degreasing.

Weathering is the cheapest method of descaling steel, but normally requires a long period of exposure, varying with the weather conditions, the steel and the adhesion of the scale. After weathering, rust and any remaining mill-scale can be removed fairly simply by wire-brushing.

Mechanical treatments include sand and grit-blasting, flame cleaning, wire-brushing and grinding (and polishing). Grinding and polishing are usually necessary before plating, the remainder being the main mechanical methods used before the application of paint or sprayed metal.

Pickling may be undertaken by chemical or electrolytic means. In the main acids are used in chemical pickling, although molten salts may also be used prior to subsequent acid pickling. In electrolytic pickling, which is far quicker than chemical pickling, the metal is made cathodic or anodic in a suitable bath.

Degreasing is a most important part of the surface treatment. It may be carried out by physical or chemical methods. In painting work degreasing by solvents is adequate, but for work in aqueous solution, electroplating, for example, chemical or electrolytic methods are necessary, as the metal parts must be sufficiently clean to be wetted by water.

(a) *Metal coatings*

A number of different metals may be used as coverings, while they may be applied in a number of different ways. It is more convenient to consider these two aspects separately.

(i) *Types*

It is important to draw a distinction between those metals used as coatings which may be cathodic and those which may be anodic to the basis metal. A cathodic coating, such as copper or nickel on steel, will not prevent corrosion of the basis metal if there are pinholes or cracks in the coating. On the other hand, an anodic coating, such as zinc or aluminium on steel, can protect the basis metal where it is exposed, provided the current density on the basis metal is sufficient. Thus, in conferring protection, the coating is destroyed. There are limits to which the anodic coating will provide such protection. Generally, protection ceases when the exposed area of the basis metal is large, although the conductivity of the electrolyte present is also important. (See also 'General considerations', 6(b), p. 53).

Noble metals. Apart from their high cost, noble metals, despite their high chemical resistance, are not generally suitable as protective coatings as they are strongly cathodic to metals such as iron, with the result that intensified attack may be expected at any discontinuity. At the same time many (gold is notable) are soft and the thin economical coatings are easily damaged. Where cost permits, thick coats free from discontinuity can be obtained mechanically. Copper-clad steel plates are obtained in this way. Composite wires having a steel core sheathed in thick copper are also manufactured, the ductility of the copper allowing bending without exposing the steel. The use of brass plating on steel is of particular value in providing a bond for rubber, itself a valuable protective coating, to steel—rubber fails to adhere to many metals, brass being the exception.

Nickel and chromium. These two metals are usually used as pairs in what is commonly known as 'chromium plating', and used mostly for the protection of steel or brass. The nickel deposits on the basis metal are covered with a thinner chromium coat. The nickel protects the basis metal against corrosion, whilst the chromium protects the nickel from fogging (dulling of the nickel on exposure to moist air containing sulphur dioxide) ; the hardness of chromium is also a further asset.

Tin. Although the main use of tin is in the canning industry (tinplate—dead-mild steel carrying a tin layer) it is used to some extent for copper or lead water pipes and brass condenser tubes. A recent development is the application of a thin electro-deposited tin coating (0.8μm thick or less) on steel before painting, to prevent the under-rusting which would cause disfigurement or even subsequent peeling of the paint coat. The thin tin coatings are believed to provide superior protection to that given by phosphate films used for the purpose of increasing the life of paint coats.

Tin-nickel alloy is notable as it is a hard, bright deposit, resistant to atmospheres polluted with sulphur compounds, and withstands salt, mustard and lemon juice ; it is, however, cathodic to steel and, therefore, fails to protect at gaps.

Lead. The resistance of lead to sulphuric acid makes it valuable as a coating to steel sections suitable for the construction of pickling tanks. Lead has been used as a coating for metal window frames. Lead is mildly cathodic to steel under most conditions and a lead coat will not prevent rusting at pin-holes. However, it has been stated that the corrosion at pin-holes stifles itself (the inhibitive properties of lead compounds may be relevant), but this does not necessarily prevent disfigurement by rust spots—an outer coat of suitable paint is required to prevent the trouble.

Zinc. A long established and common method of protecting steel is by the application of a zinc coating. In building practice such protection is applied to a wide range of steel components including sections, sheets, wires, pipes, tanks, cisterns and fixing devices. Being anodic to steel, zinc will generally provide protection at a gap (an important exception occurs in hot water at temperatures above $60°C$ when the potential difference between the zinc and steel is reversed, thus accelerating the corrosion of the steel—this reversal is notable with soft waters). In providing 'sacrificial' protection, the zinc is used up, so that if protection is to continue, thick coatings are required. However, thick coatings are apt to be brittle while thin coatings have a short life. Coat-

ings of uneven thickness (thick in some parts and thin in others) combine the disadvantages of both, so that the aim should be to ensure uniformity of thickness of the coating, if the best advantage of the applied zinc is to be obtained. (The thickness and particularly the uniformity of the coating are more important, so far as the life of the coating is concerned, than the process used to apply the zinc—various processes are, in fact, available, as explained later.) The thickness of the coating should be related to the corrosiveness of the environment, but where the coating cannot be increased in thickness, a paint coating is necessary. (Special care is required in the pretreatment of zinc to receive painting, as zinc reacts unfavourably with the ingredients of most paints, resulting in the disruption of the paint film.) Although the life of a coat is, according to tests carried out on specially prepared samples with uniform coatings, proportional to the thickness, this is not necessarily true under conditions of service. This is mainly due to the fact that, in practice, the coating is seldom completely uniform (the life would then be proportional to the average thickness). At the same time account must be taken of the fact that accelerated corrosion will occur in crevices or where water drips on to the zinc.

Aluminium. The protection of steel with aluminium coatings is a relatively new innovation. The performance of aluminium coatings has been good and protection of steel structures with aluminium coatings is used extensively. Like zinc, aluminium is anodic to steel, while the requirements of the coating in terms of thickness and uniformity are similar to those for zinc. When the thickness of the aluminium cannot be increased sufficiently to resist a given condition of exposure, a paint coating is necessary.

Cadmium. The use of cadmium has not replaced zinc, as tests originally carried out which suggested superiority over zinc coatings did not represent service conditions. However, under storage conditions of high humidity and temperature, cadmium is superior to zinc, and so cadmium coatings are preferable for articles intended for the tropics.

(ii) *Methods*

The main methods which may be used to apply metal coatings include dipping, electroplating, spraying, diffusion and cementation, vaporisation and mechanical cladding. In all cases proper pretreatment to ensure good adhesion is imperative, as outlined earlier.

Dipping. This is the oldest method of coating iron and steel. The basis metal is coated with the second ('coating') metal by dipping into a solution of the latter. A pure solution of the 'coating' metal generally gives a thin coating, affording little protection ; solutions containing deliberate additions of other elements give thicker,

and hence more resistant, deposits in what are known as 'current-less' methods. With these methods an alloy layer forms between the basis and the deposited metal ; it is often necessary for the formation of this alloy layer to be restricted. In the case of iron or steel, 'coating' metals are restricted to those with low melting points, such as lead, tin, zinc and aluminium. *Galvanised steel* is strictly speaking steel which has been protected by dipping into zinc ; the term is, however, often loosely used to refer to all steel protected by a zinc coating whatever process may have been used.

Electroplating. In this process the basis metal is coated by cathodic treatment in a solution containing a compound of the metal to be deposited. Electroplating has a number of advantages over dip coating. These include the range of metals that can be deposited (30 could be used, but about 15 are of technical interest), the saving in metal, the ability to produce thinner coats and the absence of any brittle intermediate layer. Many of the metals used are intended either as decoration or as protection against atmospheric corrosion. Plated metals are not generally used for immersed conditions (all types of water supply, for example). An important recent innovation is *brush plating.* This enables large areas of metal to be plated *in situ.* An anode, which is a tampon or brush, carries the electrolyte and is moved over the metal to be plated. In this process an extremely high current density is used.

Spraying. The 'coating' metal is applied as a shower of tiny globules (often molten) which on striking the surface flatten to give a scaly porous coating. (Porosity is no great disadvantage if the coating is anodic to the basis metal.) The coating consists, therefore, of more or less separate particles strongly bonded together. Spraying of the globules is effected by means of a 'pistol', the metal fed into the pistol as wire or powder (liquid metal is seldom used now). Protection of steel by sprayed coatings of zinc or aluminium is common. Metals sprayed with aluminium may be referred to as 'metallised'.

Diffusion and cementation. Cementation consists of heating the basis metal (usually mild steel) at high temperature in contact with a powder of the 'coating' metal (usually zinc and aluminium). Alloying of the two metals results in good adhesion, but the degree of alloying has to be limited if the coating is not to be hard and brittle. Two of the best known processes are *sherardising,* diffusion coating with zinc, and *calorising,* diffusion coating with aluminium. Sherardising is generally confined to small articles only, as the coating tends to be fissured. However, coating with aluminium has wider application. Coating metals such as chromium, copper, tungsten, beryllium, tantalum, silicon, manganese, vanadium and titanium are more commonly applied by vaporisation methods, rather than by diffusion.

Vaporisation. Metal compounds are thermally decomposed on the metal surface. An important coating prepared in this way is that by chromium diffusion, *chromising.*

Mechanical cladding. The advantages of this method include a coating completely free of porosity and one which may be of any desired thickness. Various processes are used, but that most used is *roll-bonding,* in which the coating metal at the desired thickness is rolled on to the basis metal at the welding temperature. In another method, the coating metal is clad under heat and pressure with the aid of an intermediate layer of bonding material. Coating metals are mainly copper, nickel and aluminium, although highly resistant alloys such as stainless steel have also been used. An important example of cladding is that of an aluminium alloy with good mechanical properties clad with a thin sheet of pure aluminium which has superior resistance to corrosion.

(b) *Anodising aluminium*

The process of anodising a metal produces a thick oxide film on the surface; in effect the surface is 'pre-corroded'. The much more resistant film of oxide, which is very much thicker than that formed naturally on exposure to air, is formed by electrolytic anodic oxidation. A number of metals may be anodised, but the most common in building is aluminium.

Three conditions are necessary to produce thick oxide layers, namely: (1) the solution must be able to attack the metal anode to some extent; (2) formation of capillaries in the oxide must take place; and (3) the solubility of the layer formed must be low in the electrolyte. The layer forms from the metal outwards and pores are necessary for the electrolyte to reach the metal so that the anodic process can continue. As the result of various reactions during the process the layer is not completely homogeneous being hard and dense next to the metal and soft and less dense on the outside. Nevertheless, the film is chemically stable and relatively hard. The porosity of the film enables it to form an excellent base for paint or dyestuffs.

On the pure metal the film as formed is transparent but it is often coloured for decorative effect. After formation the film is sealed. The combined anodising and sealing, not only enhances the appearance but also increases resistance to corrosion and abrasion.

Anodised and sealed surfaces, although having a high resistance to atmospheric attack, can, like the naturally protected surfaces, be destroyed locally by corrosion resulting from the deposition of dust, dirt and soot. The film then becomes perforated and the aluminium pitted. As with ordinary aluminium, washing by rain water, or artificially, minimises these effects.

The thickness of the film and the degree of sealing after anodising or dyeing are the most important factors determining the durability of the finish. Sealing reduces the porosity of the oxide film and this may be carried out physically, by means of lacquers, oils or waxes, or chemically, by the action of pure water, steam or inhibitor solutions. The results of field tests have shown that, under identical conditions, the relationship between film thickness and corrosion resistance is not linear; doubling the thickness of the anodic film more than doubles the durability of the coating. However, it should be noted that because of the variable factors which influence the rate of corrosion the relationship between the film thickness and durability has not been definitely established. For external use on buildings a film thickness of $25.4 \mu m$ is recommended, with thicker films in localities where air pollution is high. Thinner films can, however, be used on work that is regularly cleaned. The application of lacquers and waxes to the surface also help to reduce the frequency of maintenance.

(c) *Paint coatings*

As in the case of metal coatings, there is a wide variety of paint coatings from which to select. A number of different factors will influence the choice of paint coatings suitable for given conditions. In this it is important to note that it is normal for a number of coats of paint to be used (multi-coat work), while what is normally referred to as a *paint film* is, in fact, the dried state not of one coat but rather of the various coats of paint used, each of which has a particular function to perform. The combination of the requisite coats for any given conditions is better referred to as a *paint system.*

The factors which will influence the choice of paint coatings, that is the paint system, for given conditions may be viewed from different angles. *First,* there are the basic qualities which the paint coating may possess and these include: (1) Spreading power; (2) Elasticity; (3) Resistance to the environment; and (4) Compatibility with the metal being protected. *Second,* the method (or methods) by which the basis metal is to be pretreated to receive the first coat of paint (usually the primer); in this a differentiation has to be drawn between these methods suitable for (1) factory* or (2) site application. *Third,* methods of fabrication, storage, transport and erection. *Fourth,* maintenance schedule and the ease with which maintenance can be carried out. *Fifth,* compatibility of the various coats of paint. (An intermediate coat may often be used to 'link' two otherwise incompatible coats.)

The success of paint coatings is largely dependent on the thoroughness

*For new work, particularly iron and steel, the adoption of factory painting to replace site painting is probably the best guarantee of durability that there is at present—factory painting is more efficient and avoids delays from bad weather and other difficulties on site. But, it is important to note, proper pretreatment is still essential if rapid paint failure and corrosion are to be prevented.

of pretreatment in order to ensure good adhesion and application and drying under favourable conditions.* As regards the latter, painting should not be carried out under damp conditions (or when the surface to be painted is damp); under conditions which are likely to retard drying out (air temperature should preferably be at least 5°C and relative humidity not more than 80 per cent), or when significant amounts of dust, dirt and other debris are likely to be deposited on the surface, particularly prior to painting.

The basic characteristics of paint coatings, mechanisms of protection action and types of paint coatings, including recommendations of their use, are more conveniently discussed under separate headings.

(i) *The paint system*

Normally a paint system consists of a *primer,* whose main functions are adhesion to and protection of the base; *undercoats* which have a high pigment content and a low gloss to cover and protect the primer; and, *finishing coats* which provide further protection and finish. (In normal decorative work there is a clear distinction between undercoats and finishing coats, but in protective schemes this is not usually the case and the undercoat is often a version of the finishing coat, sometimes differently tinted to ensure that the subsequent coat covers it fully.) In order to ensure that each of the coats performs its special function properly, it is essential that they should be mutually compatible. There are, it should be noted, certain systems as, for example, coal-tar/epoxy paints and some zinc-rich paints, in which primers are not used.

In all multi-coat work it is essential that the paint system is considered as a whole.

(ii) *Basic composition*

A paint consists basically of two components; the pigment and the vehicle. *The pigment,* a finely divided solid constituent, is dispersed or suspended in *the vehicle,* a liquid constituent which, when spread out thinly, changes in time to an adherent dry film. The vehicle may also include 'thinners' to facilitate spreading, but which evaporate after application, and 'driers' or 'curing agents' to accelerate the reaction of the vehicle. The composition of the constituents of a paint influence its spreading power, elasticity, resistance to the environment and compatibility with the metal being protected.

(iii) *Mechanisms of protective action*

The basic mechanisms by which a paint film provides protection deserves special consideration. A paint film may affect the electrochemical corrosion reaction by inhibiting the cathodic and

*Outdoors, winterpainting is very difficult; in the United Kingdom it has been shown, according to the BRS, that there is a greater risk of corrosion of iron and steel following November site painting than at any other time.

73

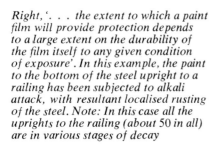

Above, corrosion of the sill member of a painted steel ground-floor window to a 10-storeyed building, where conditions of exposure are, when compared to the rest of the window, severe. This example may help to underline the advisability of using, except in mild conditions of exposure, two coats of inhibiting primer to ensure a continuous film of even thickness, free from pin-holes (see text). Note: This example has been taken from a large housing development (about 14 years old) in which nearly all the ground-floor windows are in a similar condition.

Right, '. . . the extent to which a paint film will provide protection depends to a large extent on the durability of the film itself to any given condition of exposure'. In this example, the paint to the bottom of the steel upright to a railing has been subjected to alkali attack, with resultant localised rusting of the steel. Note: In this case all the uprights to the railing (about 50 in all) are in various stages of decay

anodic reaction, or by providing a high resistive path between the anode and cathode (i.e. by insulation). Some paint systems are formulated to provide protection specifically by inhibiting the reactions (those intended for the protection of ferrous metals are particularly notable), while others have no inhibiting power and therefore protect entirely by providing a high resistive path.

In general, paint films are not completely impervious to water and oxygen. The extent to which a paint system will provide a resistive path is largely dependent on the *thickness* of the paint film, although other factors, such as the type of paint system, roughness of the metal and conditions of exposure, are equally important. However, the protective power of a paint film does increase

with its thickness. Consequently, for those paint systems which provide protection entirely by insulating, rather than inhibiting, the thickness of the paint film is extremely important. In this it is as well to note that marked differences in thickness (up to 100 per cent) do occur from point to point, even when the paint is applied by a skilled painter, while equally great differences occur as between one skilled painter and another. Thus, discretion is needed in defining film thickness solely in terms of average value.

Inhibiting properties are achieved by the incorporation of inhibiting pigments,* and those commonly used

*The majority of pigments used in paints do not have any special inhibiting effects; they merely help to exclude damp and aggressive agents.

include red lead,* calcium plumbate, zinc chrome, metallic lead and zinc dust. These are usually incorporated in priming paints, which, as already noted, must have good adhesive qualities while also providing a firm foundation for later coats. The efficiency of these pigments depends partly on the medium in which they are incorporated. Some pigments, it is important to note, although having an inhibiting effect on some metals may stimulate corrosion on others. A red lead primer, for example, should not be used on aluminium, as it stimulates corrosion. *Thickness* is also important when inhibiting primers are used, if their full potential is to be achieved. With one coat of primer it is usually impossible to achieve a continuous film of even thickness and, as important, free from pinholes—the points at which corrosion begins. Apart from mild conditions of exposure, it is always advisable to use two coats of inhibiting primer, particularly in the protection of ferrous metals.

(iv) *Resistance to the environment*

Apart from the mechanisms involved (see (iii) above), the extent to which a paint film will provide protection depends largely on the durability of the film itself to any given conditions of exposure.† In this paint systems vary markedly in their resistance. In general it is the *vehicle* which determines the durability of a paint film to given conditions of exposure, although the pigment may also be involved. In the present context a distinction may be drawn between *four* types of paint vehicle: (1) *Oil-based vehicles,* consisting mainly of vegetable drying oils, such as linseed oil, tung oil and dehydrated castor oil; (2) *Oleoresinous vehicles,* made by incorporating resins into drying oils; (3) *Alkyd-resin vehicles,* being virtually a special case of the previous type but those based on drying-oil-modified alkyd resins are particularly useful for the manufacture of weather-resistant finishing paints; and (4) *Chemical-resistant vehicles,* used for paints which have to withstand very severe conditions of exposure (chemical fumes, alkalis, or immersion in sea-water, for example), and include epoxide resin, coal tar/pitch, polyurethane, chlorinated rubber and vinyl resin.

(v) *Priming paints*

The importance of the properties of priming paints cannot be over-emphasised. A priming paint should 'wet' the surface readily and provide a

*The pigments red oxide and red lead are sometimes confused. Red oxide is an oxide of iron and has no specific corrosion-inhibiting properties. Certain types are used in the moderately effective oil primers and also in many quick-drying primers which are not always satisfactory. Red lead is an oxide of lead and has valuable corrosion-inhibiting properties. It is sometimes used with red oxide or graphite. It is not advisable to use it in paints other than primers for iron and steel.

†Alkali resistance of paints is covered in *3.06 Chemical attack,* under Alkali action (p. 23).

74

firm and adherent foundation for later coats. In addition, since paint films are not completely impermeable to corrosive agents, priming paints should contain an inhibitive pigment. This is particularly relevant in the protection of iron and steel, which, in general, corrode comparatively easily.

The commonly used inhibiting pigments may be used in different vehicles. For example, red lead and calcium plumbate paints are normally made with oil-based vehicles, which 'wet' steel well; metallic lead and zinc chrome paints are often made with more complex oleo-resinous vehicles, while zinc-rich paints are generally bound with chlorinated rubber, isomerized rubber, polystyrene or epoxide resin vehicles—there is also a type of inorganic vehicle. The characteristics of various priming paints are included, for convenience in Table 3.07/3.

Although the conditions of exposure and use will influence the choice of a priming paint, the method of surface preparation will also be an important factor. A priming paint should match the method of surface preparation. The relationship between surface preparation and priming paints for both ferrous and non-ferrous metals are summarised in Table 3·07/4.

(vi) Undercoats and finishes

The main functions of undercoats and finishes* are to provide additional film thickness, water resistance and possibly decorative appearance. Looked at in another way, undercoats and finishing coats may be said to serve to protect the primer and, when an inhibiting pigment is used, to enable the primer to retain its inhibiting effect. A highly decorative finish is rarely associated with maximum protection, although suitable colour coats for application over protective paints such as micaceous iron oxide paint are available.

Inhibitive pigments are unnecessary in undercoats or finishing coats. Inert pigments are generally more serviceable. Among the inert pigments are lamellar pigments, such as leafing aluminium, micaceous iron oxide and silica graphite, which orientate themselves in such a way as to reduce the permeability of the film and to retard its chemical degradation by sunlight. Other commonly used pigments are red iron oxide, white lead and rutile titanium oxide.

It may be noted that some undercoats act as links between incompatible priming and finishing coats.

The properties of the three main types of undercoats and finishing coats, namely oil- and alkyd-based paints, bituminous and coal-tar paints and chemical-resistant paints are summarised in Table 3.07/5.

(vii) Protective schemes

In any protective scheme, the paint system should consist of a priming

*As already noted, in protective schemes a clear distinction is not made between undercoats and finishing coats. (See (i) The paint system.)

paint suited to the metal or metal coating to be protected and undercoats and finishing coats suited to the conditions of exposure. (The primer, undercoats and finishing coats must, of course, be compatible.) These basic requirements apply equally to both ferrous and non-ferrous metals, but because the latter are more corrosion-resistant than the former, there are detailed differences which will influence the choice of a suitable scheme. The two groups of metals are, therefore, better considered separately.

Ferrous metals

Protection of ferrous metals is usually confined to iron and ordinary steel—stainless steel may need 'localised' protection at bimetallic junctions. Special care is needed in the selection of protective schemes for iron and steel due to their inherent corrosion-resistant weakness. In the United

---

Table 3.07/3. Characteristics of priming paints for metals

Priming paint	Main characteristics
Red lead	1. Should comply with BS 2523, Types A, B or C. 2. Excellent for site use, but unsuitable for spraying or dipping. 3. Fairly tolerant of imperfectly prepared surfaces, carrying broken mill-scale and rust (from weathering and hand-cleaning). 4. Slow drying. This is a disadvantage for outdoor painting in grossly polluted atmospheres or for indoor painting with limited covered space. Faster drying properties by incorporation of natural or synthetic resins in the medium usually less effective—reduction of protective properties and tolerance of imperfectly prepared surfaces. 5. Essential to comply with requirements of Lead Paint Regulations, 1927.
Metallic lead	1. Should contain not less than 25 per cent metallic lead pigment, and at least 40 per cent for maximum resistance. 2. As red lead, fairly tolerant of imperfectly prepared surfaces, but application properties better—easier to brush, flow better, pigment can be bound in quick drying media and storage properties are good. 3. Corrosion resistance in marine and chemical environments better than red lead. 4. Weather resistance good. Can be used as finishing coats. 5. As for red lead, essential to comply with requirements of Lead Paint Regulations, 1927.
Calcium plumbate	1. Specified in BS 3698 (Type A, 48 per cent; Type B, 33 per cent calcium plumbate). 2. Higher standard of surface preparation needed than for red lead. Do not perform well on rusty surfaces or where contact with water is continuous or prolonged. Good primers for hot-dip galvanised surfaces. 3. Better drying properties than red lead. 4. Not compatible with all types of undercoats and finishing coats. 5. As for red lead, essential to comply with requirements of Lead Paint Regulations, 1927.
Lead cyanamide	Limited experience in the UK.
Zinc (and other) chromates	1. Not covered by British Standard but should not contain less than 15 per cent zinc chromate, and the better types not less than 40 per cent. Often also contain red oxide. 2. Less tolerant than red lead of imperfectly prepared surfaces, but are easy to apply and dry quickly. Useful for spraying, dipping and storing. 3. Good resistance on well prepared surfaces but only in mildly corrosive environments. Inferior resistance to aggressive environments (when compared with red lead and calcium plumbate primers) due to production of thin films. 4. Etch primers (see below) also contain zinc chromate type pigments. Can be used on steel only if it is clean. Particularly suitable for aluminium and its alloys.
Zinc-rich	1. Unlike the primers above, not oil-based. Metallic zinc pigment should be bound with non-saponifiable media such as chlorinated rubber, polystyrene or epoxide resin, so as to yield a paint suitable in all respects for brush application. Dry paint film should not contain less than 85 per cent by weight of metallic zinc. 2. Often known as 'cold galvanising' paints, but their hardness and resistance to abrasion are not equal to that of zinc metal applied by hot-dipped galvanising or spray. 3. Can be used either as primers or as the main protective system. Can be rather expensive. 4. Epoxy resin based usually applied after grit blasting as thin, 'temporary' protective coats ('prefabrication' primers), and as such are much less expensive.
Zinc phosphate	1. Newly introduced anti-corrosive pigment. Experience limited but favourable. 2. Non-toxic and suitable in quick drying primers. 3. White and of low opacity. Can, unlike most other anti-corrosive pigments, be used in white or light grey primers.
Etch-primers	1. Also known as pre-treatment or wash primers. 2. Contain a resin medium, an inhibitive pigment (e.g. zinc chromate) and phosphoric acid to etch the surface. 3. Provide best possible adhesion but film produced is usually thin. Apart from mild conditions, should be followed by a coat of normal chromate primer. 4. Most supplied in two parts, each mixed in definite proportions immediately before use—remain workable for about 8 hr—and preferably applied by spray. Important to follow instructions. Subsequent coats of paint must be applied without delay. One-pack etch-primers also now available. (For aluminium two-pack types generally superior; one-pack types probably suitable for small jobs.) 5. Some are water sensitive in their early life. Modified type should be used if there is likely to be exposure to rain or dew. 6. Generally more suitable for application to non-ferrous metals (aluminium and its alloys in particular); should be applied to steel only if it is clean.
Welding primers	1. Include some 'prefabrication' primers. Specially formulated to permit welding without weakening the joint or emitting toxic fumes, i.e. overcoming one of the disadvantages of the lead-based primers. 2. As primers they are not as efficient as the fully inhibitive kind. Welded areas should be reprimed as soon as possible with fully inhibitive kind of primer.
Other primers	Recently marketed products claim to cover rust and mill-scale successfully. These claims are still being investigated (BRS). Red lead primers are the most suitable for surfaces which cannot be properly cleaned.

References: (1) Painting of Metals in Buildings: 1—Iron and Steel; and 2—Non-ferrous Metals and Coatings, BRS Digests (2nd Series) Nos. 70 and 71, HMSO, May and June, 1966, respectively.
(2) Protection of Iron and Steel Structures from Corrosion: CP 2008 : 1966.

| Metal | Preparation | | Suitable primers |
	Factory	Site	
1. *Ferrous metals* Iron and steel	Grit or shot-blasting	Grit-blasting, open or closed circuit according to site conditions	Etch, 'prefabrication' (e.g. zinc-rich type) and/or inhibitive primers
	Pickling	Pickling jellies or pastes, or acids generally: not recommended	Usually quick drying, zinc chromate types, but red lead, metallic lead, etc., for heavy gauge
	Flame cleaning	Flame cleaning	Inhibitive 'tolerant' primers
	Phosphating	Phosphoric acid washes and chemical treatments (much less effective than factory processes)	Zinc chromate and other inhibitive (non-inhibitive in mild conditions)
	Hand or power tools	Hand or power tools	Red lead, metallic lead (i.e. 'tolerant') inhibitive primers
2. *Non-ferrous metals* Aluminium (smooth surface, e.g. sheet, extrusions, aluminised steel)	Phosphating Acid or alkali-chromate baths Anodising (mainly as alternative to painting)	Degreasing compounds Emery and white spirit (not wire wool) Phosphoric acid treatments	Etch-primer (not after phosphating); Zinc chromate (not lead-based primer)
Aluminium (rough surface, e.g. castings and sprayed metal)	Smooth off nibs with emery paper. Clean off dust and dirt	Smooth off nibs with emery paper. Clean off dust and dirt	Etch-primer; Zinc chromate (not lead-based primer)
Zinc (sheet, hot-dipped galvanised or electro-galvanised)	Degrease Phosphate and/or chromate treatments	Degrease with white spirit Weathering for at least several months, plus washing Phosphoric acid treatments (not as effective as factory processes)	Calcium plumbate; Etch-primer (not after phosphating); Zinc chromate primer, zinc dust/zinc oxide primer, or zinc rich paint
Zinc (sprayed or sherardised coatings)	'Denib' Clean off dust and dirt	'Denib' Clean off dust and dirt	Etch-primer (preferably plus zinc chromate primer)
Copper (also brass and bronze)	Special processes Electro-deposited tin coating	Emery and white spirit (Do not weather. Do not abrade dry) Phosphoric acid treatments	Etch-primer; Aluminium pigmented primer
Lead	Not usual	Weathering Emery and white spirit Phosphoric acid treatments (Do not abrade dry)	Etch-primer
Tin coatings	Degreasing	Light abrasion (do not abrade through coating) Degrease with white spirit	Etch-primer; Zinc chromate
Cadium (coatings)	Phosphating	Emery and white spirit Phosphate treatments Not weathering	Etch-primer
Chromium and nickel plating	Not usual	Emery and white spirit	Etch-primer

Table 3·07/4. Surface preparation: methods and primers for metals

Reference: Painting of Metals in Buildings: 1—Iron and steel and 2—Non-ferrous metals and coatings, BRS Digests (2nd Series) Nos. 70 and 71, HMSO, May and June, 1966, respectively.

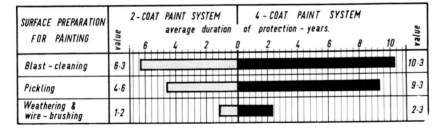

SURFACE PREPARATION FOR PAINTING	value	2 - COAT PAINT SYSTEM / 4 - COAT PAINT SYSTEM average duration of protection - years.	value
Blast - cleaning	6·3		10·3
Pickling	4·6		9·3
Weathering & wire - brushing	1·2		2·3

C.3.07/8
Results of tests on painted steels at Sheffield made by BISRA. (These results confirm that blast-cleaning and pickling are the most practical and reliable procedures for obtaining

surfaces free from mill-scale and rust). (From: 'Protection of Iron and Steel Structures from Corrosion', CP 2008, Table 2, p. 39, 1966)

Kingdom they generally need some form of protection whatever the exposure. Once a particular scheme has been selected, thorough pretreatment (particularly the importance of removing mill-scale and rust—see comparative chart C.3.07/8) and application (a thick even film is significant) are essential. Primers with inhibiting pigments should always be used for ferrous metals, and, apart from mild conditions of exposure, two coats of primer are essential for full protection.

The choice of undercoats and finishing coats will be largely determined by conditions of exposure. In some instances where conditions of exposure are severe, paint coatings may be inadequate, even if these are applied over non-ferrous metal coatings. Consequently, alternatives, either another type of coating or another material (metal or otherwise) may be essential.

Table 3.07/6 indicates the alternative schemes available for the protection of steel. Although choice will be determined by conditions of exposure, account should also be taken of the differences between site- and factory-application. The latter should provide greater durability, other things being equal.* It should also be noted that for good protection a total film thickness of at least 125μm and often up to 250μm is necessary. With air drying paints this normally means at least four coats, including two priming coats; thixotropic and chemically cured paints may require fewer coats.

Non-ferrous metals
The need for protective schemes for the non-ferrous metals is generally less important, particularly for ordinary atmospheric exposure, than in the case of the ferrous metals. However, it is often advisable to paint the surfaces of non-ferrous metals such as aluminium and zinc, particularly when these are used as coatings—see (a) Metal coatings. Because the non-ferrous metals are more corrosion-resistant than the ferrous metals the choice of a paint system is less critical except in highly corrosive atmospheres or in the special cases outlined later. Simpler paint systems, such as ordinary alkyd undercoats and gloss finishes, are usually adequate, but in chemically contaminated environments chlorinated rubber or epoxy paints may be used. Although adequate thickness is important, this need not be as great as for ferrous metals.

Serious consideration of protective schemes for non-ferrous metals needs to be given either when the contact of dissimilar metals cannot be avoided or when non-ferrous metals are in contact with or embedded in other building materials. As regards the latter, contact with materials likely to produce acidic or alkaline conditions (see

*An important aspect of factory-applied paint coatings is that they are virtually impossible to make good on site should they be damaged. This is particularly true of stove-enamelled finishes.

'Resistance to corrosion') should be avoided.

Where the contact of two dissimilar metals cannot be avoided, the aim should be to ensure that there is no electrically conducting path between them. This can be achieved by *thick* coats (adequate thickness is important —see Table 3.07/5) of bituminous paint or hot applied bitumen, inhibitive primers or pastes. The use of bituminous felts and some plastics sheets, although not paint systems, are also acceptable treatments.

Resistance to alkaline solutions (concrete, cement or lime mortar) or to acidic solutions (gypsum plaster—e.g. Keene's) may be given by *thick* coats of bitumen. For alkaline surfaces, including contact with plaster, alkali-resisting primers may be used. Contact with those timbers which may affect non-ferrous metals (especially timbers such as western red cedar, Douglas fir, oak and sweet chestnut) is better avoided by the use of bitumen or zinc chromate primers—wood primers may not be suitable.

The basic requirements for painting of the individual non-ferrous metals are summarised below.

Aluminium and its alloys. Paint treatments are the same for aluminium and all its alloys. Normally the priming paint should contain corrosion-inhibiting pigments such as zinc chromate and other chromates constituting about 20 per cent of the dry weight of the film—red lead must be avoided. Red oxide primers with about 5 per cent chromate (these primers are cheaper) may be used for dipping or spraying where the alloy is resistant to corrosion and the exposure is not severe. Etch-primers are particularly suitable for aluminium and its alloys —the two pack being superior to the single pack. Sprayed aluminium coatings may be painted as for zinc (see later), or simpler paint systems, usually with an etch primer, can be used. Hot-dipped ('aluminised') steel should be painted as for aluminium sheet.

Zinc-sheet, hot-dipped or electrolytic coatings. Corrosion-inhibiting primers are not necessary for zinc, but the primer must have good adhesion— zinc rapidly causes most oil-based paints to lose their adhesion. Good adhesion can be obtained with either etch-primer or calcium plumbate primer, and both require thorough degreasing—weathering or mordant washes are unnecessary. Calcium plumbate primers applied to a zinc coating which has weathered so as to expose the steel and rusting will help to prevent further corrosion. On weathered zinc, zinc dust/zinc oxide paints have proved successful. Red lead primer should not be used.

*In protective schemes undercoats and finishes are less differentiated than in normal decorative work.
References: (1) *Protection of Iron and Steel Structures from Corrosion,* CP 2008 : 1966.
  (2) *Painting of Metals in Buildings: 1—Iron and Steel,* BRS Digest (2nd Series) No. 70, HMSO, May, 1966.

Table 3.07/5. Properties of undercoats and finishing paint coatings*

Type	Properties
1. *Oil- and alkyd-based paints* (a) Oil-based	1. Should comply with BS 2525-32, 'Ready-mixed oil-based undercoating and finishing paints (exterior quality)'. 2. Do not give high degree of protection against corrosion. Those containing lead and other pigments are suitable for rural environments. (In badly polluted atmospheres paints liable to lose their gloss and discolour badly.)
(b) Alkyd resin (gloss)	1. Finishing paint should have full gloss, but alkyd undercoat should be about eggshell to semi-gloss. 2. Offer protection only in mild conditions and are useful where decorative appearance is important. (Available in a wide range of decorative colours; flow and gloss are good.) Dry film resists erosion well. 3. May be used, if manufacturer approves, over micaceous iron oxide paint to improve the decorative appearance.
(c) Oleo-resinous	Long oil type media in which micaceous iron oxide, silica graphite and aluminium are serviceable pigments. These paints *provide excellent protection* but have limited colour range and appearance. 1. *Micaceous iron oxide paint* (a) Should contain at least 80 per cent by weight of an approved micaceous iron oxide, and not more than 5 per cent of anti-setting agent; up to 8 per cent maximum of leafing aluminium flake may be added. Film should dry with not more than semi-gloss. (b) Extremely durable because their inert and flaky pigment gives a thick film. (c) Colours are limited to grey and some dark shades of green and brown. 2. *Silica graphite paint* (a) Should contain at least 70 per cent by weight of a suitable silica graphite, with a minimum carbon content of 55 per cent, together with aluminium and other pigments to provide the desired colour. (b) Extremely durable but with few applications. 3. *Aluminium paint* (a) Pigment should be of leafing type to BS 388 and paint should contain at least 15 per cent aluminium, and not more than 35 per cent of volatile matter. Paint should dry to a film of good lustre. (b) Give thin films, but are also very protective.
2. *Bituminous and coal tar*	1. Include a wide range of materials based on natural bitumens, petroleum bitumen and pitches derived from the distillation of coal and other organic materials. 2. Important to draw distinction between ordinary materials, i.e. simple solutions yielding dry film thicknesses of $25\mu m$ or so and high-build materials capable of giving much greater film thicknesses, about $250\mu m$. Materials may be applied hot or cold. 3. Paints are impermeable, inert and virtually non-saponifiable. Have no rust-inhibiting properties, so protective power depends mainly on coating thickness. If applied in thick films (about $250\mu m$) give good, inexpensive protection against water, salt and some chemicals. Thin coats of bitumen-based, so-called 'anti-corrosive' paints are inadequate. 4. Not durable when exposed to strong sunlight—ultimately film powders or crazes severely. Should be protected by a coat of bituminous aluminium paint. 5. The solvents in some bituminous paints tend to lift oil-based coatings, or their own protective coats, producing unsatisfactory, thin films. 6. Primers for use under these paints should have sufficient time to harden (up to one month) or to be specially formulated.
3. *Chemical-resistant*	1. For use in environments polluted with acids, alkalis, ammonia salts, strong solvents and other chemicals. Paints are required to be chemically resistant and impermeable. 2. Best performance only obtained with a high standard of surface preparation. Special primers appropriate to system should be used. Inter-coat compatibility with old paint should be checked before specifying chemical-resistant paints for maintenance.
(a) Cold-cured epoxide resin	1. Two-pack, and should not be confused with epoxyester paints (one-pack) which only have protective properties roughly equal to those of long oil alkyd paints. 2. Good acid and alkali resistance; highly resistant to solvents and, if carefully formulated and used, suitable for exposure to sea-water. 3. Tough and resistant to abrasion, and resist spillage of hot liquids. 4. High-build types, capable of yielding dry films up to $250\mu m$. 5. Available for brush or spray application.
(b) Coal-tar/epoxide	1. Two-pack. Combine in some measure the impermeability of thick coal tar films with the chemical resistance and thermal stability of epoxide resins. (More expensive than bituminous paints.) Have advantage of yielding thick films (about 25–$250\mu m$ per coat). Specially useful in marine situations. 2. Dry film develops considerable hardness and some solvent resistance. 3. Limited to black and dark colours. Limitation can be overcome by overcoating with other light-coloured chemical-resistant paints. 4. Pretreatment primers need to be specially formulated.
(c) Polyurethane	1. Two-pack most chemical-resistant form. 2. Better acid- and slightly lower alkali-resistant properties than epoxide resin paints; when applied in clean, dry conditions they have superior water resistance. 3. Adhesion to bare steel relatively poor; blast-cleaned steel requires pretreatment primer. 4. Sensitive to moisture and high humidities during application and throughout the curing period.
(d) Chlorinated rubber	1. Should consist of chlorinated rubber and a plasticizer, together with inert pigments and, possibly, extenders. 2. Good resistance to alkalis, weak acids and salt water but less solvent-resistant than epoxide resin or polyurethane paints and more effected at elevated temperatures. 3. Solvent sensitivity may lead to difficulty in overcoating some compositions to provide satisfactory thicknesses for protection. 4. Primer must be specially suited. 5. Rather difficult to apply. Thixotropic modification gives thicker, more protective films (high-build types give single films 100–$150\mu m$ thick) and easier to apply.
(e) Vinyl resin	1. Based on polyvinyl chloride/acetate resins and show outstanding resistance to acids, alkalis and water, including salt water, but should not be used where continuous or prolonged exposure to solvents is likely. 2. Only thin films can be achieved in a single application; adequate thickness requires a number of coats. 3. Application by brush is difficult. Spraying and roller coating recommended. Dry films are very flexible. 4. Demand well prepared surfaces for good results. Adhesion to bare steel relatively poor—can be remedied by use of a pretreatment primer or by using a vinyl resin modified priming coat. 5. Thick works-applied vinyl resin coatings (organosols and plastisols) have great protective power. Particularly suitable for continuous application to steel sheet and strip.

Table 3.07/6. Choice of protective system for steel

Iron and steel	Conditions (see notes below)		
	Severe	Moderate	Mild
Heavy structural	Metal-sprayed + etch primer, + MIO or AL; or 2 or 3 coats heavy duty bitumen, coal-tar or coal-tar/epoxy paints; or anti-corrosive wrappings	As severe; or 2 coats RL, ML or CP, + 2 coats MIO, CR or AL; or 2 coats ZR, + MIO	1 or 2 coats RL, ML or CP, + MIO, AL or gloss paint
Light structural	As above	As above; or galvanised and painted (CP + MIO, or CP + u/coat + gloss paint)	1 or 2 coats RL, ML or CP, + u/coat + gloss paint; or 2 coats ZC or RO, + u/coat + gloss paint
Sheet	Vitreous enamel or PVC coatings; or heavy galvanising; or thick bitumen coatings (better if factory-applied). (May be necessary to substitute with plastics, asbestos cement or aluminium)	Galvanised and painted (CP + MIO, or u/coat + gloss paint; or PVC coatings; or 2 coats RL, ML or CP, + 2 coats MIO, AL, CR or gloss paint)	PVC coatings; or galvanised (painted if desired); or 1 or 2 coats RL, ML, CP, ZC or RO, + u/coat + gloss paint
Window frames,* doors and door frames	May be necessary to substitute with aluminium, or PVC extruded on wood or aluminium	As severe; or galvanised and painted; or factory priming + additional priming + u/coat + gloss paint	Galvanised and painted; or 1 or 2 coats stoved factory primer or RL, ML, CP or ZC, + u/coat + gloss paint
Railings	Plastics (PVC or nylon) coatings, or substitute with aluminium	Galvanised and painted; or 2 coats RL or ML, + 2 coats MIO or AL; or 2 coats RL or ML, + u/coat + gloss paint	2 coats RL, ML, CP, ZC or RO, + u/coat + gloss paint
'Wrought' ironwork (i.e. usually mild steel)	PVC or nylon coatings; or 2 coats RL or ML, + bitumen or MIO; or 2 coats RL or ML, + u/coat + gloss paint (Not entirely satisfactory)	2 coats RL or ML, + bitumen or MIO; or 2 coats RL or ML, + u/coat + gloss paint	1 or 2 coats RL, ML, CP, ZC, ZR or ZO, + bitumen; or 1 or 2 coats RL, ML, CP, ZC, ZR or ZO, + u/coat + gloss paint
Rainwater goods (gutters, pipes and brackets) cast iron or mild steel	Consider substitutes for steel; or heavy duty bitumen, coal-tar or coal-tar/epoxy paints (2 or 3 coats)	Bitumen or tar coatings; or 2 coats RL, ML or CP, + MIO or AL; or 2 coats RL, ML or CP + u/coat + gloss paint; or galvanised and painted	2 coats RL, ML, CP, ZR or ZC + u/coat + gloss paint; or bitumen or coal-tar; or galvanised and painted
Gutters, internal surface	2 thick coats bitumen or coal-tar	Same as severe	Same as severe
Pipes (not buried)	Bitumen or coal-tar reinforced with wrappings	Same as severe; or 2 coats RL or ML, + bitumen or MIO; or 2 coats RL or ML, + u/coat + gloss paint	Same as moderate (though 1 coat of primer is permissible); or 2 coats ZR
Tanks,† external surface galvanised	Coal-tar/epoxy paints; or heavy duty bitumen or coal-tar paints	2 coats CP, or 1 coat etch primer + ZC, + 2 coats MIO or AL	1 coat CP or etch primer, + u/coat + gloss paint or 1 coat CP or etch primer + 2 coats MIO or AL
Tanks, external surface not galvanised	As above	As for 'severe'; or 2 coats RL or ML, + 2 coats MIO or AL	1 (preferably 2) coats RL, ML, CP, ZC or RO, + u/coat + gloss paint; or 2 coats ZR

* Extra care or additional coats of paint are desirable for bottom members. Condensation can cause severe corrosion at the internal surface of metal windows even in moderate or mild climatic conditions.

† Internal surfaces may require special chemical-resistant finishes, but for fresh water, bitumen-based coatings are usual (e.g. BS 3416, Type I or, for drinking water, Type II).

NOTES

Key to primers and finishes

Primers
RL = Red lead
ML = Metallic lead
CP = Calcium plumbate
ZR = Zinc-rich
ZC = Zinc chromate
RO = Red oxide

Finishes
AL = Exterior aluminium paint
MIO = Micaceous iron oxide paint (and u/coat)
Gloss = Exterior alkyd gloss paint
CR = Chlorinated rubber paint

Conditions

Severe
Areas affected by direct salt spray from the shore (e.g. up to 3·2km inland according to height and shelter); general heavy industrial pollution, or close proximity to chimneys and some industrial processes. Corrosion is rapid, very visible, disruptive of unsatisfactory paint films, and endangers the safety of structures.
Severe chemical attack by polluted atmosphere or liquid contact requires specialised coatings, usually chlorinated rubber, vinyl or epoxy resin based.

Moderate
Areas of high rainfall or continuous high humidity in industrial or urban conditions, or close to fresh water or calm sea water.
Interiors where condensation is heavy or there is a source of pollution (e.g. sulphur dioxide, sulphur, ammonia or weak acids). In moderate conditions corrosion is noticeable in a year or two and is a nuisance but not dangerous.

Mild
Inland areas of low rainfall and no special causes of corrosion; interiors of domestic buildings, schools, offices and factories not producing condensation, smoke or chemical pollution. Corrosion may be noticeable only over a period of several years.
Where maximum life without maintenance is important, the recommendations for conditions worse than those to be countered should be used.

Reference: Painting of Metals in Buildings: 1—Iron and steel, BRS Digest (2nd Series) No. 70, HMSO, May, 1966.

Sprayed zinc coatings. Subject to the investigation of suitable paint systems, the best appears to be a 'modified' (water resistant) etch primer plus a coat of zinc chromate primer. In mild conditions these may be followed by suitable decorative or protective top coats, but in the most severe conditions micaceous iron oxide paint is probably the best.

Copper and its alloys. The chief difficulty in conventional painting is due to chemical reactions between the metal and the drying oil paints. Green stains or poor adhesion sometimes result. Roughening of the surface before painting can be effected with fine abrasive paper, preferably used wet or with white spirit. Both aluminium pigmented primers and etch-primers are satisfactory. Indoors it is possible to paint directly with one or two coats of alkyd gloss paint. Preservation of the original appearance and prevention of discolouration or a patina is intended with a recently produced special clear lacquer ('Incralac').

Lead. New lead surfaces should be abraded or treated with phosphating solutions or phosphoric acid. Etch-primers and many ordinary metal primers, provided they do not contain graphite, are satisfactory.

Chromium, nickel and tin. These metals are usually only painted when corroded. Corrosion products should be removed with fine abrasive paper followed by an etch-primer and any decorative paint system.

Cadmium. Weathering to produce a paintable surface should not be used; instead phosphating treatments are suitable, while an etch-primer will provide a key for decorative paints.

(d) *Vitreous enamelling*

Vitreous enamel coats the surface of the metal with a continuous inorganic glaze which is highly resistant to corrosion. Corrosion resistance, particularly against acids, can be increased by additional amounts of silica and the introduction of titania. Accidental damage often causes chipping which renders the coating useless. This is particularly true of vitreous enamel on steel. However, vitreous enamel on aluminium—a comparative innovation in this country, although used extensively in the United States—has distinct advantages in that it may, if successfully prepared, be sawn, drilled, cut and punched without chipping. Nevertheless, care must be taken to seal cut edges with a corrosion-inhibitive paste so as to prevent unsightly staining by corrosion products.

The process of vitreous enamelling consists briefly of applying, to a suitably prepared surface, powdered glass of suitable composition, often suspended in a liquid, usually water; the particles, after being dried in warm air, are strongly heated so as to melt the glass, which under suitable conditions, flows over the whole surface producing a coherent coat. Generally several coats are applied; the first chosen for adhesion and subsequent coats for

resistance to corrosion or abrasion. Temperatures of between 650 and 850° C are generally required to fuse the silicate or borosilicate glass coatings. Because of the low melting point of aluminium, special frits, usually with lead-free formulations, which can be bonded to the surface at around 560° C, are used.

The heating necessary to fuse the glass causes a reduction in strength of the metal. Consequently, vitreous enamelling should be confined to non-loadbearing components.

(e) *Plastics coatings*

Plastics of various kinds are now used for coating metals, particularly steel, either by brushing, dipping, spraying or by cladding with the aid of adhesives. Provided the coatings are adherent and non-porous, the resistance is that of the plastics itself. Most of the plastics used are reasonably resistant to a number of environments although they may only withstand moderate temperature and are often soft enough to be easily damaged.

PVC has been applied, usually in the factory, mainly to sheet steel, and, for external use, to galvanised steel. PVC, like paint, may suffer in appearance from dirt deposition or colour change, although it is more durable than most decorative paints. On site, nylon may be applied by flame spraying. Some steel ironmongery and railings are given a dipped or powder-process plastics coating; in the latter form especially, epoxy resins give very good protection. Window frames may be coated with extruded PVC rather than painted, so as to give the best protection in severely corrosive environments. Steel pipes for water and gas services may be clad with extruded PVC sheathing which, among other things, has excellent electrical resistance. Where high resistance to corrosion is required from without and from within, PVC coatings can be applied to spirally welded steel piping internally or externally or both. Other types of plastics coatings include Neoprene and Hypalon.

3. Concrete

The use of concrete as a means of protection against corrosion is limited to iron and steel (more commonly the latter) and is generally applied to reinforced concrete or encased structural steelwork when the concrete must also perform other functions.

The alkaline nature of most Portland cement mixes (pH is normally about 12·5) serves to inhibit corrosion* of iron and steel, but the inhibiting

action may be reduced, if not completely negated, if, in addition to the calcium hydroxide which confers alkalinity, there are appreciable amounts of calcium sulphate (gypsum) chloride or carbonate present.

Temporary protection of steel can be given by cement washes. For more permanent protection, mortars or concretes of *good quality* which *cover* the steel adequately are essential.

The function of the concrete cover to steel is not, it should be noted, solely to prevent corrosion, important as this aspect may be,* but also to transmit external loading forces to the steel, in the case of reinforced concrete, and to provide adequate fire resistance, in the case of both reinforced concrete and encased structural steelwork.

The concrete cover may be applied to steel in one of two ways, namely, (1) by casting the concrete around the steel either on site or in a factory or (2) by spraying the concrete around the steel. The latter method is more commonly applied to structural steel or for lining steel bunkers and chimney stacks. Casting may be applied either in reinforced concrete work or in structural steelwork. These are some detailed differences in requirements between these two methods, which are more conveniently discussed separately. However, it should be noted that in either case all loose rust and all loosely adherent mill-scale should be removed from the steel—other surface preparation is generally unnecessary.

(a) *Cast concrete*

The main requirements for concrete cast around steel in order to prevent corrosion of the embedded steel may be summarised† as follows:

(i) *Quality.* In order to confer maximum protection, good quality concrete is essential. The materials used should be carefully selected and due consideration given to correct water/cement ratios; correct cement/aggregate ratios; correctly graded and good quality aggregates; correct mixing; adequate formwork; correct compaction; and correct curing. The main aim should be to ensure a concrete which is compact, that is, relatively impermeable, and free from cracks, other than fine haircracks. Construction joints designed to ensure the exclusion of water are also important.

(ii) *Cover.* For corrosion prevention the depth of cover required lies between 38mm and 76mm for outdoor

---

*If corrosion of the steel does develop, the effects may be : (1) cracking or disruption of the cover caused by the expansion which accompanies the corrosion of steel; (2) loss of strength where the steel is reduced in cross-section; (3) rust staining of adjacent areas.

---

*Corrosion cells may be set up due either to local differences in oxygen concentration or to different concentrations of anions such as carbonate, sulphate and chloride (see 'General considerations', 5(b), p. 52). It should be noted that *differences* in oxygen and/or salt concentrations may carry a significant risk of corrosion, although the *actual* concentrations of dissolved gases and solids are low.

†The importance of specifying and ensuring that all steelwork is adequately protected by concrete of appropriate quality and depth of cover are set out in the following Codes of Practice : (1) CP 114 : 1951 — *The Structural use of reinforced concrete in buildings;* (2) CP 115 : 1959 — *The Structural use of prestressed concrete in buildings;* and (3) CP 116 : 1965 — *Structural use of precast concrete.*

Adequate cover to steel by concrete is an important requirement. Both examples show cracking and spalling of concrete due to the corrosion of the steel reinforcement as a result of *inadequate cover. The photograph above shows part of a soffit to a reinforced concrete balcony (about 14 years old) and that below reinforced columns (about 4 years old)*

and immersed conditions,* while 19mm should be acceptable for indoor work. These recommendations apply generally to dense concrete. In the case of lightweight concrete the minimum cover for outdoor use should be increased by 13mm, that is it should not be less than 51mm.

In reinforced concrete work, it is important to note that adequate cover should not be confined to the main reinforcing bars but should also include stirrups, hooping and binding wire. Care is also required in the placing and fixing of reinforcement, including all the 'accessories' so as to ensure that there is no 'migration' towards the exposed surface (thus reducing the

*The actual depth of cover will be dependent on the relationship between the strength of the concrete and the conditions to which the concrete is exposed.

designed cover) during the placing or compaction of the concrete.

(iii) *Additives*. The use of additives such as calcium chloride* to accelerate the hardening of concrete should be strictly limited so as *not to exceed 2 per cent* calculated on the weight of cement. When calcium chloride within the permitted limit is used, concrete of low permeability is essential while it is equally important to ensure that the chloride is thoroughly mixed so as to avoid any uneven concentrations as these can set up corrosion currents. To achieve an even distribution of the chloride it should be dissolved in the mixing water and not added as a dry powder.

Although cases of failure are rare

*Salts aggressive to steel also may be added unwittingly to concrete by using sea water or unwashed sand or aggregate of marine sources.

when hydrochloric acid is used to wash precast concrete units, this practice should be closely controlled as variations in absorption of chloride leads to increased risk of corrosion.

(b) *Sprayed concrete*

Concrete may be sprayed by means of a high-pressure cement gun. The normal mixture for such a gun working at 0·21 to 0·28N/mm² is cement and sharp sand mixed dry. A cement/sand ratio of 1 : 3½ is satisfactory for most atmospheric conditions, but where water tightness is desired the ratio should be reduced to 1 : 3. For resistance to heat special semi-refactory materials are used. No foaming agent or other admixture is added and mixing with water takes place at the nozzle. In order to avoid the risk of shrinkage cracking, the

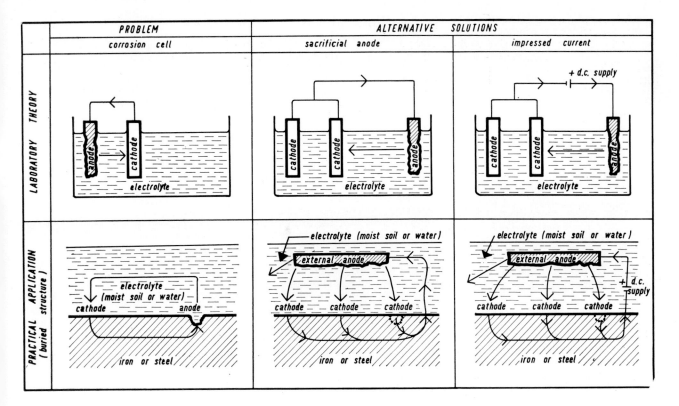

| PROBLEM | ALTERNATIVE SOLUTIONS | |
| corrosion cell | sacrificial anode | impressed current |

D.3.07/14
Principle of cathodic protection

water/cement ratio is closely controlled.

For interior work the coating should generally be at least 38mm but preferably 51mm, while for exterior work exposed to corrosive conditions the coating should be at least 51mm. Such coatings should be reinforced with welded mire mesh 4·06 or 3·66mm thick, firmly anchored to the steel surface. These thick coatings are applied in several layers, and the cement/aggregate ratio should be the same throughout, while each layer should be allowed to harden for 3 hr before being over-coated. Proper curing of the completed coating is essential.

4. Cathodic protection

(a) *Mechanism*

During the corrosion process there is a flow of current from an anodic area into the electrolyte. Cathodic protection is the application of a stronger current in the opposite direction, flowing from a specially provided anode through the electrolyte to the metal which neutralises the currents responsible for corrosion and renders the metal cathodic over its entire area. Under these conditions the anodic process occurs at the specially provided anode.

(b) *Sources of current*

The counter-current may be supplied by baser metals, that is more electro-negative metals (usually magnesium, aluminium and zinc) which undergo 'sacrificial attack' or, alternatively, by an impressed current drawn from a power supply using a transformer and rectifier to produce low-voltage d.c. (any other d.c. source may also be used). The principle upon which cathodic protection is based and the alternative methods available are illustrated in diagram D.3.07/14.

(c) *Application*

Cathodic protection is commonly applied to steel structures or containers (tanks, for example) that are immersed in water or buried in a damp environment. Continuous contact with a mass of electrolyte is generally required.

Although the principle of cathodic protection is fairly simple and straightforward, expert knowledge and experience is required in its application. The precise details of a system for a given circumstance (the current needed is notable) cannot be accurately predicted without test, although rough estimates can be based on previous experience. The conductivity of the electrolyte is important—more current is needed with electrolytes of low conductivity (fresh water) than with electrolytes of high conductivity (sea water).

As a general rule the *choice of system* will be dependent on the size of the structure, the conductivity of the electrolyte and the availability of power. Thus, sacrificial anodes may be preferred when the conductivity of the electrolyte is sufficiently high (fresh water tanks are notable) for small temporary or isolated systems; the anodes may also be preferred where the passage of a large current through the soil may be objectionable. An impressed current system, on the other hand, is likely to be preferred for large structures where a large total current is necessary, and where power is readily available.

The *choice of material* as the anode for impressed current and sacrificial anode systems will be based on different criteria. The basic requirements of each system are better considered separately.

(i) *Impressed current systems*. The requirements which the anodes should meet are: (1) reasonable working life; (2) ability to discharge the current to be used without unduly rapid disintegration of the anode connections; and (3) sufficiently low resistance to earth. These requirements determine not only the choice of material but also the form of anode and its surface area. Where a large area is required to provide high conductivity scrap metal may be used, but often materials such as graphite (if impregnated to reduce porosity), high silicon-iron, lead alloys and platinised titanium may be specifically chosen to resist deterioration because their choice will be more economical. The geometric arrangement of anodes is also important. For the protection of buried structures it is common to use a number of buried anodes connected together to form an extensive groundbed.

(ii) *Sacrificial anode systems*. The electrolytes in which the anodes are to operate governs the choice of material. In low conductivity electrolytes the e.m.f. is the primary consideration; in electrolytes with high conductivity the anode should have a reasonable working life. An anode of *magnesium alloy* has the highest driving potential and is the most universally effective in protecting buried structures. A magnesium alloy is often used for the protection of fresh water tanks. Its useful life, particularly in sea water, is reduced because it suffers natural corrosion in addition to the loss corresponding to the protection current. *Zinc and aluminium* have lower driving potentials. However, their use may be advantageous in high conductivity environments in which magnesium anodes would give more current than necessary. In certain cases it is necessary to surround buried anodes with a backfill to reduce corrosion, minimise polarisation and provide better contact with the soil.

(d) Side effects

The use of cathodic protection may, under certain conditions, produce undesirable side effects which could mitigate against the degree of protection expected or induce corrosion elsewhere. The main side effects may be summarised as follows:

(i) *Stray currents*. As a cathodic protection installation for buried structures causes a direct current to flow in the soil, adequate precautions are required in order to prevent this current from flowing along neighbouring structures, thus initiating their corrosion (see 'General considerations', 4(c)(iii)). Susceptibility to corrosion by stray currents and the magnitude of their effect will be dependent on the total protection current; the quality of any coatings on the structures, the conductivity of the soil and the relative positions of the structure and the groundbed (the anodes). However, the effect can be minimised by care at the design stage but at the same time it is advisable to notify other organisations likely to have pipes or cables buried or in contact with the soil nearby of the intention to install cathodic protection.

(ii) *Hydrogen and alkalinity*. In some cases it may be necessary, in order to achieve protection at positions where the protective effect is least, to employ potentials more negative than the protection potential over the greater part of the surface. This can result in the evolution of hydrogen gas which can disrupt coatings, or the production of a high degree of alkalinity which can destroy paint by saponification (see *3.06 Chemical attack*—page 24).

(iii) *Calcareous deposits*. In sea water and in some soils, the alkalinity causes the precipitation of an insoluble calcareous deposit. Although this may be beneficial insofar as it reduces the current needed for cathodic protection, it may be undesirable in some water installations where an excessive deposit may lead to blockage of flow channels or reduction of heat transfer.

precautions

The problems associated with the corrosion of metals are complex, while the complexity of these problems and their possible solutions, as outlined in the preceding parts of this section, are mainly due to the many variables and interactive factors involved. In practice, the difficulties that are often encountered in establishing, for any given circumstance, the precautions which should reasonably be taken to minimise the risk and/or effects of corrosion, may be due to *two* closely interrelated factors. *First,* it is generally difficult to predict, with complete accuracy, the degree of corrosion that may occur in any given circumstance. This tends to imply that such precautions as are taken should, for safety, tend to be excessive rather than minimum. *Second,* cost is invariably important, but here, too, a course must be steered between the requirements of durability on the one hand and maintenance on the other, in addition to other requirements such as strength.

Despite all these difficulties, there has been sufficient experience in the use of metals in buildings which has led to the establishment of some definite and clear recommendations particularly in the use of iron or steel. Many of the precautions that should be taken to minimise the risk or the effects of corrosion have been included in various ways in the preceding parts of this section. However, these have been included to form part of the discussion aimed at explaining not only the causes and effects of corrosion but also possible remedies. Consequently it is necessary and convenient in this part to bring together, so to speak, the more important precautions, and to set these down in outline, that is without the reasons which have already been covered, although some cross-referencing for details is desirable. For this purpose it is convenient to use the following general headings:
(1) Selection; (2) Design;
(3) Contact; (4) Protection; and
(5) Maintenance.

1. Selection

Depending on circumstances, the problems of corrosion prevention may be considered *basically* from one of two points of view. *First,* the use of a metal which is highly resistant to corrosion, or *second,* the use of some form of protection to a metal which is not resistant to corrosion. The latter course implies maintenance.

Cost will always influence which of these two approaches is adopted, but in a great many cases *strength* will be significant. However, eight other factors will influence the selection of either the basic approach or, as important, the form of protection. These may be summarised as follows:
(a) *Conditions of exposure,* that is, basic exposure plus the effects of design. In a great many cases exposure will be one of the most important factors influencing selection. Careful

analysis of exposure for any given condition is essential.

(b) *Proposed life of structure or component*. In this a distinction must be drawn between short-life and long-life buildings.

(c) *Periods required between maintenance*.

(d) *Importance of structure or component*.

(e) *Difficulty of access for maintenance*. This applies to all metal work including those components designed to be replaced, i.e. designed as short-life components.

(f) *Shape and size of structure or component*.

(g) *Protection during storage and transport*.

(h) *Fabrication methods*.

2. Design

Many details of design may seriously increase the risk of corrosion generally. Attention to such details is, therefore, important, particularly when metals of low corrosion resistance, such as ordinary steel for example, are being used. In the absence of taking the necessary steps to eliminate the use of 'corrosion increasing' details, it is necessary to ensure that some means of protection, or additional protection depending on circumstances, is provided.

In general, design includes consideration of such factors as geometry, working conditions, contact between dissimilar metals or between metals and other building materials, and accessibility for maintenance. For convenience, only geometric factors and working conditions are considered here, contact and accessibility being considered under '3. Contact' and '5. Maintenance' respectively.

(a) Geometric factors

Geometric factors may cause the initiation of corrosion, particularly local corrosion, for a number of different reasons in both atmospheric (external and internal) and immersed environments.

(i) *Atmospheric environments*. One of the most important precautions which should be taken with metals exposed to atmospheric environments is the avoidance of details which encourage the entrapment of moisture and dirt (crevices are notable). Typical examples of these and other details which should be avoided are illustrated in diagram D.3.07/15. The precautions may, however, be summarised as follows:
(1) Arrange constructional and other members so that trapping of moisture and dirt is discouraged (D.3.07/15 A). Alternatively, adequate drainage holes (sufficient diameter important) may be provided, if rearrangement of members is impracticable.
(2) Joints and fastenings should be arranged to give free and uninterrupted lines (D.3.07/15 B). Welds are generally preferable to bolted joints, with butt welds better than lap welds. If the latter have to be used, then ap-

propriate welding or filling with mastic may be necessary to avoid the entrapment of moisture and dirt.

(3) Crevices should be avoided (D.3.07/15 C) as they also allow the retention of moisture and dirt and thus increase corrosion. Where it is not possible to avoid crevices, they should be filled by welding, using a filler or mastic.

(4) Avoid structural arrangements that prevent the free circulation of air through and around them (D.3.07/15 D) so as to reduce condensation risk, particularly where thermal insulation is impracticable. *Hollow structures* such as boxed and tubular sections should preferably be hermetically sealed.

(5) Avoid sharp corners and edges or rough surfaces to metals which are to receive a protective coating, particularly if this is paint (D.3.07/15 E) All contours should be as rounded as possible in order to ensure an even coating thickness, and also to avoid the possibility of mechanical damage. Paint coatings may also break down if there is a rapid change in contour (the heads of rivets and screws and crevices) in which pickling or pretreatment solutions can become trapped.

(6) Avoid features that allow water and condensation to drip or be blown back to other parts of a structure. In this the use of drips is important, but in some cases suitable drainage with downpipes may be essential.

(7) Where it is difficult to prevent sheltered steel surfaces, such as those under eaves, where evaporation of water is retarded, ensure that the sheltered areas are given additional protection. Other metals in similar positions (aluminium and stainless steel notable) should be washed regularly.

(ii) *Immersed environments.* Some of the points made under atmospheric environments above are also applicable to metals in contact with liquids. Those features which are specially applicable to liquids are set out below; some of these are illustrated in diagram D.3.07/16.

(1) Attention must be given to the velocity of the liquid.

(2) Crevices should be avoided. These may be particularly pronounced at screwed joints. In flanged joints (D.3.07/16 A) the use of special gaskets is advised.

(3) Avoid sharp changes in direction (D.3.07/16 B), especially when high velocity liquids are being transported.

(4) Ensure that water flows from anodic metals in the system to cathodic metals.

(5) Avoid the use of storage tanks and cylinders which are difficult to drain (D.3.07/16 C).

(b) *Working conditions*

It is important to ensure that constructional procedures do not cause conditions which are likely to lead to *stress corrosion.* The highest stresses are likely to be set up by welding so adequate stress-relieving treatments are necessary. 'Force-fitting' of parts, for

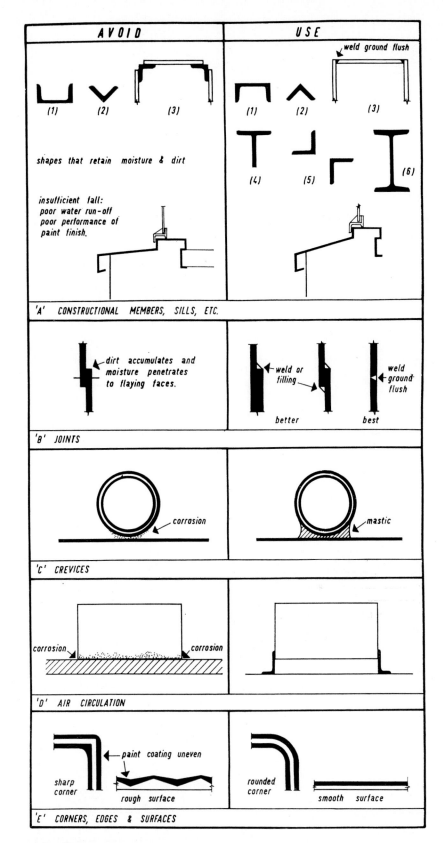

D.3.07/15

Some of the geometric factors that should be taken into account for exposure to atmospheric environments

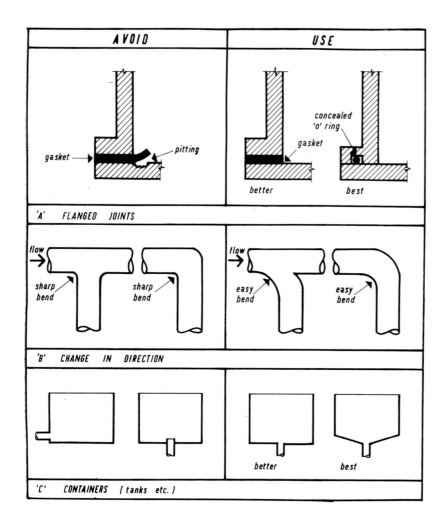

Some of the geometric factors that should be taken into account for exposure to immersed environments

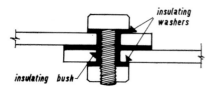

D.3.07/17

Method of electrically insulating dissimilar metals. (Courtesy: Butler, G. and Ison, H. C. K., 'Corrosion and its Prevention in Waters', Fig. 42, p. 235, Leonard Hill Books, 1966)

example, when bolt holes do not coincide, which results in the concentration of stresses should be avoided.

Despite the necessity for stress relieving treatment when welded joints are used (such treatment is also necessary with other forms of jointing), these are preferable, as riveted joints and expansion fits, for example, will tend to loosen on heat treatment.

3. Contact

In general it is safest to avoid contact between metals and absorbent building materials or contact between dissimilar metals. Where this is impracticable, then it is necessary to provide some form of insulation. This must, in most conditions, be electrically resistant and non-absorbent, consisting of suitable paints, linings, gaskets or washers.

When considering contact, it is always important to remember that this might also be caused when water flows from one surface on to another. Corrosion of aluminium gutters and pipes, for example, is often caused by copper bearing water from roofs or pipes in a water system. The same also applies to water which first passes over building materials containing corrosive agents and then over a metal. Dripping water can often be particularly damaging.

(a) *Contact with other building materials*

Conditions which are likely to lead to corrosion of metals when in contact with other absorbent building materials are included in 'Exposure conditions, 3. Other building materials' (p. 59).

Most non-ferrous metals (copper is a notable exception) are susceptible to attack by alkalis and acids. When these are in contact with alkaline concrete, cement or lime mortar, or with acidic gypsum plasters (e.g. Keene's) they (the metals) should be protected by *thick* coats of bitumen. Alkali-resisting primers may be used on alkaline surfaces and will also suffice for plaster contacts.

Wood, especially western red cedar, Douglas fir, oak and sweet chestnut, may affect metals and contact may be prevented by the use of bitumen or zinc chromate primers. Wood primers may not be suitable.

(b) *Contact between dissimilar metals*

This is a particularly important cause of corrosion. The metals which are most vulnerable when in contact and typical examples of contact in building construction are included under 'Exposure conditions, 5. Contact between dissimilar metals' (p. 59). Contacts that should always be avoided are those between copper, nickel, and their alloys (for example, brass and bronzes) with aluminium or zinc, and of aluminium or zinc components with steel.

In order to avoid contact it is important that the insulating medium is electrically resistant. Suitable treatments include *thick* coats of bituminous paint or hot-applied bitumen, inhibitive primers or paints, while bituminous felts and some sheet plastics are acceptable alternatives.

When fixing devices are used, insulating gaskets, washers, etc. (see diagram D.3.07/17) may be more convenient—the use of coatings may be undesirable due to the ease with which they may be damaged.

In water systems it is essential to ensure that *all debris*, including steel drillings, etc., is removed from tanks, particularly galvanised steel tanks, before they are filled with water.

(c) Soldering, brazing and welding

It is important to ensure that fluxes used with soldering or brazing material are thoroughly cleaned off. Weld metals which differ substantially from the base metal should be avoided, while the preparation, welding techniques and finishing should be carefully carried out so that not only is the final weld relatively smooth and well-shaped, but also excludes the presence of porosity, voids, crevices, scale inclusions or changes in structure.

(d) Aggressive water

In all types of water systems check the compatibility of the water with any metal it is proposed to use. Aggressive waters include waters from water supplies which may be soft or those containing free carbon dioxide, while acids, alkalis and salts may be derived from a number of sources (see also Table 3.07/1, p. 60).

Galvanised steel should not be used for hot water cylinders, nor should the internal surfaces of steel pipes be galvanised if the temperature of the water is likely to exceed 60° C. Above this temperature the zinc coating may no longer protect the steel pipe—see C.3.07/3, note 14 (p. 61).

(e) Flue gases

The use of boilers for heating and hot water makes it important to ensure that metals (flue linings significant) are selected for their resistance to the gases to be encountered in any particular situation. In some cases metal components may be completely inadequate.

Two examples where accessibility for repainting steelwork is extremely limited. The end of the top rail (right-hand picture) is badly corroded after six or seven years

4. Protection

The four main methods by which protection may be achieved, namely (1) Treatment of the environment, (2) Protective coatings, (3) Concrete, and (4) Cathodic protection, are covered in detail under 'Protection'. Treatment of the environment is excluded here.

(a) Coatings

A decision to use a coating to increase corrosion resistance means that the coating must be considered during design (see '1. Selection' earlier). The factors which need to be taken into account include the success of the application of a coating to a particular metal (some metals are restricted in the coatings they can receive successfully);

possible damage to the coating during storage, transport and assembly; the probable life of the coating and whether the coating can be renewed *in situ*. At the same time, consideration must also be given to the resistance of the coating to its 'working condition' which may include the need for resistance to abrasion, impact, chemicals, sunlight, etc., or thermal stability and effects on heat transfer (the latter would be important in water systems). Alkali softening of paint applied to steelwork, for example, is a common cause of corrosion.

In all cases, it is imperative that the metal to be coated is thoroughly clean, free from grease, dirt, mill-scale, rust, etc. This requires good pretreatment. Correct application of the coating is

also essential, while surfaces which are likely to lead to differing thicknesses of the coating (see diagram D.3.07/15 E) should be avoided.

Ordinary steel, it is important to note, can seldom be used without some form of protection. Selection of the coating is important, but proper pretreatment and subsequent application should not be neglected (see Table 3.07/6, p. 78).

(b) Concrete

(i) *General*. Whenever steel is embedded in concrete (reinforced concrete work, encasing of structural steel members or pipes, for example), the following precautions are essential:

(1) There must be adequate depth of cover. In reinforced concrete work

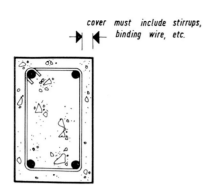

D.3.07/18

Adequate cover in reinforced concrete work needs to include stirrups, binding wire, etc.

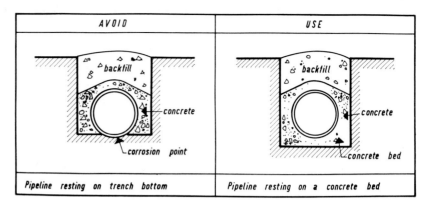

D.3.07/19

Illustrating the need for complete encasement of steel pipes buried below ground

this means cover to all steel, including stirrups, hooping and binding wire, and not merely that to the main bars (diagram D.3.07/18). In those cases where it may be difficult to comply with the amount of cover required (by BS. CP 116 for example) particularly in lightweight concrete work, consideration should be given to the use of zinc-coated reinforcement. (See *Zinc-coated reinforcement for concrete,* BRS Digest No. 109, HMSO, Sept. 1969.) Pipes encased in concrete below ground must not rest on the soil but on a concrete bed (diagram D.3.07/19).

(2) The concrete must be of good quality. This means attention must be given to the quality of the aggregates (shrinkable aggregates should be avoided); correct water/cement ratio; and correct compaction.

(3) Avoid the excessive use of chlorides (calcium chloride should not be added in excess of 2 per cent by weight of cement). When chlorides are used, ensure that these are thoroughly mixed and ensure that a concrete of low permeability is achieved by specifying well-graded aggregates, low water/cement ratios and thorough compaction.

(4) Additional precautions will be necessary if corrosive substances are present in ground waters and in marine and industrial environments. (Sulphate attack may be significant—see *3.06 Chemical attack,* p. 27.)

(5) Ensure that cracks in the cover to the steel are not deep enough to allow moisture, etc., to penetrate to the steel. In this quality control is vital, but also formwork should not be undersized or badly made, while it is important to ensure that a good bond is achieved at all construction joints—badly made honeycombed joints are likely to lead to trouble.

(ii) *Reinforced concrete floors.* Special consideration is required with reinforced concrete floors, particularly in the following circumstances:

(1) Where the finish itself is unaffected by corrosive liquors but does not provide sufficient protection of the underlying structure. Examples are: (a) concrete surfaces permeable to saline wash waters which do not affect the concrete itself; (b) epoxy and polyester floorings sold for use in corrosive situations and laid up to 6mm thick. Many liquids that do not affect these floorings may leak through them, particularly when some wear has occurred. The risk may not be recognised when they are laid by firms with little chemical engineering experience.

(2) Where the finish, e.g. granolithic concrete, may disintegrate. Here the user might carry out repairs to the concrete yet not recognise that the steel below is corroding.

(3) Where the floor finish can disintegrate to produce a corrosive chemical. In this category there is only magnesium oxychloride. This flooring has been responsible for at least one collapse of a reinforced concrete floor caused by the action of magnesium chloride on the reinforcement. The Code of Practice for *in situ* flooring, CP 204, points to the need for protecting the metalwork of gas, water and electrical services by 25mm of dense concrete when this flooring is used *even in dry conditions.* In wet conditions the flooring should never be used because the reinforcement cannot be protected by bitumen or galvanising.

(4) In corrosion-resistant flooring where detailing at channels, gulleys, upstands, etc., is defective.

(5) Where there is a change of use in a factory and it passes unnoticed that a corrosion-resistant floor *designed to resist other chemicals* may not be suited to the new use.

(6) Where, before laying epoxy resin flooring, washing with hydrochloric acid to remove laitance is recommended. (Hydrochloric acid may also be used to make concrete floors less slippery.)

(iii) *Exposure.* The vulnerability of copings, sills and other projections and of large plane-surfaced walls of reinforced concrete must always be taken into account.

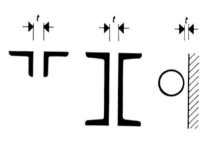

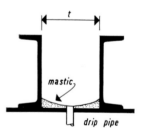

Detail shown above is difficult to maintain; detail shown below is preferable.

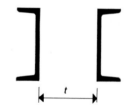

NOTE: In all cases 't' should provide adequate access for painting.

D.3.07/20

Adequate provision for access is important for all painted metalwork

(c) Cathodic protection

Cathodic protection can be applied to any parts of a structure that are immersed in water or buried in a damp environment. The choice of system and details of design require expert knowledge and experience; it is therefore important that such advice is always sought.

Factors which need to be taken into account include the following:

(1) Continuous contact with a mass of electrolyte.

(2) Resistivity of the electrolyte to determine probable corrosion risk to structure.

(3) Field tests to determine groundbed locations, and the requirements of the groundbed and current supply.

(4) Provision of permanent and accessible insulated test leads at representative points to enable electrical tests to be made of the structure.

(5) Provision of insulation from any neighbouring structures. Other organisations likely to have pipes or cables buried or in contact with the soil near a cathodically protected structure should be notified.

(6) Provision should be made for subsequent inspection and maintenance.

5. Maintenance

Maintenance may, depending on circumstances, include regular washing, replacement of a protective system or replacement of a metal or other component (sealants notable).

(a) Inspection

Maintenance is required whenever systems of protection against corrosion with short lives are used. However, it is always wise to ensure that, subsequent to the completion of a building, all metalwork, including the structures in which metal may be embedded or concealed, is regularly inspected.

(b) Accessibility

It is important at the design stages to ensure adequate accessibility. This would include physical access to the metalwork or structure as such, access by means of removable panels, etc., to conceal metalwork and, as important, access to enable coatings such as paint to be applied. As regards the latter, details of design may seriously hinder this; some typical examples are given in diagram D.3.07/20. If it is impracticable to provide access, additional protection is important.

(c) Frequency

This will be largely governed by the durability of the metal used (if unprotected that is) or the durability of the protective system. In this details of design as outlined earlier under '1. Design' can increase the intervals between maintenance.

(d) Washing

Regular washing of unprotected and sheltered metals, such as aluminium and stainless steel, for example, can greatly increase their durability.

3.08 frost action

Changes in temperature play an extremely important part in frost action, but the deleterious results of freezing would not take place if water was not present. Thus, despite the close relationship, insofar as the mechanics of frost action is concerned, with factors that are to be considered under *4.00 Heat and its effects*, it is more convenient to include this problem in this section.

Frost action is only associated with porous materials, but there are two quite distinct problems which need to be considered. First, the durability of porous materials during the life of the building and, second, the effects of low temperatures on materials and processes during construction. The latter are generally included under what is known as 'Winter building', and are better considered separately.

The frost resistance of materials is dependent on the interrelationship of three factors, namely: (1) the properties of the material, (2) the position in which the material is used, and (3) climatic conditions. In general, the plain wall surfaces of buildings are not subject to the deleterious effects of frost action; heavily exposed parts which are likely to be saturated are more commonly susceptible to attack, and so it is these parts which need special consideration.

Various attempts have been made to devise laboratory tests in order to establish the frost resistance of materials, particularly the resistance of brick and stone. A reliable method would be invaluable for those who wish to use new materials or existing materials in new ways or positions. However, as yet no reliable method has been found, although the results of some tests may offer partial guidance.

Greater attention has been given in recent years to the problems of winter building so that the suspension of building operations might be avoided when temperatures are low. The various precautionary measures which have been recommended are directed not only at minimising the effects of low temperature and frost on materials, but also at providing better conditions for building operatives.

It is convenient to consider the problems of frost action under three separate headings, namely, (1) *General considerations,* dealing with the basic mechanisms and freezing in materials; (2) *Practical considerations,* covering effects on materials, likely positions, assessment of resistance and precautions; (3) *Winter building precautions.*

General considerations

1. Basic mechanisms

Unlike most other liquids, water ceases to contract just above the freezing point (4° C) and begins to expand again. On conversion to ice at the freezing point there is a further sudden expansion of 9 per cent by volume. Thus weight for weight, ice is bulkier than water. However, the effects of pressure are equally significant. Ice will melt with the application of pressure; the degree of pressure required being dependent on the temperature of the ice below freezing point—the lower the temperature, the higher the pressure required. Looked at in another way, the application of pressure reduces the freezing point of water.

If, before freezing takes place, water only partially fills a closed container, then it follows that there is room in which the expansion that occurs on freezing can be accommodated, as shown in diagram D.3.08/1A. (In this it is assumed that the air can be evacuated.) If, on the other hand, a

BEFORE FREEZING	AFTER FREEZING
air / water	ice
91% full of water	100% full of ice

A   BASIC EXPANSION – partially filled container

water	pressure of walls of container sufficient to resist freezing.	deformation of walls of container.	wall of container broken
100% full of water	water	ice	ice

B   POSSIBLE EFFECTS OF EXPANSION – completely filled container.

D.3.08/1

Diagram of the basic mechanisms and possible effects of freezing water in a container

closed container is already completely full of water before freezing takes place, then the subsequent expansion will result in pressure on the walls of the container with one of three possible effects, depending on the strength properties of the walls as shown in diagram D.3.08/1B. Subject to the temperature involved, the walls of the container may be strong enough to resist the pressure; alternatively, the walls may undergo deformation and, provided this is within the elastic limit, the shape of the container will be restored when the ice subsequently melts; finally, the walls of the container may be broken.

2. Freezing in materials

The pores in porous building materials are the containers which may be filled, in varying degrees, with water. However, the arrangement of the pores presents an extremely complex pattern of containers, as shown in diagram D.3.08/2. Whether or not expansion of the water within the pores during freezing is likely to cause damage to the walls of the pores depends on a number of different factors chief of which include moisture content, moisture gradient, rate of freezing, temperature gradient, freezing/thawing cycles and pore structure. The relationship between these factors is extremely complicated. However, it is convenient to discuss the significance of each separately, indicating as far as possible the relationship between them.

(a) *Moisture content*

By definition, moisture content (see *3.03 Moisture content*, Vol. 2) is the moisture which a material contains at a given time and expressed as a percentage of its dry weight. Values of moisture content only express the amount of water that is present in a material, but do not indicate the manner in which the moisture is distributed, nor the extent to which the pores are filled. However, in general terms, materials with high moisture contents (generally saturated) subjected to freezing are more likely to suffer from frost action than those under similar conditions with low moisture contents.

(b) *Moisture gradient*

Moisture gradient (see *3.03 Moisture content*, Vol. 2, p. 70) is the variation of moisture content between the outer and inner part of a piece of material (or construction).

In external wall elements, there is generally a drop in moisture content across the thickness of the element, with high moisture contents near the exposed faces. Warmth from within the building also helps to maintain low moisture contents at or near the internal face. In general, but subject to pore structure, a moisture gradient is advantageous, in that there is room in the interior into which water being squeezed out by the expansion caused

by freezing at or near the exposed external face may escape (diagram D.3.08/3).

In the more heavily exposed parts of a wall, such as parapets for example, there may not be a moisture gradient across the construction, although there may be a moisture gradient down the construction. In the absence of a damp-proof course under a coping stone, saturation of a considerable part of the parapet may occur. Under such conditions the initial freezing of water in the coping may not result in any deleterious effect on the material of which the coping is made. However, it is possible for water to migrate from unfrozen to frozen parts, as is known to happen in the formation of ice-lenses and the consequent heaving of soils, for example, under freezing conditions. Water drawn from the underlying masonry may then contribute to subsequent splitting or breakdown of the coping, when this additional water also freezes (diagram D.3.08/4). In this the ease with which water will migrate from the underlying masonry will depend more on the bedjoint than on the elusive differences in character between one stone and another. Nevertheless, it is important that damp-proof courses are inserted under copings as *one* way of increasing the durability of the coping stone.

(c) *Rate of freezing*

Rate of freezing and the tensile strength of the walls of the pores in a material are closely interrelated. In this it is important to note that the tensile strengths of the materials normally subjected to frost action, such as bricks and stones, are in general low.

If the rate of freezing is slow, the pressure exerted is gradual and, as important, may be well within the tensile strength of the material. If this is so, then it is possible for the ice which may be formed to be liquefied. The surplus water may thus be extruded, either to the outside, that is above the surface of the material, or to empty pores within the material. This liquefaction enables the material to relieve stresses.

If the rate of freezing is rapid, and particularly when freezing occurs at low temperatures, the pressures exerted, in addition to being rapid, are often of a magnitude far in excess of the tensile strength of the material. Consequently, liquefaction and thus relief of stress is not possible, and this in turn leads to damage of the material.

(d) *Temperature gradient*

In most buildings there is a drop in temperature across the thickness of the enclosing elements. The extent of the drop is dependent on the relative internal and external air temperatures, while the distribution of temperature is dependent on the thermal properties of the materials that make up the element

D.3.08/2

The complex pattern of containers that may occur in porous materials

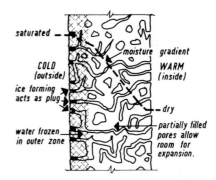

D.3.08/3

Illustration of moisture gradient and the advantage this may have in leaving room into which water squeezed out by expansion caused by freezing at or near the exposed external face may escape

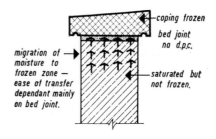

D.3.08/4

Migration of water from unfrozen to frozen parts as may occur in a parapet. The durability of copings may be increased by inserting a d.p.c. under the coping

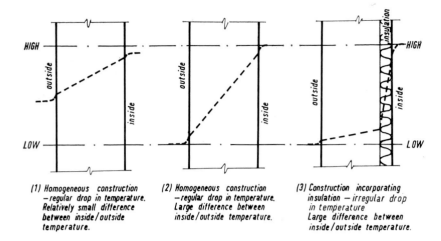

(1) Homogeneous construction — regular drop in temperature. Relatively small difference between inside/outside temperature.

(2) Homogeneous construction — regular drop in temperature. Large difference between inside/outside temperature.

(3) Construction incorporating insulation — irregular drop in temperature Large difference between inside/outside temperature.

D.3.08/5

Illustration of temperature gradient

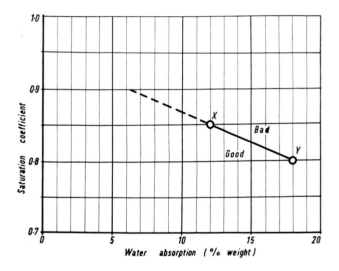

D.3.08/6

Illustrating relation between frost resistance of bricks and their water absorptions and saturation coefficients. (Courtesy: Butterworth, B., 'Bricks and Modern Research', Fig. 23, p. 95, Crosby Lockwood, 1948)

(see *4.00 Heat and its effects*), as shown in diagram D.3.08/5. The significance of the temperature gradient is that the zone of freezing is generally restricted and cannot take place, except in rare circumstances, throughout the thickness of a construction. The risk of frost action may be increased if, under saturated conditions for example, the depth of the freezing zone is considerable. However, as already noted in (b), warmth from inside a building may help to reduce the moisture content of those layers near the inside face

sufficiently to allow room into which water squeezed out by expansion in the outer zone may pass.

(e) *Freezing/thawing cycles*

Severe damage may occur if water is trapped between two layers of ice. This kind of condition can occur in heavily saturated walls subjected to severe frosts between which there are partial thaws.

Brickwork, for example, may, under conditions of severe frost, freeze to a depth of 76mm to 102mm during one

night. During the day following the frost, the sun may thaw the surface and moisture from melted snow trickle over it. There may be a severe frost during the night following the partial thaw. Thus, water is trapped between two layers of ice at different depths.

(f) *Pore structure*

Pore structure plays an extremely important part in determining the resistance which a material may provide to frost action. The arrangement and size of pores influence two of the factors already outlined, namely, moisture content and moisture gradient. These, in turn, are associated with absorption and the saturation coefficient of a material, both of which have been used in the past as possible guides to the frost resistance of materials. As a result of work carried out in both the United States of America and the United Kingdom, a relationship between these has been shown to exist, but because of the wide variation in pore structure between materials of the same kind, the relationship cannot always be universally applied in practice. However, it is of interest to outline this relationship. (Absorption and saturation coefficient are both covered in *3.03 Moisture content*, Vol. 2, p. 72.)

The amount of water absorbed by a material is usually expressed as a percentage of the weight of the material, while the saturation coefficient is the ratio of the volume of water absorbed and the total volume of voids in a material. Values of either do not, however, indicate the zones of a material which actually contain water, nor whether pores are completely or partially filled nor whether there is any room for expansion. However, it has been shown, in laboratory tests, that materials with high saturation coefficients were of poor durability, while those with low coefficients were of high durability. This, in fact, proved to be a generalisation, as it was not possible to draw a line which clearly demarcated the good from the bad. Tests carried out on the basis of absorption and crushing strength tended to yield the same result. However, if all three tests were taken together, it was possible to separate the good from the bad. In the absence of reliable artificial frost tests, this method has provided a useful empirical generalisation.

Simple charts based on the relationship between absorption and saturation coefficient alone (strength has been found to add little to the accuracy with which durability can be predicted) have been suggested, as shown in diagrams D.3.08/6 and 7. D.3.08/6 illustrates the 'give and take' that was found possible in assessing the durability of a brick. For example, a brick with an absorption of 12 per cent and a saturation coefficient of 0·85 is likely to be as durable as one with an absorption of 18 per cent and a saturation coefficient of 0·80. D.3.08/7 illustrates

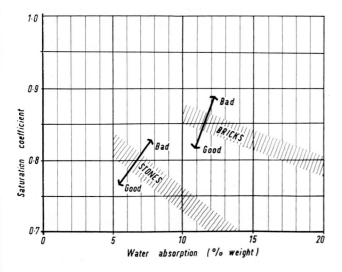

D.3.08/7

*Illustrating the different relations
between frost resistance and water
absorption and saturation coefficient
for bricks and certain limestones.
(Courtesy: Butterworth, B., 'Bricks and
Modern Research', Fig. 24, p. 96,
Crosby Lockwood, 1948)*

the different relations between frost
resistance and water absorption and
saturation coefficient for bricks and
certain limestones. In this the pore
structure between the materials is
significant, although differences in
strength should also be included.

Practical considerations

Emphasis is given here to the problems
related to the durability of materials
as the problems of winter building are
dealt with separately later.

It is convenient to discuss under
separate headings the following: (1)
The effects of frost action on materials,
including soils; (2) The positions in
which damage is likely to occur; (3)
Methods of assessing the resistance of
materials to frost action; and (4) The
precautions which should be taken in
order to reduce the possibility of frost
action causing damage.

1. Effects on materials

Damage due to frost action is generally confined to the shattering of the
surface of materials.* Under extremely severe conditions of freezing,
as often occur in laboratory freezing
tests, the whole or a substantial part
of a material may be shattered. Some
examples are shown in the accompanying photographs. The degree of shattering and the manner in which it takes
place depends largely on the pore
structure and strength of the material
and the conditions during freezing as
outlined under 'General considerations' earlier. Materials such as stone,

*The considerable expansion which accompanies
freezing may result in the overall expansion of an
element of construction. This expansion is generally
not seen to be a major cause of cracking but may, in
some cases, be an important contributory cause. For
this reason, shattering of materials is given as the
chief deleterious effect of frost action on materials.

for example, with a laminated structure tend to fail at the boundaries of
the various layers of which the material
is composed. Effects such as this can
be seen on slate roofs which have been
subjected to frost damage. In stone
walling, delamination can occur if the
beds are laid parallel to the external
face.

A rather different effect may result
with sandy soils under concrete ground
floors, particularly when the soil has
been used as a fill. Heaving of the soil
resulting from expansion may lift a
building or part of a building differ-
entially out of the ground, giving rise
to cracking of the structure. On thaw-
ing, the building may settle to its
original position in the ground. However, this settlement does not repair the
cracks formed during freezing, which
means that the structure remains permanently weakened.

2. Likely positions

In general, damage as a result of frost
action is mostly confined to those parts
of a building which may be saturated
with water when exposed to frost.
Saturation with water immediately
before freezing is, of course, an
extremely significant requirement if
damage is to occur. Thus, conditions
for frost action in external walls are
usually only found when there is
exposure to damp conditions with little
or no protection. Such conditions are
likely to arise in parapets, parts of
walls below damp-proof course level,
retaining and free-standing walls and
especially horizontal surfaces such as
copings, cornices, string courses and
sills, as shown in diagram D.3.08/8.

Roofs finished in tiles or slates may
suffer damage from frost action.
Attack is generally more severe in low-
pitched tiled roofs because the tiles

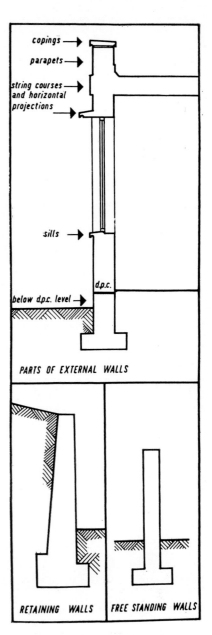

D.3.08/8

*Illustrating the positions in which frost
action is likely to occur. All these
positions may be saturated with water
when exposed to frost*

remain wet for longer periods than
when steeper pitches are used. In
general, tiles or slates at or near the
eaves are more susceptible to damage
than those in the rest of the roof slope.

Although the incidence of frosts is
an important climatic factor to be
taken into account, the likelihood of
frosts following immediately on a
rainy spell also needs to be considered.
In the United Kingdom it is unusual
for sudden changes from heavy driving rain to severe frosts to occur. This,
plus the fact that warmth from within
a building tends to encourage sufficient
drying out, explains why external walling between damp-proof course level
and eaves generally remains unaffected
by frost action. The important exceptions are those parts which may be

The result of frost heave of chalk used as hardcore under oversite concrete from a house that was unoccupied and therefore unheated. Freezing of the chalk while water-logged lifted the oversite concrete and brickwork above it (Courtesy: BRS, Crown Copyright)

Icicles extruded from a damp brick wall during frosty weather. Extrusion of this kind is more likely to take place if the rate of freezing is slow—see text (Courtesy: BRS, Crown Copyright)

Examples of frost shattering bricks of low frost resistance. The two photographs below show retaining walls and that on the left a coping (Courtesy: BRS, Crown Copyright)

saturated, as already noted. It is in these parts, because of their vulnerability, that care in the selection and use of materials is important.

3. Assessment of resistance

Ideally, it would be most useful if frost resistance could be measured on some sort of scale of numbers, like thermal resistance or electrical resistance. Unfortunately, frost resistance cannot be measured in this way, as the term is only meaningful in the context of a particular form of construction, in a particular location, and in a particular climate. Thus, it is normally only possible to make a broad distinction between 'normal' exposure and 'severe' exposure, the latter implying saturated conditions prior to freezing. Despite these difficulties, it is useful to outline the present position generally and that relative to bricks.

(a) General

The simple charts based on the relationship between absorption and saturation coefficient outlined earlier (General considerations 2(b)) may provide, in the absence of reliable artificial frost tests, some guide as to durability. For many years attempts have been made to develop reliable freezing tests in the laboratory. In the main these tests consist of subjecting saturated samples to freezing conditions with some form of freezing cabinet. Experience has shown that tests of this kind do not simulate natural conditions accurately enough, with the result that a number of anomalies have been found.

The unreliability of artificial freezing tests has led to the comparatively recent development of the 'tray-test' method at the Building Research Station. This method adopts a natural freezing test in which samples stand out-of-doors, partially immersed in water in shallow trays and exposed to the natural climatic conditions. Observations extending over many years have shown that it is possible to differentiate materials that normally show good frost resistance in copings, sills and other exposed features from those that are susceptible to frost damage in similar conditions. The 'tray-test' method also gives information on the broad relationship that exists between frost resistance and the *easily*-measured* water-absorption properties, so that, when necessary, tentative deductions can be made on that basis.

In general, it would seem that there is, as yet, no way in which materials may be tested quickly in order to establish, with great reliability, their resistance to frost action. Some tentative deductions may be obtained, while some use can be made of the results of tests previously carried out on similar materials. Despite the variability of both natural stones and clay

*In this connection it is worthwhile noting that the measurement of saturation coefficient cannot be carried out with the same ease as absorption.

Table 3.08/1. Susceptibility of materials to deterioration as the result of frost action	
Class of material	*How affected*
Natural stone	Variable. Best stones unaffected. Some stones with pronounced cleavage along the bedding planes are unsuitable for copings or cornices.
Clay products	Variable. Best bricks and tiles unaffected. Some products, insufficiently fired, or with flaws of structure originating in the machine, may deteriorate, especially bricks in copings, and tiles on flat-pitched roofs.
Cast stone, concrete, asbestos cement	Material of good quality is rarely affected.

Note: A laminar structure usually makes a material more liable to deterioration.
*Reference: Principles of Modern Building, Volume One, HMSO, 3rd Ed., Table 9.1, 1959.

---

products in the resistance they may provide to frost action, the susceptibility of materials to deterioration is summarised in Table 3.08/1.

(b) Bricks

Despite the amount of information available on the results of tests on some hundreds of varieties of bricks undertaken both in the laboratory and in many years of exposure to natural weathering, BS 3921 : 1965* only gives partial guidance on the choice of frost-resistant bricks. This appears to be due to the fact that the evidence available still presents a number of anomalies.

Understandably, the British Standard does not require bricks and blocks for *internal walls* to be frost resistant, although they may need protection if stacked on the site during winter. Bricks of *ordinary quality* are only required to resist frost for one winter, whilst stacked on a building site. This assumes that bricks of this quality will not be used in situations (severe exposure) for which bricks of special quality should be used.

For bricks and blocks of *special quality*, three methods of identification are provided and the onus of providing evidence of frost resistance is placed upon the manufacturer, as follows:

'The best evidence of ability to withstand frost damage is provided by buildings which have been in service for some years, and bricks and blocks of special quality shall be deemed to be frost-resistant if they satisfy *one* of the following requirements *a. b* or *c*.

'(*a*) The manufacturer shall provide evidence that bricks and blocks of the quality offered have been in service under conditions of exposure at least as severe as those proposed for not less than three years in the area or locality in which their use is now to be considered, and that their performance, by inspection, has been satisfactory.

'(*b*) Alternatively, in the absence of buildings constructed from the bricks or blocks in question in the area concerned, manufacturers should arrange for sample panels of their products

*BS 3921 : 1965, *Bricks and blocks of brick-earth, clay or shale.*

. . . . to be built in an exposed position under the supervision of some independent authority, e.g. the local authority of the area in which the works are situated, so that independent testimony to their quality shall be available. Bricks or blocks which give satisfactory performance after not less than three years' exposure in panels built in accordance with the above paragraph are deemed to satisfy the frost resistance requirements for bricks or blocks of special quality.

'(*c*) Where it is not possible to provide evidence of frost resistance by either of the above methods, for example if the brick to be offered is essentially a new product, or if it has to be used for the first time in a certain area, a brick or block which is of engineering classification either as regards strength or as regards water absorption shall be deemed to be 'frost-resistant'.'

4. Precautions

Although there are relatively few situations in which damage from frost action is likely to occur, it is nevertheless important that these are carefully considered. The precautions necessary may be summarised as follows:

(a) Selection of materials

Careful selection of materials is imperative in all vulnerable positions, that is those subjected to severe exposure, such as occurs in parapets, parts of walls below damp-proof course level, retaining and freestanding walls, and especially horizontal surfaces such as copings, cornices, string courses and sills.

In general, experience of the performance of particular materials used over a number of years in particular constructions in particular positions and under particular climatic conditions is likely to provide the best guide. In this the importance of climate cannot be overlooked, even in the United Kingdom there are quite wide variations in exposure to driving rain, for example (see diagrams D.3.02/3 and 4, Vol. 2). Thus materials which may perform quite satisfactorily in the less exposed parts of the country may suffer from frost damage if used in the more

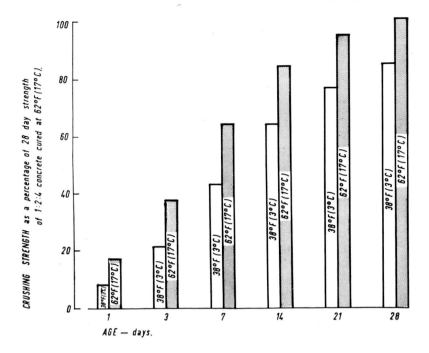

C.3.08/1

Effect of temperature upon the rate of hardening of a typical concrete made with ordinary Portland cement

heavily exposed parts of the country.*

(b) *D.p.c.'s under copings*

Ensure that a suitable damp-proof course is incorporated under copings (see diagram D.3.08/4).

(c) *Direction of bedding planes*

It is advisable to ensure that the bedding planes of stone are laid at right-angles to the external face of a wall.

(d) *Roof pitch*

Flatter pitches than those recommended in CP 142† may be used, subject to good quality of tiles *and* the ability of design features of the tiles to exclude water.

(e) *Fill of sandy soils*

The use of sandy soils as a fill under ground-floor concrete slabs is better avoided particularly in poorly heated

*The BRS Scottish Laboratory has reported recently that exposure in the Glasgow area has caused frost damage in situations (between ground and damp-proof course and in window reveals) where it is rarely seen in other parts of the country. In addition, some facing bricks sent to Scotland from England have sometimes been used, with disastrous results, in free-standing walls, apparently in the mistaken belief that a facing brick is necessarily a brick of special quality.

†British Standard Code of Practice: CP 142 : 1958 (amendment added June, 1961) (general series), *Slating and tiling.*

94

buildings, as these soils may be subjected to frost-heave.

winter building precautions

Bad weather conditions may delay or otherwise affect work on building sites at any time of the year and at all stages of construction. Low temperatures in particular may, at best, interfere with the hardening of mortar, plaster and concrete (see comparative chart C.3.08/1) or, at worst, actually cause disintegration of materials used in the wet trade processes. The considerable amounts of water used in mortars, plasters and concretes (see Table 3·02/2, Vol. 2) make these materials particularly vulnerable to damage by frost action before they have developed sufficient strength to resist the expansion which accompanies freezing. In this it is important to note that subsequent strength of a material is considerably reduced if expansion takes place while the material is in a wet or 'green' state.

In this part particular consideration is given to the precautionary measures which should be taken if work is to proceed when temperatures are low. Emphasis is given to the wet trade processes, although some reference is also made to other materials which may be affected by low temperatures. It is important to note that no reference is made to the protective measures which may be used for the comfort and convenience of building operatives, such as protective tents and screens which

provide temporary cover over whole or part of a building site. These coverings may, of course, also be used in certain circumstances to protect materials.

It is convenient to deal with the precautionary measures related to specific materials separately.

1. In situ concrete

If concrete is to be placed in cold weather it is important to ensure that the concrete is at a temperature of at least 4° C and that its temperature is maintained above 2·5° C until it has thoroughly hardened. In order to meet these requirements the following means may be used:

(a) *Protection of aggregates*

All aggregate should be so stored or covered as to prevent freezing. The reason for this precaution is due to the fact that sand and aggregate which have been left unprotected will contain moisture and will, during periods of frost, acquire coatings of frost or ice and contain lumps of ice. Concretes made with aggregates in this condition are generally weak with high porosity and poor durability due mainly to the fact that mixes are improperly proportioned and the formation of voids that result from the presence of frost or ice.

(b) *Protection of plant*

The concrete mixing plant should be covered with screens and roof and, if possible, a sheltered position on the site should be selected. In some cases it may be necessary to defrost equipment, shuttering reinforcement, etc.

(c) *Planning*

In order to avoid excessive heat loss and also to ensure a mix at a satisfactory temperature after compaction in the forms, the process of mixing, transporting and placing should be carefully planned.

Ready mixed concrete conforming to BS 1926 is required to be delivered at a temperature not less than 4° C.

(d) *Accelerating setting and hardening*

It is generally advantageous to use rapid-hardening cement. Setting and hardening may be accelerated by the addition of calcium chloride (not more than 2 per cent of the weight of the cement) to either ordinary or rapid-hardening Portland cements. Calcium chloride *must not be added to* extra rapid-hardening Portland cement, nor to high alumina cement. Some 'cold-weather' cements incorporate anti-freeze additives.

It may be noted that acceleration of setting and hardening is accompanied by an increase in the heat of hydration.

Thus, not only does the concrete attain its frost resistant strength sooner, but also it is warmer, particularly in its early stages.

(e) Protection of concrete

Immediately concreting is stopped the exposed surfaces should be covered, for example with tarpaulins, sheet polythene or building paper. This is a basic precautionary measure; more elaborate methods of protection may be required as discussed under (f) below.

(f) Heating and insulation

If concreting has to continue in very cold weather, special heating arrangements may be needed. The technique may involve preheating of materials (the cement itself should not be heated) and formwork and insulating the placed concrete to reduce heat loss, or it may include warming the concrete whilst it is setting and hardening. In general, when frosts occur only at night it is necessary merely to provide insulation to the finished concrete, and to adjust the time for stripping the concrete.

For convenience, Table 3.08/2 summarises recommendations for cold weather concreting; Table 3.08/3 summarises the assessment of heating treatment required and Table 3.08/4 methods of heating; and finally Table 3.08/5 deals with insulation.

(g) Stripping of formwork

Formwork should not be stripped until the concrete has hardened sufficiently (i) to resist subsequent freezing without damage, and (ii) to carry the loading asked of it. For beam sides, walls and columns (unloaded) it is generally only necessary to satisfy (i). The length of time required before formwork is stripped will depend on weather conditions and the type of concrete involved.

2. Precast concrete

Precast concrete is relatively free from the influence of frost. All precast concrete products should be properly matured before they are delivered to a site or incorporated in a building. Insulation and covering is normally only necessary at joints as a protection against frost.

3. Brickwork

(a) Protection of bricks

It is important that the moisture content of the brickwork should be as low as possible. In order to achieve this it is necessary to ensure that the bricks are dry. Consequently, bricks should not be wetted before laying and, as important, they should be suitably protected during storage on the site by ensuring that they are kept off the ground, stacked and covered with light protection such as tarpaulins (see Vol. 2, pp. 86-88).

(b) Protection of sand

Precautions should be taken to ensure that particles of ice are not included in the sand. In severe frosts, both materials and plant should be housed in an enclosure.

(c) Accelerating hardening of mortar

In order to accelerate the hardening of mortar mixes during cold weather it is normal to use mixes which are richer in cement than those used in the summer. Mortar mixes should not be weaker than 1:1:6 (cement:lime:sand), or 1:6 (cement:sand, with plasticiser). In some conditions it may be necessary to use slightly stronger mortars as summarised previously in Tables 3.04/4 and 5 (Vol. 2). Apart from these conditions, the recommendations for using mortars in frosty weather may be summarised as follows:

(1) If the bricks can be kept dry before laying, use either:

(a) 1:5–6 cement:sand mortar with an air-entraining plasticiser *free* from calcium chloride or similar salts, *or*,

(b) a 1:1:5–6 cement:lime:sand mortar, *or*,

(c) a masonry cement:sand mortar

Table 3.08/2. Recommendations for cold weather concreting (with ordinary Portland cement)

	Air temperature for commencement of special measures	Preheating	Insulation	External heating
Urgent work, i.e. work which has to carry its loads as soon as possible	3° C with prospect of falling. The rate of hardening of concrete is retarded when air and materials are below 10° C. When early strength development is required, it is desirable to start preheating at temperatures below 10° C if aggregates are chilled by hard frost at night	Sufficient to give 10° C or over in concrete when placed	Cover as soon as possible. Supply ample insulation to conserve heat for three days. Temperature of surface of concrete should not fall below 4° C at any part. If it does, extend period and apply external heating if necessary. If temperatures at any surface of concrete are near 0° C expose portions most likely to be coldest and test with hot water or blow-lamp to see whether frozen. Frozen work must be removed	To be used in very cold weather to maintain stipulated temperatures
Less urgent work	3° C with prospect of falling	As above but 4° C	As above but seven days and 2° C minimum	As above

Reference: *Winter Building*, Interim Review by the Committee on Winter Building, HMSO, Table 3, p. 17, 1963.

Table 3.08/3. Assessment of treatment required

Example	Temperature required in placed concrete	Assured temperature drop in transportation etc.	Minimum temperature at mixer	Condition of aggregates	Treatment required
A	10° C	13° C	13° C	Frost free at 2° C	Water heated to 71° C
B	4° C	7° C	11° C	Aggregate defrosted but not heated (say 0° C)	Water heated to 71° C
C	16° C	8° C	24° C	Coarse aggregate defrosted, sand heated	Water heated to 71° C Sand heated to 49° C
D	13° C	8° C	21° C	Sand and coarse aggregate to be heated	Water heated to 71° C Sand and coarse aggregate heated to 16° C

Notes: a. Specific heat capacities assumed: Water 4186·8J/Kg°C. Sand and Coarse Aggregate 9211J/Kg°C
b. Temperature of cement assumed: 0° C
c. Moisture content assumed: Sand 7%. Coarse Aggregate 2½% by weight
d. Water content of mix assumed: 18 kg/m³ (approx. 1:2:4 mix)

Reference: *Winter Building*, Interim Review by the Committee on Winter Building, HMSO, Table 4, p. 17, 1963.

Table 3.08/4. Preheating (with ordinary Portland cement)

Item to be heated	Maximum heated temperature	Methods of heating	Remarks
Water	71° C	Domestic types of water heater—(small jobs). Water passed through coil in large coke stove. Steam coil in supply tank. Steam jet in supply tank	Heating of water is the most economical method of getting the requisite heat into the concrete. The supply tank should be large enough to maintain the temperature of water fed to the mixer
Aggregate	49° C	Heating on corrugated iron sheets over coke fires—(small jobs). Stock piles tented over and braziers or other heaters placed in the enclosure. Passing aggregate over heated plates. Banking aggregate over large metal pipe in which fire is built. Steam jets in stock piles, preferably by means of perforated pipes. Steam coils in or under stock piles. Electric heating pads	Care is necessary in all the methods to ensure uniform heating. It may prove difficult and expensive to raise temperature of aggregates much above 15° C. Aggregates must be thawed out before being placed in mixer. Covering over with tarpaulin helps to conserve heat and keeps stocks dry. High steam pressure in jets is more effective than low pressure. When using steam jets the effect upon the water content should be considered. Dry heating of aggregates is liable to be uneven, and in the case of porous aggregates may lead to some absorption of mixing water
Concrete in mixer	38° C	Steam jet or hot water heating prior to use	
Wheelbarrows, skips, chutes, dumpers, etc.		Steam jets or hot water heating prior to use	Runs to be as short as possible, since 6 to 11° C may be lost between mixer and forms. Open chutes lose a good deal of heat and also present difficulties owing to ice formation between runs
Forms and reinforcing steel		Steam jets or hot water heating or braziers to thaw out immediately before use	

Reference: *Winter Building*, Interim Review by the Committee on Winter Building, HMSO, Table 2, p. 16, 1963.

Table 3.08/5. Insulation

Type	Materials	Remarks
Shuttering	Timber board as normally used. Forms backed with straw, etc. Forms backed with closed air space formed by building paper, etc., tacked over battens	Where timber formwork is used, this may provide sufficient insulation in itself to the surfaces it contains. Steel shuttering has very low insulating value and readily conducts heat away to other parts of structure as well as losing it to the air. Back with straw, etc.
Top cover	Several layers of building paper, sacking, cement bags, etc. 152mm or more of straw or similar materials. Boards with canvas over. 152mm to 610mm air space over slabs and pavings formed by stretching canvas over wood frames	Adequate lapping and tacking down at edges is important. Sacks, etc., kept dry by sheeting over with tarpaulin or building paper provide better insulation. Considerably improved by tarpaulin over. Heat sometimes applied under the enclosure
Enclosures	Complete covering of the job by thick canvas sheeting, etc., allowing 456mm air space all round the work. Enclosure is heated	For severe conditions care must be taken to avoid all unnecessary openings

Reference: *Winter Building*, Interim Review by the Committee on Winter Building, HMSO, Table 5, p. 18, 1963.

of equivalent strength (e.g. 1½ : 4, see Table 3.04/5).

(2) If the bricks are wet when laid, use an aerated mortar as in 1(a).

(3) *Note:* Mortars containing air-entraining plasticisers do *not* need calcium chloride as well. In any case the addition of this salt (to *compo* or masonry cement mortars) cannot be relied upon to prevent frost damage and, further, it introduces a risk of permanent dampness with eventual defects in plaster and decoration. The use of 'anti-freeze' compounds is not advised, many of which have calcium chloride as the basis of 'frost proofing' additives. The heat generated by such additives is rapidly dissipated into the adjacent cold bricks, and much of the additive in the mortar is drawn with the water into the surrounding bricks.

(d) Heating of materials

When night temperatures fall no lower than −4° C only very simple precautions such as those mentioned in (a)–(c) above plus protection of the completed work at night, need be used. In extreme conditions, however, when the temperature falls to the region of −10° C, heating will be needed to ensure that the mortar sets and hardens sufficiently for work to continue. The techniques are similar to those used for *in situ* concrete (see 1. *In situ* concrete), the simplest being to preheat the mixing water (temperature required 49–66° C), the sand and perhaps the bricks. The mortar used

should be at a temperature of 16–27° C and should still be above freezing point when the work is completed and covered.

(e) Protection of completed work

On completion, new brickwork should be covered and protected for three to seven days, according to the extent of frost. The temperature of the brickwork must not be allowed to fall below freezing point, and the provision of heat under the covers may be necessary. The rate of hardening of the mortar will be affected by low temperatures in the same way as concrete, and the period of protection has to be related to achieving the required strength.

4. Plastering

Two basic problems are associated with plastering at low temperatures. First, the rate of drying out is considerably reduced (high humidities during winter are important in this) thus delaying the following trades and, second, the risk of the plaster freezing, in which the coldness of the surfaces to be plastered is significant.

(a) Choice of material

The plaster used should be suitable for the weather conditions. Special plasters are now available which obviate the need to wet high-suction backgrounds. The rapid hardening properties of gypsum based plasters make these plasters more suitable for winter conditions than those containing lime and cement.

When it is not possible to avoid the use of lime and cement plasters, consideration should be given to ready-mixed mortars which may be made up under conditions free from frost. An aerated cement/sand undercoat will help to isolate the finishing coat plaster from any moisture in the wall, and will reduce the risk of subsequent efflorescence.

In some cases it may be desirable to use a dry lining technique in preference to traditional plastering.

(b) Enclose building

The part of the building to be plastered should be completely enclosed. If glazing has not been completed, then some form of translucent sheet should be used over the window openings. All external door openings should also be suitably covered, while the number of entrances should be restricted; these should be fitted with self-closing devices.

(c) Heating and ventilation

Sufficient heating should be introduced to raise the air temperature to a level at which plastering may safely and satisfactorily be carried out, and to increase the rate of drying out. The heat should be maintained at least until the completion of hydration, which normally takes 24 hr. Care is required in the provision of heat to ensure that excessive localised drying out does not take place.

In order to minimise condensation introduced by gas fuels, to aid drying out, and in the interests of safety, it is important to ensure that there is adequate ventilation.

5. Flat roof work

All flat roof decks are liable to become wet as a result of their exposure to rain unless some elaborate form of protective covering is provided before the impervious finish is laid. Roof decks of concrete and screeds contain, without the aid of rain, considerable quantities of water. Consequently, unless situably insulated they are vulnerable to frost attack. In addition, they do take a long time, even if suitably protected, to dry out. Methods by which the impervious roof finish may be laid prior to complete drying out are covered in detail in *3.04 Exclusion*, 'Entrapped water', Vol. 2, pp. 156-161.

6. Floor finishes

(a) General

Although special care and precautions must be taken when dealing with most types of floor finishes in winter, it is usually possible to provide the correct atmospheric conditions, as the floor laying usually takes place inside a nearly completed building. Dryness of the subfloor is commonly an important requirement, but particularly when moisture sensitive flooring such as linoleum and PVC are used. Attention must be given to the proper storage of timber if problems associated with moisture movement are to be minimised (see *3.03 Moisture content*, Vol. 2).

(b) Screeds and cement-based finishes

Screeds are common to most types of floor finish and the precautions given under '1. Concrete' earlier are applicable. Where it is impossible to provide heat for the laying and curing period, the use of rapid hardening cement may be of assistance in marginal temperature conditions. Screeds should not be laid when the air temperature is falling below 3° C. The same conditions apply to granolithic topping. The setting and hardening of ordinary or rapid hardening Portland cement may be accelerated by adding not more than 1·0kg of calcium chloride to 50·0kg of cement, dissolved in the mixing water (calcium chloride should not

exceed 2 per cent of the weight of cement); alternatively, an extra-rapid hardening Portland cement or high alumina cement may be used (calcium chloride must not be added to these cements). Finally, the freshly placed concrete or screed should not be allowed to freeze and, if necessary, should be covered with sacks, tarpaulins or plastics sheeting supported from 152 to 457mm above the surface.

7. Painting

During winter painting may be seriously restricted due to the presence of moisture on or under the surfaces to be painted and to the delayed drying out of the paint itself due to low temperatures. The latter problem may be overcome by the use of special quick drying paints, some of which are now available even for outside work. Care is required in the selection of paints suitable for early decoration in new work when the background on which

the paint is to be applied may not have dried out thoroughly. The paint selected should be porous—see Table 3.08/6.

References

(1) Butterworth, B., *Bricks and Modern Research*, Crosby Lockwood, 1948. (2) BS 3921 : 1965, *Bricks and Blocks of Fired Brick-earth, Clay or Shale*. (3) *The Selection of Clay Building Bricks : 1 & 2*, BRS Digest (2nd Series), Nos. 65 & 66, HMSO, December, 1965, and January, 1966, respectively. Useful appraisal of BS 3921 (see ref. (2) above). (4) *Some Common Defects in Brickwork*, National Building Studies, Bulletin No. 9 HMSO, 1950. (5) *Principles of Modern Building*, Volume One, 3rd Ed., HMSO, 1959. (6) Schaffer, R., *The Weathering of Natural Building Stones*, Building Research, Special Report No. 18, HMSO, 1932. See also reference (7). (7) *The Weathering, Preservation and Maintenance of Natural Stone (Parts 1 & II)*, BRS Digests (1st Series), Nos. 20 & 21, HMSO, July, 1950 (revised March, 1965, and August, 1950, repectively). These two digests help to bridge the gap in time since reference (6) above was published. (8) *Winter Building*, Interim Review by the Committee on Winter Building, HMSO, 1963. (9) *Concreting and Bricklaying in Cold Weather*, National Building Studies, Bulletin No. 3, HMSO, 1948. (10) *Working in Winter or Bad Weather*, BRS Digest (2nd Series), No. 3, HMSO, August, 1950. (11) *Mortars for Jointing*, BRS Digest (2nd Series), No. 58, HMSO, May, 1965. (12) *Soils and Foundations : 1*, BRS Digest (2nd Series), No. 63, HMSO, October, 1965.

Table 3.08/6. Porous paints suitable for early decoration

Name	Type	General properties	Conditions of use
Distempers	Oil-bound washable	Can be used as a permanent decoration Can be redecorated with distemper or oil paints Will withstand light washing if allowed to harden for some time Most of these distempers are somewhat liable to alkali attack (in severe conditions)	Mainly for interior use, but some are made for exterior use Should not be used where alternate wetting and drying, e.g. due to condensation is likely. This may cause flaking, especially on highly trowelled surfaces
	Oil-free non-washable (size bound)	Not fast to dry rubbing Can readily be washed off, and must be removed before redecorating	Used where rubbing is unlikely, e.g. on ceilings
Flat oil paints (some)	Porous, i.e. flat finish due to high-pigment-filler content	Provide a serviceable permanent decoration or a suitable base for redecoration More permanent than distempers Most are not resistant to alkali attack	Can be used on all surfaces, but an alkali-resistant primer may be needed Preferable to distempers where resistance to alternate wetting and drying or greater permanence is required The primer must also be porous
Cement paints		Provide a hard durable matt surface Resistant to chemical attack Can be redecorated with cement paint, but are liable to cause chemical attack on oil paints applied over them, unless precautions are taken	Mixing must be carried out strictly according to the manufacturer's directions Especially suitable for use on exterior or interior surfaces of concrete, cement rendering or asbestos cement sheet Should NOT be used on damp materials containing excess sulphates, e.g. gypsum plasters and some bricks
Textured paints	Sometimes called 'plastic paints'	In spite of the thick coat usually applied, plastic paints are fairly porous, unless a glaze coat is applied	Mixing and application must be carried out strictly in accordance with the manufacturer's instructions
Emulsion paints	Polyvinyl acetate (matt or with slight gloss)	Porous (except gloss finish) and resistant to alkali attack. Can be used as a permanent decoration	Suitable for interior and, if properly selected, for exterior use. Resistant to alkali attack, but not always to efflorescence, and never to powdered surfaces. Washability good as a rule, and one of the best general coats for early application to new plaster

Reference: Winter Building, An Interim Review by the Committee on Winter Building, HMSO, 1963.

H

3.09 weathering

Geologically weathering is associated with the disintegration and decay of solid rock. In building, the term is normally associated with changes in appearance of the exposed external surfaces of materials due to the action of the weather—rain, wind and sun. For the present purposes, the term is being used to include not only superficial changes in appearance, but also the disintegration and decay of materials used externally. Whereas weathering is traditionally more commonly associated with materials such as brick, stone and concrete, all types of materials are included here.

The main purpose of this section is to act as a summary of the more commonly found problems in which water plays a major part. However, it has been convenient to include some examples of weathering due to other causes.

On exposure, all materials change their appearance to some extent. In most cases the degree of change is most important from both the maintenance and general appearance points of view. In a great many cases weathering effects produce what appear to be 'stains' which inevitably alter the *designed* appearance of buildings. These 'stains' may be due to the washing effect of rainwater concentrated on certain areas of the surface or to deposits left on the surface. In this there are a number of variable factors involved, such as the nature of the surface and the degree of exposure. Consequently some materials 'stain' more readily than others—in some cases the 'stains' may not show. Traditionally, the 'soot and whitewash' effect on sedi-

mentary stonework was thought to improve appearance by giving a light and shade effect. Such an effect cannot be obtained if the weathering details —the mouldings, such as cornices, strings and dripstones, on traditional buildings—are removed. At the same time plane surfaces do not necessarily weather evenly, while differential staining is often accentuated if projections and recessions are inadequately designed. In many post-war buildings uncontrolled flow of water over the surfaces of materials has inevitably marred the appearance of the buildings.* Some of the methods which may be used to control the flow of water have been included in preceding sections and are not repeated here. However, in the examples which follow the causes of the staining and their possible solutions are included.

It has been considered more convenient to present weathering by means of suitably captioned photographic examples. In the preceding sections examples from buildings of all ages have been included to illustrate certain aspects. In this section, however, all the examples are from buildings erected in the *post-war period,* that is from 1947. At the same time not all the possible weathering effects have been included. The exceptions are chiefly alkali attack, sulphate attack and frost action. None of the examples are repeats of those included in other sections. Examples of the same type of weathering effect are not different views of the same building, but are examples from different buildings.

Weathering effects may be classified in a variety of different ways. What-

ever classification is used there is bound to be overlapping. The classification used here does not follow the headings used in the preceding sections. Instead weathering effects have been related to specific problems and the general headings used are: (1) Geometric factors; (2) Solubility; (3) Soluble sales; (4) Parapets; (5) Condensation; (6) Failure of joints; (7) Movement; (8) Corrosion of metals; and (9) Miscellaneous. The captions to each example include wherever possible the lessons which can be learnt from the weathering shown. To this end all the examples are of failures rather than successes, although it is possible that some effects were anticipated or were design intentions. It is beyond the scope of this study to include expectations and intentions. Instead the examples have been interpreted 'as found', bearing in mind the lessons they might teach others.

geometric factors

The way in which water flows over the surfaces of buildings is primarily influenced not only by the geometry of the surfaces of materials but also by the geometry of the face of the building. Geometric factors do influence exposure. (*3.01 General considerations,* Vol. 2, and *3.02 Exposure,* Vol. 2.) Increases in exposure are associated with (1) omission of drips, (2) inadequate projections, (3) no projections to throw off or disperse water or provide shelter, (4) building details, and damage to details, as shown in the examples that follow.

*It has been suggested that the 'soot and whitewash' effect common in traditional stone building was a design intention. Plane surfaces also appear to be a design intention, particularly after Dr. Holden felt 'that every Portland stone building should wash its own face' and (about 1935) that, as far as mouldings were concerned, 'when in doubt leave them out' (NBS Special Report No. 33). Although these views have been shown to have been rather optimistic, it does not necessarily follow that buildings should not have plane surfaces or that there should be a return to the use of mouldings. Instead a positive approach to the problems of the flow of water is needed, in which selection of materials and detailed design are, as always, significant.

1. Omission of drips

Water will flow along the underside of horizontal surfaces if it is not checked by a suitable drip. The effects of the flow pattern the water follows may produce some unsightly results, particularly if the surface of the soffit is soluble. Water may also flow from the soffit on to a vertical surface.

1

1. *Reconstructed stone coping. In this case a drip would have been required not only at the front edge but also to the return at the open joint. The stonework in this example has been* painted to improve appearance since the photograph was taken. 'Staining' of the soffit of the coping is beginning to be visible again after six months

2

2. *Water has not only flowed over the underside of this rendered reinforced concrete canopy (projection about 0·75m) but also down the vertical surfaces of the column and glass on which soluble matter has been deposited*

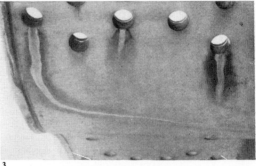

3

3. *This is one of those unfortunate examples where drips are basically unnecessary but where their inclusion (around each of the circular openings) would have prevented the staining which has been caused by leakage of the roof lenses. Quite a number of lenses in other parts of the rather long canopy have also leaked*

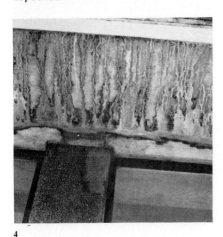

4

4. *Detail of another part of the same canopy (2 above). Here too some water has flowed on to the column*

5

5. *The drip to this balcony slab is a small downstand and has proved to be inadequate especially where there are heavy concentrations of water such as at the uprights to the balustrade. At the returns water has flowed down the wall surface. (Building is about 10 years old)*

2. Inadequate projections

Sills, copings and similar details of many post-war buildings are characterised by their lack of adequate projections to throw water clear of wall surfaces or to disperse the water and thus avoid undue concentrations of water. The result is very often to disfigure these surfaces particularly when they are of porous materials. Among materials which appear to be readily affected are limestones, concrete, renderings, and sand-lime bricks.

6

6. *Staining and discoloration of sand-lime bricks underneath all projections none of which exceeds 12mm. Note the effects of over-* *flowing at the returns to the sill (bottom left-hand corner of photograph)*

7

7. *A traditional looking projection which has failed to afford protection due mainly to the omission of suitable drips. Facing is Portland stone. Effect after about five years*

8

8. *Painted steel sill with about 12mm projection. Concrete edge beam. Water appears to have been able to get underneath the sill*

9

9. *Aluminium parapet capping with about 12mm projection. Sand-lime bricks to wall*

100

10. *Painted steel sill member with 12mm projection. Concrete beam. Note also cracking of part of the left-hand column*

11. *Aluminium sill with about 12mm projection and little fall to the sill. Limestone spandrel. Washing effect after 12 months*

12. *Aluminium sill with less than 12mm projection. Concrete infill*

13. *Aluminium sill with about 25mm projection. Rendered spandrel. The fall of the sill appears to be uneven while wind action has tended to blow the water laterally across the rough rendering*

15. *Painted steel sill with about 25mm projection. Concrete spandrel. Generally the sill projection has been succesful but there are zones where complete cleaning has not taken place. This is noticeable at the joints in the sill which are slightly raised. Note that there has been a flow of water along the soffit of the spandrel due to the omission of the drip*

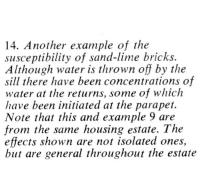

14. *Another example of the susceptibility of sand-lime bricks. Although water is thrown off by the sill there have been concentrations of water at the returns, some of which have been initiated at the parapet. Note that this and example 9 are from the same housing estate. The effects shown are not isolated ones, but are general throughout the estate*

3. No projections

The omission of projections to sills, parapets, etc. but without any means of dealing with the flow of water from horizontal ledges (such as forming the ledge into a concealed gutter with suitable drainage, for example) is another characteristic of detailing on many post-war buildings. As in the case of inadequate projections, the result is uncontrolled disfigurement of vertical surfaces, notably of porous materials such as limestone, concrete, renderings and sand-lime facings.

16

16. *Black sand-lime facings projecting about 19mm in front of the concrete parapet beam and without any form of protection to the exposed horizontal ledge of the facings. As a result the facings have been stained both by* *seepage of water via the unprotected horizontal ledge and by the uncontrolled flow of water over the ledge. The building is about three years old*

17

17. *Lead flashing with no projection. Painted rendered edge beam*

18

18. *Lead flashing. No projection. Limestone 'sill'*

20-21. *The front (20) and side view (21) of a concrete gargoyle which has become disfigured due to the uncontrolled flow of water over the flat top ledge onto the sides. The drip incorporated to the soffit at the front edge has been of no value. The disfigurement may have been overcome if the top ledge had a steep fall inwards or if it had a suitable capping and drip*

19

19. *Portland stone spandrel with 10 floors above it. The building is located in a heavily polluted atmosphere. After about six years*

20

21

102

22

22. In this example the disfigurement of the concrete could have been prevented if the projections had been made into 'hopper heads'

23

23. This example shows quite clearly the important part played by exposure to driving rain in the staining effect when projections are omitted. Those surfaces which are more heavily exposed to driving rain have remained clean due to the efficient washing effect of the wind-driven rain. The same thing has not occurred on the less exposed face of the building. The cladding in this case is exposed granite aggregate. Although granite is a relatively impervious material, the rough surface tends to hold atmospheric deposits

24

24. This example shows quite clearly how a projection can help to avoid the washing effect of the concentration of water that occurs over a horizontal ledge without a projection to give shelter or to throw the water sufficiently clear of the vertical surface. The spandrel is of Portland stone. The photograph was taken about 12 months after completion of the building, although the effect began to show about a month after completion

25

25. The shelter provided near the corner of this Portland stone faced building has prevented the stone from becoming excessively washed in one zone. However, elsewhere the lack of projections to the sills has resulted in uncontrolled disfigurement. The example also shows the effects of rising moisture with soluble salts in the plinth where the necessary damp-proofing has not been carried out. The building is about 10 years old

26

26. Another example of a projecting sand-lime brick infill panel. The rendered fillet to the exposed top ledge affords little or no protection due to cracking and loss of adhesion of the rendering. The joint in the aluminium parapet capping has allowed a concentration of water which has also affected the concrete beam. The photograph was taken about three years after completion of the building, but the general staining effect could be seen within about three months after completion. The rendered fillet was made good after six months, but without success

4. Building details

Certain building details tend to concentrate the flow of water over particular parts of a façade. This usually results in a washing effect in the zone or zones of greatest flow.

Accidental or other damage to details such as projections can cause disfigurement as shown in both examples of sills that have been damaged, the result of which has been to wash the Portland stone facings under them.

28

27. *The recessed painted steel channels provide an efficient flow line for water. The washing effect of the Portland stone faced beam may have been avoided if the base of the channel had a proper drainage system. This would have preserved the general line of the beam, Alternatively, a continuous sill above the beam with adequate projection could have been used*

27

28. *Although each sill has an upstand to the return to prevent water flowing over the sides and an adequate projection, there is still a concentration of water down each painted steel mullion which has washed the stone*

faced edge beam. This effect could have been avoided if the sills had been continuous. Alternatively the mullion could have been extended to the underside of the stonework

29

30

29. *Another example of the concentrated flow of water and resultant washing effect at the junction of a projection and the vertical face. The stone is Portland stone*

30. *Some concentration of water has occurred at the returns of the sills. More general is the concentrated flow which has occurred down the returns of the projecting brick panels*

31

32

31-32. *The general geometry of this precast concrete 'grille' has concentrated water fairly consistently in the same places thus giving rise to a general overall weathering effect*

33

33. *Concentrated flow from the gargoyle in particular has disfigured the black sand-lime facings*

34

35

34. *The drip to the balcony slab is generally adequate but it cannot function at the junction with the wall. Here again the flow line may have been controlled if there had been a vertical groove or channel in line with the junction of the edge of the slab and the wall. This example also shows the sheltering effect afforded by a projection—a large one*

35-37. *Three different examples of the returns of projections in which concentrated flow is revealed by lime washing from the surfaces on to the brickwork. In these cases it is usually difficult to overcome the concentrated flow. When lime washing can be anticipated (or any other form of deposit), then it might be better to incorporate suitable vertical grooves or channels in the walls so as to contain the flow within a predetermined 'line'*

36

37

38

39

40

38. *The results of a poorly detailed and executed mullion/sill junction*

39. *Portland stone sill the front edge of which has been slightly chipped*

40. *A slate sill which has cracked diagonally*

Solubility

Water flowing over one material on to another in juxtaposition may contain soluble matter derived from the first material and this soluble matter may then be deposited on the second material. The latter is then disfigured. Although soluble matter, such as lime, is more commonly derived from the surfaces of materials, such as limestones and cement-based products, it may also be derived from within a material if water has access to the interior. In some cases water-soluble pigments may give rise to staining. (See also 'Corrosion of metals' later for another source of deposits.)

41

41. *Lime washing from concrete surface on to black sand-lime facings after about three years*

42

43

42-45. *Four examples of lime washing from Portland stone on to brickwork which tends to hold the deposits. In some of these cases the staining may have been reduced or eliminated if water flowing over the stonework had been thrown clear of the brickwork. An adequate projection is required*

44

45

46

46. Soluble salts from behind the concrete cladding deposited on the painted steel window frames

47

47. Staining of the granite apron by the water-soluble pigment of the teak window frames which has been washed out by rain, because the teak was not treated (by proper oiling) initially. The two examples which can be seen in the photograph are not isolated cases but are typical of hundreds of granite aprons similarly affected on the same building. The pigment is extremely difficult to clean off—it is not washed away by rain

48

49

50

48-49. Lime derived from a concrete roof slab has been allowed to drip on to the vitreous mosaic facing on which it has become encrusted. As the water is dripping fairly regularly, stalactites have formed on the underside of the concrete lintel as can be seen in the detailed photograph (49)

50. Soluble salts derived from the concrete under the vitreous mosaic works its way to the surface and eventually crystallises

Soluble salts—efflorescence

Soluble salts may be derived from a number of sources. Efflorescence, the crystallisation of salts (*3.05 Efflorescence*), on the surface is usually unsightly, rather than harmful, and unless there is a 'perpetual' source of salts, is only temporary, often only lasting a few years after the completion of a building on which it occurs. In some cases efflorescence that takes place under the surface of a material may cause some exfoliation or pitting. Soluble sulphate salts may cause disintegration or damage to certain cement-based products due to attack of some of the constituents of the cement. (*3.06—Sulphate attack.*)

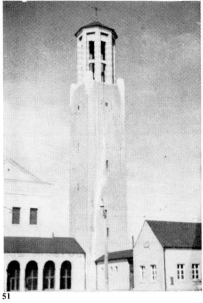

51

52

51. *This brick tower was apparently built with sea sand mortar and is perpetually efflorescing. (A Belgian example. Photograph by Ian Mathew)*

52. *Efflorescence on the brickwork of a newly completed building which should disappear within a few seasons*

53

54

53. *Water with soluble salts splashed from the pavement and from the fill and ground under the pavement has risen to an exceptional height in the Portland stone. Efflorescence has caused some damage to the stonework. This problem can only be solved by suitable damp-proofing and using an*

impervious stone such as granite for the plinth. Effect after about 11 years

54-55. *Another example of the rise of water and soluble salts in Portland stone taken down to pavement level without adequate damp-proofing, after about eight years. The damage caused by efflorescence can be seen in the*

detailed photograph (55)

56. *A difficult example to understand, but one which shows, by comparison, that Portland stone should not be taken down to pavement level. The granite plinth detail performs its function properly. Ideally the plinth should have been continuous*

55

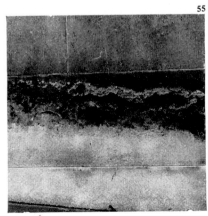

56

57

58

59

57. *The marble facing used as a 'plinth' has not prevented the rise of water and soluble salts up the Portland stone it is masking. The marble has however masked the splashing from the pavement*

58-59. *Brown staining of newly built (or newly cleaned) Portland stone is usually due to an alkali reaction between the mortar and organic salts in the stone. Usually the stains disappear after a while except in* sheltered areas. *The stains in 58 have persisted for at least 10 years. Note that the stains mostly occur in the vicinity of joints—the source of alkalis is in the mortar*

Parapets

Failure to take adequate precautions in parapets to prevent the downward penetration of water—use of proper copings and d.p.c.'s important—usually results in disfigurement and/or decay (efflorescence, sulphate attack or frost action).

60. *Dampness has resulted in some efflorescence and some discoloration of the clay brickwork*

61. *Dampness has resulted in discoloration of the black concrete bricks and some efflorescence*

62. *The failure of each joint in the coping has accentuated the staining effect. (Not a post-war building)*

Condensation

Condensation is dealt with fully in *Part 4.00 Heat and its effects.* In view of its growing incidence, selected examples are included of both surface and interstitial condensation illustrating some of the deleterious effects that the water involved may have.

Below, two examples of condensation that has taken place behind sheets of glass cladding

63

65

63. *Coloured glass panel. Condensation seems to have formed or at least to have run down the face of the backing to the glass. Where interstitial condensation is anticipated it is wise to allow the condensate to drain away. No such provision has been made in this example*

Two examples from domestic buildings. In both cases (65-66) the condensation has formed and had deleterious results at junctions or corners where thermal bridges exist. Note the formation of mould growth. (Courtesy: (65) London and Essex Guardian Newspapers Ltd.; (66) BRS, Crown Copyright)

64

66

64. *The condensation that has occurred behind the glass cladding appears to have caused some distortion to the material behind the glass*

Failure of joints

Joints are required to perform a number of different functions (*3.04 Exclusion,* Vol. 2, p. 41) one of which is to exclude the weather. The failure of a joint may at one extreme only cause disfigurement due to concentrations of water while at the other allow the penetration of water within a wall or roof. In a great many cases the performance of the sealant used in the joint is particularly important.

67

68

67. Poor joint design accounts for the failure of this mastic

68. Failure of a mastic used in an expansion joint to a wall built in sand-lime bricks, partly due to insufficient backing to the mastic and partly to deterioration of the material as a result of exposure to sunlight

69

70

71

69-73. In these five examples, all the sills are of slate, itself an impermeable material. In each case there has been a failure of the mortar joint between lengths of the sill to remain intact. Either the mortar has cracked, lost its adhesion to the slate or simply fallen out, thus breaking the 'impervious' continuity of the sill, and allowing water to concentrate at the joints with resultant cleaning of the spandrels whether of textured rendering, Portland stone or brickwork. The problem arises chiefly from the fact that it is extremely difficult for continuity to be maintained particularly when butt joints (as in the examples) are used. Due to movement and other causes, the mortar invariably fails mainly where it has no support, that is at the overhang of the sill. A mastic used instead of mortar may fail for the same reason. However, a lap joint filled with mastic is likely to prove more successful (see 76 for the results when the lap joint is not sealed). Note effects shown in 72 and 73 are as found about two years after completion of the buildings

72

73

74

75

76

74. *Junction of a canopy and main wall of the building 'sealed' with a mastic. There has been loss of adhesion at the interface of the canopy and the mastic (left-hand of the joint) and water has percolated downwards, eventually to run along the underside of the canopy. As a safety precaution it might have been wise to return the drip (Photograph taken 12 months after completion of the building and soon after a spell of rain)*

75. *Failure of the mortar joint to a precast concrete coping. Lime leached from the concrete has been washed on to the brickwork below. A properly inserted d.p.c. would have helped to overcome the problem*

76. *A slate capping with a lap joint. The joint has, however, not been sealed with any type of jointing material. Water finding its way through the joint has washed unevenly over the Portland stone facing below. Dirt collected from the top of the capping has also been washed on to the facing where it has been deposited causing the dark streaks. Note the photograph was taken on a cold day (the joint is therefore wide) about seven years after completion of the building*

77

78

77. *Mastic which has been poorly applied to the junction between a window frame and precast concrete sill. In some places there has been loss of adhesion, in others there is hardly any mastic at all. This is another case when a backing to the mastic and some protection may have helped*

78. *Water percolated down this joint where the mastic has failed bringing corrosive products and lime with it to stain the glass, sill and vitreous mosaic facing. Effect after about 18 months*

79. *Failure of this mastic joint between a window frame and sill at ground floor level occurred within one year of the completion of the building. Not only has the mastic been badly applied but also appears not to have been given an adequate backing*

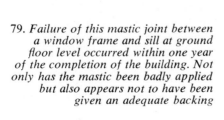

79

K

Movement

Movements may occur for a number of different reasons (see particularly *2.03 Cracking in buildings*, Vol. 1, p. 114) one of which may be moisture. The deleterious results of movement, namely cracking, are often due to restraint while one or more factors often 'operate' simultaneously. Movements may also result in loss of adhesion.

80

80. *A rather clumsy way of making good to cracking of the mortar joint in sand-lime brickwork. In long lengths of walling built in sand-lime* *bricks it is necessary to make provision for moisture movement which normally takes place during the first year of a new building's life*

81

82

83

81. *Loss of adhesion of rendering to concrete at an expansion joint. The rendering elsewhere to concrete columns on the same building are all sound. This failure appears to be due to bridging across the expansion joint which has helped to loosen the rendering on either side of the joint*
82. *Lifting of a coping with cracking of the mortar joint due to the lack of an expansion joint in a wall which is over 61m long*

83. *Exfoliation of the surface of a stone facing due probably to the combined effects of moisture movement and frost action. An isolated example from a building where the same cladding has been extensively used*

84. *Cracking which could be due to corrosion of reinforcement or some chemical action. Note the collection of soot*

84

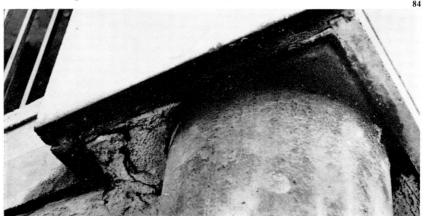

85-86. *Crazing of the surface of reconstructed stonework. The reasons for the crazing are complex but are associated with curing of the slabs and differences between the surface layer and the interior of the material. The cracks are normally confined to the surface, that is they do not penetrate deeply into the interior*
87. *Crazing of rendering to concrete, due probably to moisture movement. The widest distance between cracks is about 25mm*
88. *This example of small cracks in a reconstructed stone facing shows the way in which the appearance of cracks can be accentuated by dirt and soot deposits that collect within the cracks*
89. *Cracking of terrazzo to a concrete column. Cracking of this kind sometimes occurs due to moisture movement of the terrazzo and/or the movement of the background*

85

86

87

88

89

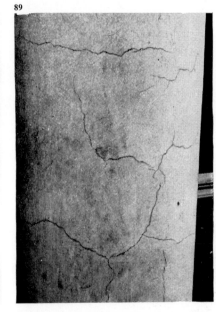

90-91. *Two examples of cracks which have occurred at joints due probably to moisture movement either of the stonework, the joint or the background. In 91 there has been*

some spalling of the Portland stone facing

92. *Loss of adhesion of the vitreous mosaic facings which appears to be*

due to movement of the concrete background—probably moisture movement if the mosaic was applied before the concrete had cured properly

90

91

92

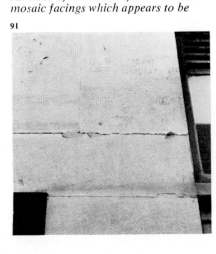

115

Corrosion of metals

The corrosion of metals may have basically two effects if deterioration of the metal itself is not taken into account. First, staining of the surfaces of materials in juxtaposition, and, second, cracking or spalling of the material in which a metal (usually steel) is embedded (reinforced concrete notable). Staining by corrosion deposits from ferrous metals can be prevented by suitably protecting the metal and ensuring that the protection is maintained; with non-ferrous metals such as copper and aluminium it is usually necessary to ensure that water does not flow from the metal over other materials. Cracking and spalling are best prevented by ensuring adequate cover. (See also *3.07 Corrosion*.)

93

94

95

Staining

93-95. Under certain conditions the results of corrosion of aluminium and its alloys in polluted atmospheres can stain materials over which water containing the corrosive products can flow. In 93 the flow of water down the aluminium lightning conductor is concentrated at the fixing positions from which it flows downwards carrying corrosive products with it. This has resulted in staining of the vitreous mosaic after about six months. It is difficult to overcome this kind of problem but a vertical groove in the mosaic would at least have contained the staining along a controlled line. In 94 staining of the Portland stone from *the vertical aluminium channel section has occurred mainly from the exposed top of the channel. Water flowing within the channel from a height of 20 floors has tended to clean the stonework, particularly the left-hand side. The staining effect could have been overcome, either by continuing the aluminium to the bottom of the stone spandrel or by providing a drainage arrangement at the base of the channel. The photograph was taken about four years after completion of the building. (95) The geometry of the roof fascia ensures concentration of deposits at particular locations. Portland stone facing stained after about 12 months*

96-97. Two examples of staining from poorly protected or inadequately maintained steelwork. In 97 corrosion products from the painted steel railings have stained the vitreous mosaic facing to the balcony balustrade. Water has tended to concentrate at the uprights. The steelwork has been exposed to a marine atmosphere for about three years. All the 15 balconies to this building have generally stained in the same way—the degree varies slightly. In 96 the cantilevered painted steel supports to the sign are in an advanced state of corrosion after about 10 years despite the fact that there is adequate clearance for repainting. There is similar staining of the concrete column from all the other supports in the same shopping precinct

96

97

 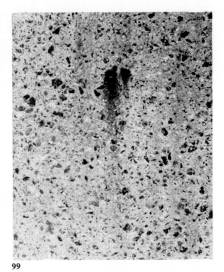 

98-100. *These three examples illustrate the results of small iron particles which may sometimes be present in aggregate used for concrete*

  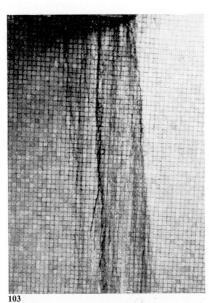

101. *Staining of concrete from steel fixing devices used in connection with the formwork after about eight years*

102-103. *Spalling of the concrete slab shown in 102 may have been due to corrosion of embedded steelwork. However, water has gained access to the steel reinforcement the corrosive products of which combined with lime*

leached from the concrete have caused a wide band of staining of the vitreous mosaic facing for a considerable distance down the wall as can be seen in 103

Cracking and spalling

104-109. Inadequate concrete cover to steel reinforcement leads to corrosion of the steel and cracking and subsequently spalling of the concrete. In practice it is more difficult to ensure that steelwork is adequately covered in thin reinforced concrete sections. The six examples are all of thin sections of reinforced concrete. 104 A boot lintel which has already been repaired but to no avail. 105 Isolated spalling of a r.c. floor slab. The dark horizontal lines in 106 are zones of cracking due to corrosion of steel reinforcement in the r.c. wall. The cracks are accentuated by the fact that they have collected dirt and soot. There are also same vertical cracks due to corrosion. These cracks are generally more severe than the horizontal ones as can be seen in the close-up photograph 107. As yet there is no staining from the corrosion. The building is about 17 years old. In 108 spalling of all 12 balcony balustrades of reinforced concrete with applied render has occurred in about two years from completion of the building. There is already some staining. 109 Spalling of a r.c. wall

104

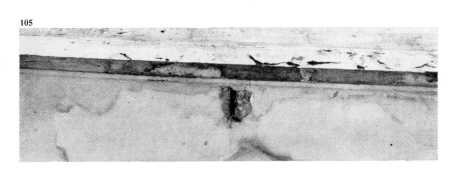

105

106

107

108

109

110. *Cracking of concrete due to corrosion of steelwork embedded in the joint. Note also cracking of the glass due to corrosion of the steel frame. Building is about 14 years old*

110

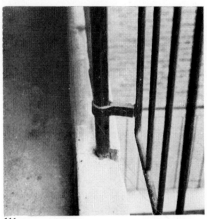

111

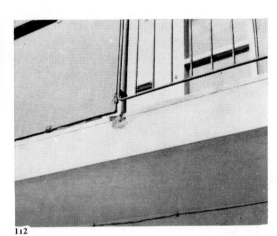

112

111-112. *Spalling of concrete of two different steel uprights in the same balcony due partly to corrosion and partly to movement. Building is about 10 years old*

113

114

113. *The washing effect on a Portland stone spandrel from water splashed from the horizontal projection. In* *cases such as this an impervious material such as granite, slate or a metal should be used as a 'plinth'*

114. *Movement of an asphalt skirting leaving a vulnerable opening for the ingress of water*

115

116

115. *Weathering of reconstructed stone facing after about 15 years. The weathering pattern is fairly consistent, although dirt and soot has tended to collect in recessions particularly at the joints—the slabs are obviously not* *truly flush but there are no horizontal ledges to cause a washing effect. A further point is that the wall is fairly sheltered from driving rain. There are some corrosion stains*

116. *The grinning of joints through render (or plaster) is usually due to differences in absorption of the components of the background, in this case the mortar joint and the blockwork. Differences in absorption are usually due to variations in porosity*

118

118. *Deterioration of the finish applied to timber cladding. It is important that timber claddings such as Western red cedar are treated if disfigurement is to be avoided but it is equally important that the treatment is maintained*

119

119. *The messy result of spillage of another liquid—oil*

117

117. *This building shows some of the more commonly found weathering effects*

Index

Index

Index

Index

Index

Index

Index